THANKS TO OUR CONTRIBUTORS

To obtain for our readers gourmet recipes, easy to prepare, we contacted the producers of such convenience foods as frozen foods, powdered mixes, freeze dry foods, powdered foods, canned goods, and other packaged foods on which the manufacturer does all or part of the work ordinarily done in the kitchen.

We asked for tested recipes using wine with their products. A generous number of recipes was received. These were further tested by our home economist. Only when they resulted in a gourmet dish relatively easy to prepare were they approved for inclusion in this book.

Aided by excellent commercial equipment, producers of convenience foods not only remove peels from vegetables, excess fat and bone from meats, shells from seafood, and so on, but in many instances they do it more efficiently and economically than can be done in the home. As the result, the cook often realizes savings with convenience foods.

As many of the convenience food producers will tell you, add wine to their foods and they become festive.

Producers and promoters of convenience and other foods who contributed recipes are listed toward the end of this book under the heading "Brands Used in Testing Recipes" and "Contributors Not Specifying Brands."

Our thanks go to them for combining their foods with wine for savory recipes that we can share with you.

D. C. Turrentine, *Manager*
WINE ADVISORY BOARD

GOURMET WINE COOKING
the easy way

BY WINE ADVISORY BOARD

Production Editor: DAVID R. WILCOX · *Recipe Editor:* NIELSINE H. GEHRKE

Designer and Illustrator: FRANCIS E. REDMAN

Editorial Assistant: SHEILA KAUFMAN

Food Consultants: MARJORIE LUMM, DOROTHY CANET

CONVENIENCE foods and wine

Good cooks the world over have been using wine to flavor their foods for hundreds of years. Many of the old recipes have become classics. They are worth every minute of the time it takes to chop innumerable ingredients, simmer slowly for hours, and season intricately.

When these great dishes were originated, there were no convenience foods. There was no other way than to start from scratch. Busy Americans are finding that there are acceptable short-cuts to producing good food through the combination of some of the prepared foods found in our markets—the frozen, canned, dried, partially-mixed or fully cooked specialties. Over the years these convenience foods have been vastly improved. Today their flavors are excellent, and the steps required to prepare them are shorter and easier. These foods are readily available and easily stored.

Experiment with Wine

One of the most imaginative and compatible approaches to experimenting with convenience foods is the use of wine. It can turn any one of these foods into a dish that has sparkle and character. Frozen carrots simmered in Sauterne and butter taste much better than carrots boiled in water. Yet preparing them with wine takes no more effort or time than boiling them in water. The addition of Sherry transforms canned pea or bean soup into a rich and aromatic menu item. Port turns raspberry-flavored gelatin into a distinctively fresh dessert.

Like convenience foods, wine is readily available and easy to use. It does not have to be cleaned, chopped, sliced, sauteed, etc. before you can use it. You simply measure it and pour it into or over the food.

Most seasonings provide flavors of their own that sometimes overpower the flavor of the food. Wine, on the other hand, brings out the basic food flavors and blends them together. The alcohol evaporates during cooking to leave nothing but an over-all enhancement of the food. Where a more pronounced wine flavor is desired, more wine may be added to the dish just before serving.

Some Helpful Guides

Dry white wines are generally more compatible with delicately flavored foods, such as chicken, fish, cream soups, and cream sauces. With robust foods, such as beef, meat sauces, meat and vegetable soups, dry red wines are most often used. Rosé goes well with ham, veal, and fruit. Use dessert wines, such as Port and Cream Sherry, in desserts, dessert sauces, and gelatin salads.

The recipes in this book illustrate how many of the new convenience foods can be enhanced with wine—the wines produced in California. And more and more Americans are discovering that a glass of wine, served as the meal-time beverage, makes even the simplest food taste festive.

CONTENTS

Recipes

helpful facts about wine

Alcohol Boils Away

Do wine cooked foods contain alcohol? The answer is "no." Alcohol boils at a lower temperature than water, 172°F, at the simmering point, to be exact. If you cook foods with wine at or above boiling for as little as 10 minutes, there will be no alcohol remaining, but the fine flavor and delicate aroma and bouquet of the wine will be left behind to add to your enjoyment of the foods.

All-Purpose Glasses

What about wine glasses? Your best buy is a 6–9 oz., all-purpose stemmed wine glass. You may obtain information on availability of such glasses by writing to the Wine Advisory Board. This glass has a large diameter bowl, is tapered inward toward the top to collect the aroma and bouquet of the wine. It has been recommended by the Wine Growers of California as being proper for the service of all wines including dessert, appetizer, white table wines, red table wines, and sparkling wines. If you don't mind the extra cost and storage, you can get traditional glasses for each of the wine classes named above.

Pronounced Wine Flavor

Wine is used sparingly in the recipes contained in this book so that its flavor will blend subtly with the flavors of the other ingredients and not overpower them. Many enjoy more pronounced wine flavor. Where a more pronounced flavor is desired, add more of the specified wine to suit your taste just before the soup, meat, or other dish is served.

Cooking Wines

In many areas there are wines on the market especially designated on their labels as "cooking wines." Most of these wines have been salted so that they cannot be used as beverages. Government regulations specify the amount of salt they must contain to qualify as non-alcoholic beverages. As the name implies, it is perfectly satisfactory to use a dry cooking Sherry in place of a California Dry Sherry or a white table cooking wine instead of Sauterne, etc. However, in using those that contain salt as stated on the label, you will want to reduce the amount of salt called for in the recipe.

Can You Substitute?

If California Sauterne or other dry white table wine is specified in a recipe and you do not have it, don't hesitate to use Chablis or another dry white table wine. Where dessert or appetizer wines are specified in a recipe, substitution of a different wine type is likely to cause a measurable difference in flavor of the final dish.

Taste Many Types

The fun of wine is in exploring its wide range of colors, aromas, bouquets and flavors by tasting many different wine types. Suggestions from others with wine experience can be helpful but treat them only as guides—not rules. Your own eyes, your own sense of smell, your own taste buds are your best guides to enjoyment. Develop confidence in them and you will not go wrong.

Stand Up Feature

Gourmet Wine Cooking the Easy Way is designed to lie flat when open so you can keep your place while cooking. If desired, it will stand up and let you "look while you cook." A rubber band slipped around each cover and the pages is another aid to keeping the book open to your recipe while it stands up.

No Sugar Added

California State law prohibits the addition of cane or other sugars to traditional California table or dessert wines. The long, gentle, sunlit seasons in this state ripen the grapes fully, developing the natural grape sugar to the optimum point for wine making. Thus, the cane sugar added in some other wine growing areas is not needed for California wines.

Bottle Capacity

When the word "bottle" is mentioned in this book without further explanation, it refers to a wine bottle of 25.6 fluid ounces. This size is also referred to as a "fifth," meaning one-fifth gallon, or four-fifths quart.

Left-Over Wines

Tables wines once opened are perishable and should be used within several days even though stored in the refrigerator unless rebottled in smaller containers.

Re-Bottling

Fifth-gallon and tenth-gallon bottles of wine with screw caps can be purchased from most retailers and saved when empty for rebottling wines left over from larger containers. Fill the bottle well up into the neck to eliminate as much air space as possible. If corked bottles are used, corks slightly larger than the bottle neck may be softened by soaking in boiling water for a few minutes so they fit easily.

From Brittanica

This book outlines uses of wine for the consumer. Additional uses are found in this writeup which appeared in Encyclopedia Brittanica: "Wine is as old as civilization, and no drink except water and milk has won such commendation through the ages. It is used to perform rites in churches; to observe memorable occasions; to launch ships; to administer to the sick; to welcome guests; and to inspire the mind."

Flaming Brandy

When lights are low, flaming a dish with California Brandy presents a spectacular sight while adding a memorable flavor. Brandy of 100-proof lights and flames easily. With Brandy of 80-proof, it is best to warm it in a double boiler (caution: do not put pan with Brandy directly on heat). Remove from heat as soon as water in bottom of double boiler begins to simmer to avoid loss of alcohol. For even better flaming, add a few drops of lemon or orange extract (they are high in alcohol) to a sugar cube, place in center of dish with Brandy and light. Spoon Brandy gently over this flame with tablespoon.

Testing of Recipes

All recipes for food and drinks appearing in this book have been thoroughly tested by home economists and given high ratings.

CHAMPAGNE-aperitifs

for a festive START

Today's smart young hostesses are civilizing the cocktail hour—to the relief of their husbands and most of their guests. At the best planned parties, one or two interesting drinks, chosen with care and served with style, now replace the "What-would-you-like-to-drink?" routine that used to keep the host as busy as a short-order cook. Now he opens and pours Champagne for everyone, or he serves a mixed wine drink from a chilled pitcher.

Inspiration for this trend came from such gourmet groups as the Wine and Food Society, and the so-called Gourmet Clubs that flourish in many neighborhoods. With the promise of a memorable meal to come, the members of these groups keep the aperitifs in their proper perspective. The pre-dinner drink relaxes the guests, starts the flow of conversation and stimulates the appetite for the dinner. Wine serves superbly in each of these roles.

Selecting the wine: The tremendous increase in the production and consumption of California Champagne suggests that this festive wine is often the type chosen. The appetizer wines—dry Sherry and Vermouth—offer other possibilities. Gaining popularity fast are the flavored wines, relatively new to this country, but familiar and popular in Europe. Sometimes the same wine to be served with the first course in the dining room is poured earlier to accompany the appetizers in the living room. Still another trend among wine enthusiasts is a small-scale pre-dinner wine tasting. Then the cocktail hour becomes a party with a purpose—a time to become better acquainted with several different wines. A selection of three California red table wines is one possibility; or two or three different brands of dry Sherry is another. Along with critical tasting and evaluation, there is much conversation and a feeling of camaraderie that carries over to the dining room when the short, but lively, tasting is over.

TO A dinner party

Champagne: As an appetizer, choose a dry Champagne. The label may specify "Brut," meaning very little sweetness, or "Natural," indicating none at all. Chill it well, at least two hours in the refrigerator. When the size of the party will require several bottles, and the refrigerator is full of food as it is likely to be at this time, look around for other means of chilling. Plenty of ice cubes in a big tub will be satisfactory. It will take from 30 minutes to an hour to chill a number of bottles to the desired temperature. Portable camping ice chests, styrofoam picnic containers, and paper or plastic paint buckets are good make-shift Champagne coolers. Long contact with the ice or water will sometimes wrinkle or disfigure the labels on the bottles. Enclosing each bottle in a plastic bag will prevent this. The amount of Champagne to buy will vary with the group, the period of time it is to be served, and the size of the glasses. A four-ounce serving is the average size. A bottle holding approximately 26 ounces will pour six servings. Here's a Champagne party formula: *Number of guests x number of drinks for each = total number of drinks to be served. Total number of drinks ÷ 6 drinks per bottle = number of bottles to buy.*

Sherry and Vermouth: Dry Sherry is the aperitif form of this popular wine, although many people enjoy the medium Sherry before meals, too. These days it is most often served lightly chilled, and sometimes is offered over ice with a twist of lemon. Either dry or sweet Vermouth—or a mixture of the two—is a pleasant appetizer over ice. The herb flavors of the Vermouth seem to alert the palate for the food to come. The usual serving of Sherry or Vermouth is 2 or 3 ounces.

Flavored wines: Natural Flavored Wines are made by private formulas in which pure flavors (not synthetic), such as herbs or citrus fruit flavors, are added to the wine. These sometimes are labeled "aperitif wines" and often bear unique names. Mixed with sparkling water or flavored soda—or served over ice—these wines are excellent as appetizers, refreshing as wine drinks and as a base for wine coolers whenever you entertain.

MENUS FOR FOUR
of RECIPES

SPRING

Champagne Brunch

California Champagne

Cheese and Wine Quiche 74

Sherry Walnut Ham, sliced 50

Croissants*
(Ready-baked from freezer cabinet)

St. Helena Fruit Cup 116

FALL

Buffet Supper

California Port and Tonic 19

Easy Stroganoff on Rice 38

Broiled Tomatoes with Sherry 83

Wine Marinated Artichokes 82

Pimiento Biscuits 87   Butter

California Burgundy

and

California Sauterne

Toddy Gingerbread 101

California Port

* Recipes for all dishes listed appear in this book on pages indicated except that the two marked by an asterisk are not included.

SEASONS
from this book*

* Recipes for all dishes listed appear in this book on pages indicated except that the two marked by an asterisk are not included.

# of GRapes and WiNES

The winemaking process begins when grapevines are planted.

There are more than 8,000 known and named varieties of vinifera (Old World) grapes, but only a few of them make really good wines. Not more than 60 or so varieties of grapes are important for winemaking in California, for example.

Grape Variety Is Important

Winemaking begins with the grapes because the variety is important and the number of bunches on each vine is equally so. Pruning the vines to control the yield means that the remaining fruit will reach the highest degree of ripeness and full flavor.

Any grape will make wine of a sort. The natural yeasts on the skins see to that. But the wines of California are grown today from selected varieties that are picked at the right moment. That moment comes when the grapes reach an ideal balance between acid (which decreases as the grapes ripen) and natural grape sugar (which increases with maturity).

In California Grapes Mature Every Year

In many parts of the world, some years are not warm and dry enough to bring the grapes to full, balanced maturity. The natural grape sugar in such years must be augmented with other sugars to produce a palatable wine. (In California, wine must be made from the grape alone — no sugars, other than from the grape, may be added.) In many places the so-called "vintage years" are of significance, for they are the years in which grapes ripen fully. Vintage dating of wines obviously matters more in these other areas than in California, where growing conditions invariably produce mature grapes before the winter cold and rains.

The growing season begins in early spring when the first warm weather brings out new shoots on the pruned vines. It ends as early as August in some parts of California, and continues until November in the northern regions.

The Grape Families

All the grapevines used for winemaking in California (as well as table and raisin grapes) are of the family Vitis vinifera. This is the classic species, the one used in Europe, South America, Africa, Asia and Australia.

The only other major species are native to North America, and are used for wine, jelly, canning and table grapes in the rest of the U. S. and Canada. These American vines also supply disease-resistant rootstock for the vinifera vines of much of the rest of the world. Best known of the native species is Vitis labrusca, of which the Concord is the most prominent variety. Hybrids of native and vinifera grapes also are used to make wine in the Eastern states.

bEVERAGES

Wine mixes so compatibly with fruit juices, sherbets, carbonated drinks — even ice cream — that it is possible to concoct interesting specialty beverages using these conveniently packaged, frozen, bottled or canned ingredients. They're easy to produce in all sizes — a wine "cup" is an individual serving, good before a meal; a "cooler" is tall, contains ice cubes, refreshing in warm weather; a punch is for a party, large or small. The traditional punch bowl is spectacular, but not essential. Any of these punches can be served from a pitcher.

Sauterne with Sherbet Punch
(About 60 3-oz. servings)

Because it is so beautiful to look at, delicate and light, this punch is recommended for a ladies group. Perhaps use it as a brief refreshment, served with cookies or little cakes, after a lecture or fashion show. Of course there's no law against men appreciating this combination too.

> 4 (4/5-qt.) bottles California Sauterne, well chilled
> 2 quarts sherbet, raspberry, pineapple, orange or lemon

Pour wine into punch bowl; add sherbet and stir carefully until no lumps of sherbet remain. Serve at once in punch cups. Garnish with a sprig of mint.

Fruited Sherry
(About 10 servings)

For the young crowd this drink is inexpensive and appealing. Serve it after a good swim or during quiet after-dinner conversation.

> 1 (4/5-qt.) bottle California Sherry
> 2¼ cups orange-grapefruit, orange-apricot or
> pineapple-apricot drink
> Ice cubes

Chill all ingredients well. Combine Sherry with the fruit juice of your choice. Pour over ice cubes in tall glasses and serve at once.

California Champagne Punch
(25 4-oz. servings)

Colorful, light and gay enough for any lively occasion is this refreshing wine punch. Originally it was made with California Champagne, but Sauterne will do very well too, uniting with the fruit-flavored drink mix.

> 2 packages raspberry or strawberry flavored drink mix
> 1 cup unsweetened lemon juice
> 1 (4/5-qt.) bottle California Champagne or
> Sauterne, chilled

Combine ingredients in chilled punch bowl. Serve immediately.

Cranberry Sparkler
(18 5-oz. servings)

Offer this long and cold drink to the thirsty. The two "fifth" bottles of California Burgundy or other red table wine may be replaced by one-half gallon, if desired. This changes the proportion of the wine slightly but not enough to influence the flavor.

> 2 (4/5-qt.) bottles California Burgundy, Claret or Rosé
> 1 (1-pt.) bottle cranberry juice cocktail
> 2 (12-oz.) cans lemon-lime carbonated beverage

Refrigerate all ingredients for several hours. Just before serving, combine in a large pitcher or punch bowl. Serve over ice cubes in tall glasses.

American Beauty Punch

(About 40 3-oz. servings)

With this punch recipe you can keep one eye on the budget while serving confidently a large number of guests at a gala party occasion. California Rosé is refreshing, pink, and delightful with grenadine syrup and citrus juices. California Champagne, not an expensive addition used in this way, adds sparkle.

       2 (4/5-qt.) bottles California Rosé, chilled
       3 cups orange juice or 1 (6-oz.) can frozen orange
         concentrate diluted according to package directions
    ½ cup lemon juice
       1 large bottle California Champagne, chilled
       3 limes, sliced (optional)

Combine all ingredients in a punch bowl, adding California Champagne last; stir to blend. Add block of ice, or tray of ice cubes and serve at once. Punch may be garnished with lime slices.

Apricot Pitcher Punch

(About 12 6-oz. servings)

One of the best thirst-quenchers ever stirred together in a large pitcher is this combination of California Sauterne and apricot nectar. It looks cool and delicate and tastes delightful. Instead of Sauterne you might use Chablis or Riesling.

       1 (4/5-qt.) bottle California Sauterne or
         other white table wine, chilled
       2 (12-oz.) cans apricot nectar, chilled
    ¼ cup lemon juice
    ½ cup sugar
       1 (1-qt.) bottle gingerale, chilled

In large pitcher combine Sauterne, apricot nectar, lemon juice and sugar; stir until sugar is dissolved. Chill pitcher and contents. Just before serving, pour in gingerale. Pour over ice cubes in tall glasses.

Iced Cranberry Rosé

(6 servings)

After all ingredients have been chilled and assembled, it's fun to do the drink mixing before your guests. This California Rosé and cranberry juice concoction is easy to make and good to drink.

    ½ cup California Rosé
       2 cups bottled cranberry juice cocktail
       1 egg white
    ¼ cup sugar (approximately)

Combine chilled Rosé, cranberry juice cocktail and egg white in cocktail shaker. Stir until well blended, then add sugar to taste. Add a generous amount of cracked ice and shake vigorously. Strain into chilled Champagne or cocktail glasses.

Champagne Sparkler

(About 40 3-oz. servings)

Keep this recipe ready for an event that calls for a light-hearted approach, perhaps a house-warming, to launch a new career, or a definitely feminine luncheon. The resulting punch is colorful and can be combined (except for the California Champagne) in advance.

       1 (6-oz.) can frozen limeade concentrate
       1 (46-oz.) can unsweetened pineapple juice
       1 (10-oz.) package frozen strawberries
    ¼ cup lemon juice
    ¼ teaspoon salt
       3 (4/5-qt.) bottles California Champagne, well chilled
       1 lime, thinly sliced

Combine undiluted lime concentrate, pineapple juice and slightly thawed strawberries; stir in lemon juice and salt. Turn into punch bowl over small chunk of ice or ice cubes. When ready to serve, add chilled California Champagne. Garnish punch bowl with lime slices.

Strawberry Rosé Punch

(60 3-oz. servings)

Little short of spectacular is this fruited, pink punch. It's ideal for an afternoon gathering, perhaps in a garden setting. California Rosé makes the wine base to which strawberries are added. Then the treasure of the wine cellar, California Champagne is added to give elegance and flavor.

       4 (12-oz.) packages frozen sliced strawberries,
         partially thawed
       1 cup sugar
       4 (4/5-qt.) bottles California Rosé
       4 (6-oz.) cans frozen lemonade concentrate
       2 (4/5-qt.) bottles California Champagne, chilled

In a bowl combine strawberries, sugar and 1 bottle of Rosé; cover and let stand at room temperature 1 hour. Strain mixture into punch bowl, add frozen lemonade concentrate and stir until completely thawed. Add remaining bottles of Rosé, then the California Champagne. Add a block of ice or a tray of ice cubes and serve at once.

Wine Lemonade Punch
(25 servings)

Gather around the punch bowl and be delighted before and after sampling. The lemonade, made from a concentrate, is first frozen and then crushed and molded before it is turned into the punch bowl with the California Champagne and Sauterne. Strawberries make it gay whether it's June or January.

1 (6-oz.) can lemonade concentrate, thawed
1 (4/5-qt.) bottle California Champagne, chilled
1 (4/5-qt.) bottle California Sauterne, chilled
2 (10-oz.) packages strawberry halves, thawed
  or 2 cups fresh strawberries, halved
  Fresh mint leaves

Reconstitute concentrate as directed on can; pour into two ice cube trays and freeze. Crush lemonade ice cubes and press firmly into a small bowl. Invert molded ice in punch bowl and pour wines around it, stirring gently around ice to blend. Add strawberries and juice; garnish with mint leaves. Serve in punch cups with some of the crushed lemonade ice in each cup.

Wine Punch Hot or Cold
(22 5-oz. cups)

This is good to have on hand for all occasions when you would like to offer a hospitable cup of punch. The coffee syrup blends delightfully with California Sherry to make either a hot or cold punch. California White Tokay may be used as the wine too.

Syrup: Combine and bring to a boil, stirring constantly ½ cup instant coffee, ½ cup water and 1½ cups light corn syrup.

To serve hot: Combine all of the syrup with 1½ quarts boiling water and 2 cups California Cream Sherry. Add and mix slightly, 1 cup heavy cream, whipped until stiff. Serve at once in punch cups.

To serve cold: Combine all of the coffee syrup, chilled with 1 quart ice water and 2 cups California Cream Sherry. Add and mix slightly 1 cup heavy cream, whipped until stiff. Pour over tray of ice cubes and serve at once in punch cups.

Champagne Wedding Punch
(About 50 4-oz. servings)

Inspire the wedding toast with this sparkling punch, a happy combination of California Champagne and Chablis with fruit juices. It's delightful for the occasion and gay enough to revive happy memories later on. For variation in the wines you might like to try Champagne with one of the other white table wines, like Sauterne, Pinot Blanc, or Riesling.

3 (4/5-qt.) bottles California Chablis or
  other white table wine
2 (46-oz.) cans pineapple or pineapple-grapefruit juice
2 (6-oz.) cans frozen lemonade concentrate
2 (4/5-qt.) bottles California Champagne

Have all ingredients well-chilled. Combine Chablis and fruit juices in punch bowl with small block of ice. Pour in chilled Champagne just before serving.

Burgundy Apple Punch
(About 35 servings)

California Burgundy and apple juice just naturally go together to make a cool and cheerful beverage. With the addition of gingerale we are reminded of a country apple cider made glamorous. Instead of California Burgundy you might use Cabernet, Red Pinot or Claret.

2 (4/5-qt.) bottles California Burgundy or
  other red table wine, chilled
1 (1-qt.) bottle apple juice
2 tablespoons lemon juice
1 cup sugar
1 (1-qt.) bottle gingerale

Combine Burgundy, apple and lemon juices and sugar in punch bowl; stir to dissolve sugar well. Pour in gingerale and stir lightly to blend. Add block of ice or tray of ice cubes. Serve at once.

Rosé Lemonade for a Party
(12 to 14 servings)

Just as good as lemonade is this California Rosé and lemon cooler. You'll never miss the bother of squeezing and straining the citrus fruit, and best of all, it's deliciously pink in tall glasses.

½ gallon California Rosé
2 (6-oz.) cans frozen lemonade concentrate
  Ice cubes

Pour California Rosé into a large pitcher or punch bowl; add lemonade concentrate and stir until well mixed. Place 2 or 3 ice cubes into each tall glass. Fill glasses with wine lemonade and serve at once.

Star Syllabub
(About 30 4-oz. servings)

Light and airy, this mixture presents a handsome appearance in the punch bowl with the garnish floating on top. The diet-conscious may drink it without worry for it is not rich in calories.

    4⅔ cups instant nonfat dry milk
    3½ quarts water
     2 cups sugar
    ⅓ cup finely grated lemon peel
    1 cup California Sherry

    ½ cup cold water
    ¼ cup lemon juice
    ½ cup instant nonfat dry milk

Combine 4⅔ cups nonfat dry milk and 3½ quarts of water in a large bowl; stir to blend. Add sugar and lemon rind; beat with rotary or electric beater until sugar is thoroughly dissolved and mixture is frothy and foamy. Stir in Sherry. Pour into large glass punch bowl. In small deep bowl, combine the ½ cup cold water, lemon juice and ½ cup nonfat dry milk. Whip at high speed in electric mixer 6 to 8 minutes, or until stiff. Drop by spoonfuls on top of milk-wine mixture. If desired, sprinkle lightly with nutmeg.

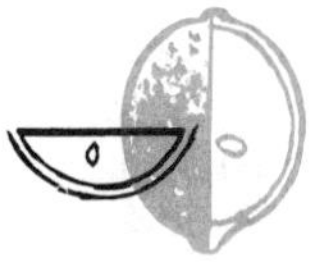

Sherried Apple Eggnog
(About 12 4-oz. servings)

Call this frothy mixture perfect for an evening refreshment, or perhaps as a light dessert after a satisfying luncheon. To give extra tang, add about 2 tablespoons lemon juice.

    3 eggs, separated
    ⅓ cup sifted powdered sugar
    ¼ teaspoon nutmeg
      Pinch salt
    2 cups California Sherry, chilled
    2 cups apple juice, chilled
    1 cup heavy cream

Beat egg yolks with half of the sugar, nutmeg and salt until thick and lemon colored. Stir in chilled California Sherry and apple juice. Beat egg whites to soft peaks; add remainder of the sugar gradually continuing to beat until stiff meringue forms. Fold into chilled Sherry and egg yolk mixture; fold in cream, whipped until stiff. Serve in cups, with a light sprinkle of nutmeg. Accompany with a teaspoon.

Sauterne Sparkle
(40 4-oz. servings)

If you are looking for a punch that is light, not too sweet and very easy to make, stop right here. Add to its list of virtues the fact that it's economical, making it nice for a large group gathering.

    1 (4/5-qt.) bottle California Sauterne
    2 packages lime flavored drink mix
    2 quarts water
    ¼ cup unsweetened lemon juice
    ¼ cup unsweetened orange juice
    2 quarts lemon sour, chilled

Combine Sauterne with all ingredients except lemon sour. Chill. Just before serving add lemon sour. Garnish with twists of lemon peel.

To Serve It Forth. Lacking a punch bowl, create a container for a large amount of cold beverage from an out-size mixing or salad bowl. Set the bowl in a wreath of greens, with perhaps a few floaters. Freeze a fruit block or ring to float in the punch.

Frosty Orange Cooler
(1 serving)

Delightful to serve from its own orange shell container is this cool and refreshing drink.

    ½ cup California Dry Sherry, chilled
    ½ cup orange juice, chilled
    1 tablespoon each honey and lemon juice
    1 drop mint extract
    1 cup crushed ice

Place all ingredients in blender and whirl to frappé consistency. Fill into orange shell and garnish with mint leaves. Serve with straw.

Vermouth Frost
(1 serving)

For that special person who loves daiquiries, here's a way to make the cold drink with an added flavor of California Dry Vermouth.

    ¼ cup (2-oz.) California Dry Vermouth
    2 tablespoons frozen daiquiri mix
    ⅓ cup crushed ice

Place all ingredients in blender and blend briefly, about 10 seconds. Serve at once in chilled glass.

Try one of these three magic cold drinks, designed for quick, colorful creation by combining wine with liquid diet food. The blender does a neat whirl-away job for smoothness, but you may use an electric or rotary beater at high speed to get the same effect.

Ported Strawberry Freeze
(About 2 7-oz. servings)

1 (10-oz.) can strawberry liquid diet food
½ cup California Port
½ teaspoon grated lemon peel
Maraschino cherries for garnish

Pour liquid diet food into ice tray and freeze until almost firm in center. Put into blender with Port and lemon peel; blend until well mixed. Serve immediately in parfait glasses; garnish with cherry. (You may want a spoon with this.)

Sherried Mocha Chocolate
(About 3 4-oz. servings)

1 (10-oz.) can chocolate liquid diet food
½ cup California Sherry
¼ teaspoon cinnamon
½ teaspoon instant coffee

Chill liquid diet food in ice tray until slushy. Combine in blender with Sherry, cinnamon and instant coffee; mix until light and frothy. Pour into glasses; garnish with light sprinkle of cinnamon. Serve at once.

Sherry and Pineapple Nog
(About 3 4-oz. servings)

1 (10-oz.) can pineapple liquid diet food
½ cup California Sherry
1 egg

Chill liquid diet food in ice tray until slushy; combine with Sherry and egg in blender and mix until light and frothy. Pour into glasses and dust with nutmeg.

Port Cranberry Refresher. Blend together one part California Port with two parts cranberry juice cocktail. Pour over ice cubes in wine glass or tall glasses and serve. Good for afternoon drop-ins or late evening.

Syrup or Honey Sweetens Summer's Iced Drinks: A hostess who serves tall cool drinks to her summer guests knows that there is quite a difference in tastes where sweetness is concerned. This is especially true of wine coolers—some like them refreshingly tart, others prefer to add sugar. For everyone's enjoyment, it's a good plan to have a small pitcher of simple syrup made up in advance and chilled in the refrigerator. Use two parts sugar to one of water and heat just until the sugar is completely dissolved. Or, use honey, nature's own sweetener. It stirs into a cold beverage easily and adds a pleasant flavor of its own. Chances are, a wine cooler made with California Port, mixed with an equal amount of sparkling water and poured over ice cubes in a tall glass, will be sweet enough for anyone. Port is a fruity dessert wine. The dry red or white wines, also often used in this way, sometimes call for extra sweetness.

Strawberry Sangria
(12 4-oz. servings)

Pink and pretty like an old-fashioned shrub is this strawberry and wine punch. Serve it in tall glasses with crushed ice and garnish with strawberries, lemon and mint leaves.

2 pints fresh strawberries
1½ cups sugar
3 cups water
1½ cups lemon juice
2 cups California Claret or Rosé

Puree strawberries in electric blender or force through food mill; sieve to remove seeds. Combine sugar and water in saucepan, stir and heat slowly until sugar dissolves. Mix with strawberry puree and lemon juice, then the wine. Chill thoroughly.

California Tomato Juice Cocktail
(4 servings)

The bright good flavor of tomato juice is considerably enlivened with the addition of California Chablis and just a hint of dill. Other white table wines such as California Sauterne or Rhine Wine may be used as a change from the Chablis.

1 cup California Chablis
1 cup tomato juice
¼ teaspoon Worcestershire sauce
Cracked ice
Dried dill
Thin lemon wedges

Measure wine, tomato juice and Worcestershire sauce into shaker; add cracked ice, cover and shake well. Strain into chilled serving glasses. Sprinkle lightly with dill and serve with lemon garnish.

Orange Sherry Flip
(4 servings)

For those who like their beverages very cold, add ½ cup cracked ice or 6 ice cubes to the recipe ingredients before blending, then strain into glasses. To make a Cream Sherry Flip, add ½ cup cream.

- 1 cup California Sherry
- 1½ cups orange juice
- 2 eggs
- ¼ teaspoon salt

Have all ingredients well chilled. Whirl in blender until well mixed and frothy. Serve in chilled glasses with a sprig of mint to garnish.

A Unique Summer Refresher: Here's liquid ambrosia which serves 8 delighted people. In a good-sized pitcher, combine 1 large bottle California Sauterne or other white table wine with ⅓ cup lemon juice, ½ cup sugar and several crushed mint leaves. Chill 3 hours. Remove mint, add a 6-ounce can frozen pineapple juice concentrate. Stir well, add 2 cups chilled sparkling water. Pour over ice in tall glasses. Garnish as desired.

The Bamboo
(1 serving)

Well-chilled, this simple wine drink can be perfection—not too sweet, not too dry. Be sure to pour it into a cold, cold cocktail glass. Mix 1 jigger California Sherry, 1 jigger California Sweet Vermouth and a dash of bitters; stir well. Strain into cocktail glass and garnish with green olive or small pickled onion.

Sherry Banana Shake
(3 to 4 servings)

Pretty up the glasses in which this cold rich drink is served. Rim the edges of tall glasses lightly with egg white, then twirl in powdered sugar and let dry.

- ⅓ cup California Sherry
- 2 bananas, peeled and sliced
- ¾ cup milk
- 1 pint chocolate or coffee ice cream

Combine Sherry with bananas and milk in blender and whirl until smooth. Add ice cream and blend a few minutes longer. Pour into glasses and serve at once. If a blender is not available, mash bananas and beat all ingredients thoroughly with an electric or rotary beater.

California Burgundy Refresher
(4 servings)

Another quick but easy to make drink is this California Burgundy and fruit juice combination with excellent color and flavor.

- Crushed ice
- 2 cups California Burgundy
- 2 cups cranberry-apple drink
- Mint sprigs for garnish

Fill glasses half full with crushed ice. Add Burgundy and cranberry-apple drink in equal parts (½ cup each) in each glass. Stir gently. Garnish glasses with springs of mint.

Peaches and Wine Cooler
(5 to 6 servings)

Something quite different, cool and temptingly flavored, this drink would be especially pleasant some warm afternoon.

- 1 (10½-oz.) package frozen peaches, partially thawed
- 3 or 4 drops almond extract
- 1 tablespoon lemon juice
- 1 (4/5-qt.) bottle California Chablis
- Nutmeg

Whirl peaches, almond extract, lemon juice and half the wine in blender until smooth. Stir in remaining wine. Pour into chilled glasses and fleck with nutmeg.

Snappy Tomato Juice
(16 4-oz. servings)

Extremely commendable is this bright and nourishing pick-me-up creation designed for any chilly weather occasion or for a brunch warm up.

- 2 cups California Dry Sherry
- 1 (46-oz.) can tomato juice
- 1 (10½-oz.) can beef bouillon
- 2 tablespoon each Worcestershire sauce and lemon juice
- ¼ teaspoon red pepper sauce

Combine all ingredients. Heat slowly to boiling, stirring now and then. Pour into heat-proof glasses or mugs.

Sherried Tea Flip
(4 servings)

A well chilled drink that is made frothy by beating ice cream and California Sherry into it. There's a whisper of spice too.

    ¼ cup instant tea
    ¼ cup sugar
    ⅛ teaspoon cinnamon
      Dash mace
    3 cups cold tap water
    1 pint vanilla ice cream, softened
    ¾ cup California Cream Sherry

Combine instant tea, sugar and spices; add cold water and stir briskly. Beat in ice cream and Sherry until smooth and frothy. Pour into tall glasses and serve.

Sherried Spiced Tea. The little tea bag makes it easy to make a cup of good relaxing tea. Add California Sherry and spices to make it even better. Rinse mug or glass with hot water. Pour about ⅓ cup boiling water over tea bag and let stand about a minute. Remove tea bag, add ⅓ cup California Dry or Medium Sherry, a dash of nutmeg and cinnamon.

Swedish Glogg
(About 20 4-oz. servings)

The Swedes have a name for this hot spicy wine drink that warms from head to toes. They call it Julglogg (Christmas Wine). The cardamom should be cracked and tied with the other spices in a little cheesecloth bag. Then it is easy enough to retrieve from the glogg before it is poured into the punch bowl. Stud a few cloves into the orange peel for decorative effect and be sure to serve a little fruit in each glass.

    1 (4/5-qt.) bottle California Burgundy
    1 (1-qt.) bottle California Port
    1 (3-inch) strip orange peel
    2 (2-inch) cinnamon sticks
    8 whole cardamom, cracked
    12 whole cloves
    ¼ cup sugar
    ½ cup dark seedless raisins
    1 (4-oz.) bottle maraschino cherries
    1¼ cups California Brandy
    1 cup whole blanched almonds

In large saucepan combine Burgundy and Port with the rest of the ingredients, except ¼ cup Brandy. Heat slowly, just to simmering; pour into punch bowl. Heat remaining Brandy in double boiler; ignite and pour into punch.

Hot Wine Cranberry Cup
(About 28 3-oz. servings)

For a speedy serving of a hot drink, prepare the special, spiced cranberry syrup ahead and store it in the refrigerator. It takes only a moment to combine it with California Burgundy or Claret to make this stimulating drink.

    2 (1-pt.) bottles cranberry juice cocktail
    2 cups water
    1½ cups sugar
    4 inches stick cinnamon
    12 whole cloves
      Peel ½ lemon
    2 (4/5-qt.) bottles California Burgundy or Claret
    ¼ cup lemon juice

Combine all ingredients but wine and lemon juice in saucepan; bring to boil, stirring until sugar is dissolved. Simmer gently 15 minutes, then strain. Combine syrup with wine and lemon juice; heat, but do not boil. Serve in preheated mugs or cups; serve with a sprinkling of nutmeg.

Mulled Burgundy Punch
(12 4-oz. servings)

The origin of the word "mull" is uncertain, but we do know it means to heat, sweeten and spice. That's what we do with this punch combination of California Burgundy, cranberry and pineapple juices.

    2 cups California Burgundy
    1 pint bottle cranberry juice
    1 (1-pt. 2-oz.) can pineapple juice
    ⅓ cup brown sugar, firmly packed
    ¼ teaspoon each cinnamon, cloves, ginger
    ⅛ teaspoon salt
      Butter or margarine

Combine all ingredients except butter, and heat slowly to simmering, stirring occasionally. Ladle into mugs or heat-proof glasses, dotting each serving with a bit of butter.

California Port and Tonic
(4 servings)

When the occasion presents itself for an interesting drink, one not too complicated, California Port does very well combined with quinine water.

    1 cup California Port
    2 cups quinine water (tonic mixer)
      Crushed ice
      Lemon wedges for garnish

Pour ¼ cup Port and ½ cup quinine water over crushed ice in each serving glass. Stir lightly, and garnish with lemon wedges.

Holiday Chocolate
(6 to 8 servings)

Of course you don't have to wait for any special day to make this delicious hot chocolate, generously laced with California Sherry. Use it for brunch, or depend on its warmth to liven guests some chilly evening on the patio or garden.

    ½ cup semi-sweet chocolate bits
    1 cup California Sherry
      Dash of salt
    ¼ teaspoon cinnamon
    3 cups milk
    ½ cup light cream

In top of double boiler place chocolate bits, Sherry, salt and cinnamon; cook over hot water, stirring occasionally, until chocolate is melted. Heat milk and cream to scalding point; add to Sherry and chocolate mixture and beat well until foamy. Pour into mugs or cups, top with whipped cream (if desired) and dust lightly with cinnamon.

Winter Warm-up
(12 4-oz. servings)

Just the thing to warm the hearts of those coming in from the cold. California Sherry or Muscatel joins with orange juice to make this special hot mug.

    1 (4/5-qt.) bottle California Sherry or Muscatel
    6 cups orange juice
    1 teaspoon ground cardamom

In saucepan heat all ingredients to simmering. Remove from heat and pour into heat-proof mugs or glasses.

Hot Sangaree. Well tested and approved is this hot spiced wine drink. For each serving rinse mug or glass with very hot water. Pour in about ½ cup California Port and 1 teaspoon simple syrup (if desired), following quickly with about ⅓ cup boiling water; stir. Add dash of nutmeg.

APPETIZERS

These appetizers, as their name implies, are intended to tease the appetite, not satisfy it. All are flavored with wine, a fact that improves their taste and suggests that they will be particularly good combinations with a beverage wine. Here are several answers to the question: "What do I serve with Champagne?" Also included are ideas for the go-alongs for a mid-afternoon Sherry Hour, or an evening glass of Port. Space out these "made" appetizers with such all-time favorites as salted nuts and some of the excellent new crackers that are appearing on the market as snack foods.

Sherried Seafood Appetizer

(6 servings)

The delicious, pert sauce makes this an outstanding appetizer. The California Sherry smooths and tones down the catsup-mayonnaise combination just enough to bring out the wonderful flavor of crab meat and avocado. If you wish, other seafood such as lobster, shrimp or tuna may be used instead of crab meat.

- ½ cup catsup
- ¼ cup mayonnaise
- ¼ cup California Dry Sherry
- 1 teaspoon lemon juice
  Dash of cayenne
- 1 (6½-oz.) can crab meat or 1½ cups fresh crab meat
- 1 cup diced avocado
- ½ cup finely diced celery

Mix catsup, mayonnaise, wine, lemon juice and cayenne. Beat until well blended. Chill one hour or more. Shortly before serving time, mix sauce with other ingredients.

To accompany this seafood: **California Dry Sherry** or **Dry Sauterne**

California Marinated Mushrooms

(20 to 25 mushrooms)

Because they are to be used whole, choose fresh mushrooms carefully, selecting only small perfect caps. Keep the mushroom stems for other cookery purposes, chopped and added to sauces, sandwich fillings or vegetable salads. Lacking fresh mushrooms, there's no reason why the small whole canned mushrooms cannot be marinated for a most attractive appetizer. Afterwards, the marinade may be used as a dressing for a tossed green salad.

- 1 pound fresh mushrooms
- ¼ cup California Burgundy or other red table wine
- ½ cup salad oil
- 1 tablespoon garlic salt

Rinse mushrooms well under running water; remove stems; drain caps. Combine Burgundy with oil and garlic salt; pour over mushrooms, and allow to marinate for several hours or overnight. Stir occasionally. Serve on cocktail picks.

To accompany this appetizer: **California Dry Sherry** or **Dry Vermouth** or **Port and Tonic**, *page 19*

Little Links Hawaiian

(About 80 appetizers)

Small sausages are heated with pineapple chunks in a piquant sauce, made with California Sherry and pineapple juice. If you wish, make the sauce in advance and refrigerate until serving time. Then assign it to a chafing dish or electric skillet and cook to showy advantage before your guests.

    2 tablespoons each brown sugar and cornstarch
    ¼ teaspoon each salt and powdered ginger
    1 (1-lb. 14-oz.) can pineapple chunks
    ½ cup California Dry Sherry
    2 (5-oz.) packages small smoked sausage links
    3 (5½-oz.) packages small wieners

In saucepan combine brown sugar, cornstarch, salt and ginger. Drain pineapple, reserving syrup. Add enough water to pineapple syrup to make 1½ cups; pour into saucepan. Stir in Sherry and cook over medium heat, stirring constantly, until sauce boils and thickens. (Refrigerate the sauce if you are preparing in advance.) Pour into chafing dish or electric skillet to keep warm. Add pineapple chunks and heat two or three packages of links or wieners at one time (takes about 5 minutes). More may be added later. Use cocktail picks for serving pineapple and sausages.

To accompany this appetizer: **California Dry Sherry** *or* **Sauterne Sparkle,** *page 16*

Braunsweiger Paté

(1 cup)

Tiny bits of crumbled bacon add a salty crispness to this smooth liver paté, making it more interesting. Present the paté on a tray with crackers or other spreadables to accompany glasses of California Dry Sherry, or use it as a late evening snack. Makes a nice little gift too, packed in a decorative pottery jar.

    6 slices bacon
    8 ounces liver sausage
    2 tablespoons California Dry Sherry
    2 tablespoons softened butter or margarine

Sauté bacon until crisp, then crumble into small bits. In bowl, start to mash liver sausage and butter with a fork; add wine gradually and continue mixing until smooth and well blended. Stir in crumbled bacon. Line small bowl with waxed paper or foil; pack liver paté into bowl and chill well. Turn out on serving tray and garnish with sliced toasted almonds. Spread on thin toast strips or crackers.

To accompany this appetizer: **California Dry Sherry** *or* **Dry Vermouth** *or* **Cranberry Sparkler,** *Page 13*

Sherried Chicken Liver Paté

(4 cups)

Small packages of frozen chicken livers are available now in most markets, and they do very well in making this special paté a creditable likeness of the continental paté de foie gras. Be careful not to overcook the chicken livers. It will take only 5 to 7 minutes of simmering, and they should still be slightly pink. Lacking a blender, force the hot cooked mixture through a sieve and beat well to smooth.

    1 (8-oz.) package frozen chicken livers
    1 (10-oz.) can consomme
    1 cup butter or margarine
    1 envelope unflavored gelatin
    2 tablespoons California Medium Sherry
      Pinch of white pepper
      Pinch of monosodium glutamate

Thaw livers and trim carefully. Heat undiluted consomme and butter in saucepan, add chicken livers and simmer carefully until livers turn a pale pink. Remove from heat and stir in gelatin which has been softened in wine; add white pepper and monosodium glutamate. Cool slightly and turn mixture into blender; whirl to blend into smooth paste. Pour into serving bowls and chill until firm. Serve with crackers or toast triangles.

To accompany this appetizer: **California Champagne, Dry Sherry, Dry Vermouth** *or* **California Burgundy Refresher,** *page 18*

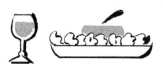

Blue Cheese Wine Spread

(1 cup)

Here's something a little different in cheese spreads for small crackers or strips of thin toast. The soft cream cheese assures a smooth blend when the blue cheese is beaten with it. The California Port stirred into the spread isn't too apparent, but it does add a certain mellowness you will enjoy.

    2 (3-oz.) packages cream cheese
    ½ cup blue cheese spread
    ¼ teaspoon Worcestershire sauce
    ⅛ teaspoon paprika
      Dash salt, cayenne
    3 tablespoons California Port

Blend together well cheeses, Worcestershire sauce and seasonings; beat until creamy. Gradually blend in Port. Place in serving bowl and chill until serving time.

To accompany this spread: **California Dry** *or* **Medium Sherry** *or* **Port** *or* **Hot Sangaree,** *page 20*

Chicken Ham Paté
(64 servings)

When there's a large buffet to consider, this chicken and ham paté will serve you well. It can be made some time in advance and refrigerated, then about 64 guests can help themselves to this smooth attractive spread. For a smaller amount, cut the recipe ingredients in half. Good for a sandwich spread too.

    1 envelope unflavored gelatin
    ¾ cup California Sauterne or other white table wine
    ⅓ cup chopped green onion
    1 cup finely chopped mushrooms
    2 tablespoons butter or margarine
    1 (10½-oz.) can condensed cream of chicken soup
    2 (4¾-oz.) cans chicken spread
    2 (4½-oz.) cans deviled ham

Soften gelatin in ¼ cup Sauterne and set aside. Cook onion and mushrooms slowly in butter until soft, but not browned. Add remaining Sauterne and simmer about 5 minutes, or until the wine is reduced to about ¼ cup. Add undiluted chicken soup and heat to boiling; remove from heat and stir in softened gelatin, stirring to dissolve. Add chicken spread and deviled ham; mix well. Turn into 1-qt. mold and chill until firm. When ready to serve, unmold on plate or tray and accompany with crisp crackers or thin toast.

To accompany this appetizer: **California Champagne** *or* **Dry** *or* **Medium Sherry, Dry** *or* **Sweet Vermouth** *over ice or* **Champagne Wedding Punch,** *page 15*

Gouda Cheese and Port
(8-oz. cheese)

Use a small Gouda cheese (the round one coated with a cheerful red wax) to make an attractive bowl for a special cheese spread. Cut the top off the cheese and hollow it out carefully, leaving a rim about ½ inch, sides and bottom. Place the cheese bits in blender with ¼ cup California Port and whirl until cheese and wine are blended smooth. Fill cheese bowl and replace top. Wrap with foil or waxed paper and keep in refrigerator. Allow to warm up at least 30 minutes before serving. For a party, use two or three of the small cheeses or the large Gouda cheese, increasing the wine for the spread in proportion. Serve with crackers or on toast points.

To accompany this spread: **California Dry Sherry** *or* **Port** *for an evening snack; or* **Brut Champagne** *before a meal*

Party Cheese Spread
(2 cups)

This is really a delicious spread, but it will taste even better if you serve it in large orange shells (oranges halved then hollowed out). And if you like a very smooth product, whirl it all (except the grated orange peel) in the blender. Fold the peel in last so the little golden flecks will decorate the spread.

    2 (5½-oz.) containers (about 1 cup)
        Cheddar cheese spread
    ½ teaspoon grated orange peel
    ¼ cup California Dry Vermouth
    1 cup small curd cottage cheese

Beat Cheddar cheese with orange peel and Vermouth until smooth. Stir in cottage cheese (press through a sieve if you prefer a smoother mixture). Cover and let stand an hour or longer to mellow flavors.

To accompany this spread: **California Dry Vermouth** *or* **Dry Sherry** *or* **Champagne Sparkler,** *page 14*

Three Cheese Spreads

Good cheese spreads are made better by the addition of a little wine and judicious seasoning. The wine not only makes the cheese more spreadable, but adds to the flavor. These spreads may be made into dips by adding wine to thin them.

Cheddar Port: Blend 1 (5-oz.) jar Cheddar cheese spread with 1 or 2 tablespoons California Port. Offer as a spread for crisp crackers or melba toast. California Dry Sherry may be added to Cheddar or American cheese spread with delicious results.

Sherry Deviled Ham: Blend together 2 (3-oz.) packages cream cheese, 2 (4½-oz.) cans deviled ham, ¼ cup California Dry Sherry, ¼ teaspoon Worcestershire sauce and a dash of garlic powder; beat well to smooth. Spread on crackers or serve in small bowl accompanied by crackers or potato chips.

Blue Cheese Sauterne: With a fork mash ½ pound blue cheese; blend in 1 (3-oz.) package cream cheese. Gradually beat in ½ cup California Dry Sauterne or other white table wine, whipping until mixture is light and fluffy. Add 1 teaspoon Worcestershire sauce, a dash of garlic powder and 1 tablespoon minced parsley. Mound into serving bowl, and accompany with several crackers or small rounds of fresh rye bread.

To accompany these spreads: **California Dry Sherry, Brut Champagne** *or a tall wine cooler made with red or white table wine or* **Apricot Pitcher Punch,** *page 14*

Crab Dip Elegante

(2 cups)

Occasionally it is pleasant to serve a hot dip, particularly when it is one like this crab meat and cheese mixture that takes only a brief cooking period.

1 (8-oz.) package cream cheese, softened
¼ cup evaporated milk
1 (6½-oz.) can crab meat, drained and flaked or
1½ cups fresh crab meat
3 tablespoons California Sauterne or
other white table wine
1 teaspoon prepared mustard
⅛ to ¼ teaspoon garlic powder

In saucepan blend together cheese and evaporated milk until smooth; stir in remaining ingredients. Place over low heat and cook until steaming, stirring now and then. Do not boil. Serve hot with potato chips or corn chips.

To accompany this dip: **California Dry Sherry** *or* **Dry and Sweet Vermouth** *mixed half and half over ice*

Raisin Curry Slices

(About 36 appetizers)

Spicy with curry, these delicate little pastry rounds are a delightful surprise to serve with a glass of California Sherry, either as a before dinner appetizer or later in the evening for a small snack. The packaged mix makes it very easy to be an expert in handling pastry.

2 tablespoons butter or margarine
4 teaspoons curry powder
⅔ cup finely chopped onion
2 cups seedless raisins, chopped fine
⅔ cup California Dry Sherry
1 (9½-oz.) package pastry mix

In small saucepan melt butter with curry powder; add onion and cook lightly, then add raisins and Sherry. Cover pan and simmer 5 to 10 minutes, until liquid is absorbed; cool. Prepare pastry mix according to package directions. Divide in half; roll out each piece to 9 x 10½-inch rectangle. Spread half of cooled raisin mixture on each piece of pastry. Roll up from long side, to make two 10½-inch rolls, pinching edges to seal. Bake on ungreased baking sheet in moderate oven (375°) 25 to 30 minutes, until browned. Cool and cut into thick slices.

To accompany this appetizer: **California Dry** *or* **Medium Sherry** *or* **Fruited Sherry**, *page 13*

Cheese Pastry Twirls

(36 twirls)

You can make these gay little pastries in less time than it takes to tell. The pastry comes from a package, easy to mix and roll out. The cheese is ready to blend with California Sherry. Refrigerate the rolls in advance, then it's simple enough to cut off slices and bake them quickly to perfection. Rush them hot to your guests.

1 (9½-oz.) pie crust mix
1 (5-oz.) jar Cheddar cheese spread
2 tablespoons California Sherry
¼ teaspoon Worcestershire sauce
Dash cayenne

Prepare pastry according to directions on package. Roll out into rectangle about 10 x 15 inches; cut crosswise in halves. Blend cheese spread with Sherry and seasonings; spread evenly over pastry rectangles. Roll up each rectangle, jelly roll fashion from one wide side to the other. Wrap rolls in waxed paper and refrigerate 1 hour or longer. Slice about ¾ inch thick; place slices on lightly greased baking sheet; bake in hot oven (425°) about 10 to 12 minutes or until golden brown.

To accompany this pastry: **California Champagne, Dry Sherry** *or a* **Flavored Appetizer Wine** *or* **The Bamboo**, *page 18*

Valley Special Dip

(2 cups)

Clams and cottage cheese mixed together have always made a good dependable dip that's easy to put together and acceptable for many occasions. In this recipe, cottage cheese with chives forms the basis of the dip and California Sauterne is added along with clams and other seasonings to make this spirited variation.

1½ cups cottage cheese with chives
2 tablespoons mayonnaise
3 tablespoons California Sauterne or
other white table wine
1 teaspoon each lemon and onion juice
¼ teaspoon Worcestershire sauce
Dash garlic powder
Salt and pepper to taste
1 (7½-oz.) can minced clams, well drained

In blender combine all ingredients except clams; whirl briefly to blend and smooth. Taste, and adjust seasonings. Fold in minced clams. Serve with potato chips or crisp crackers.

To accompany this dip: **California Dry** *or* **Medium Sherry** *or* **Dry Vermouth** *over ice*

Hot Cheese and Sauterne Dip

(1⅔ cups)

This smooth and golden combination really does have a zippy flavor, imparted to the cheese mixture by a packaged horseradish dip mix and a little red pepper sauce. The California Sauterne adds its share of subtle flavor and, of course, blends it all together.

    ½ pound (about 2 cups) shredded process
        American cheese
    ⅓ cup milk
    1 (⅜-oz.) package horseradish dip mix
    3 tablespoons California Medium Sauterne
    ¼ teaspoon red pepper sauce

Mix all ingredients in small saucepan. Place over low heat and cook until cheese melts and mixture smooths, stirring constantly. Serve hot with tortilla chips or crackers.

To accompany this hors d'oeuvre: **California Medium Sherry**

Ham and Cheese Spread: A delicious compliment to thin slices of rye bread is a wine-flavored ham and cheese spread. Combine equal portions of deviled ham and cream cheese. Moisten to spreading consistency with California Sauterne or other white table wine.

Swiss Dip Sonoma

(3½ cups)

If you are searching for a creamy, wine-flavored dip, one that will be relatively inexpensive to put before a group of hearty eaters, consider this one. The mixture goes together easily and is served hot with small pieces of garlic-buttered and toasted French bread.

    1 (10½-oz.) can condensed cream of mushroom soup
    1 tablespoon flour
    1 pound (about 4 cups) shredded process Swiss cheese
    ⅓ cup evaporated milk
    ¼ cup California Sauterne or other white table wine
    4 drops red pepper sauce

In medium saucepan, mix soup and flour; stir in cheese, evaporated milk, Sauterne and red pepper sauce. Cook and stir over low heat until cheese melts and mixture is thick enough for dipping, about 10 minutes. Pour into serving bowl, sprinkle with parsley flakes or paprika.

To accompany this hors d'oeuvre: **California Dry Sauterne** *or* **Dry Sherry** *or a* **Riesling** *in the Swiss Fondue tradition*

Surprise Puffs

(16 to 18 servings)

You will know there's a stuffed green olive inside each one of these crisp little cheese puffs, but your guests will be delighted by the unexpected when they take a bite.

    3 tablespoons California Dry Sherry
    1 cup grated process Cheddar cheese
    2 tablespoons melted butter or margarine
    ½ cup all-purpose flour
    1 teaspoon dry mustard
        Dash cayenne
    1 (3-oz.) jar pimiento stuffed olives

Combine Sherry with all ingredients, except olives. Pat mixture around each drained olive to cover completely. Arrange on lightly greased baking sheet and bake in hot oven (400°) 10 minutes. Serve at once.

To accompany this appetizer: **California Dry Sherry** *or* **California Champagne Punch,** *page 13*

Rumaki

(About 36 appetizers)

Here is something quite different, and because it tastes so good, well worth trying. Remember to cook the chicken livers briefly and gently, until they are still a bit pink on the inside. If it is inconvenient to use the broiler, bake the little bacon wrapups in a hot oven (400°) for 20 to 25 minutes.

    ½ pound chicken livers, fresh or frozen
    2 tablespoons butter or margarine
    2 (5-oz.) cans water chestnuts
    ½ pound sliced bacon

    1 cup California Medium Sauterne or
        other white table wine
    ¼ cup soy sauce
    ¼ cup water
    ½ teaspoon powdered ginger

Cook chicken livers slowly in butter for 5 minutes; cut into quarters. Slice water chestnuts into two pieces. Cut each bacon strip across in half and wrap around liver and water chestnut pieces; secure with toothpick. Prepare sauce by combining Sauterne with soy sauce, water and ginger; marinate bacon wrapups in mixture for at least an hour. Broil about 3 inches from source of heat, turning as necessary, until browned.

To accompany this appetizer: **California Champagne** *or* **Dry Sherry** *or a wine cooler (half red or white table wine, half soda over ice)*

Savory Appetizer Pastries

(4 to 5 dozen pastries)

Use these crisp pastries plain, or spread them with your favorite mixtures when you want something to go with a glass of wine for an afternoon or evening snack. As a variation, sprinkle pastries with sesame or poppy seeds before baking.

    1 (9½-oz.) package pie crust mix
    1 (2¼-oz.) can deviled ham or liver paté
    2 or 3 tablespoons California Sauterne or other white table wine

Turn pie crust mix into mixing bowl; add deviled ham or liver paté and wine and mix lightly but thoroughly. Roll out on floured board to about ⅛-inch thickness. Cut into 2-inch rounds or 4 x 1-inch strips. Bake on ungreased baking sheets in very hot oven (450°) 8 to 10 minutes or until lightly browned. Cool before storing.

To accompany these pastries: **California Champagne** *or* **Medium Sherry** *Note: Port goes well with these pastries for an evening snack*

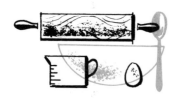

California Fruit Cocktail

(6 servings)

A good beginning to the meal is this combination of fruits, made interesting and unusual with California Port and currant jelly. Allow time for the fruit to absorb the wine flavor and for a thorough chilling.

    ½ cup California Port
    ¼ cup currant jelly
    1 tablespoon lemon juice
    Dash of salt
    1 cup pitted canned Royal Anne cherries
    1 cup pineapple tidbits
    1 cup diced orange sections

Heat Port to simmering; add jelly and stir until melted. Remove from heat, add lemon juice and salt. Cool. Combine fruits, well drained, in bowl and pour on wine mixture. Cover and chill several hours. To serve, heap fruit in sherbet glasses or dessert dishes and spoon some of the wine mixture over the top.

To accompany this fruit appetizer: **California Champagne** *or* **Rosé**

Anchovy Cheese Spread

(1½ cups)

It's simple to make but a delight to all who spread it on crisp crackers or buffet rye bread. If time allows, chill the mixture well for several hours to allow the flavors to blend, but allow to warm up slightly before serving.

    1 (2-oz.) can anchovies, drained
    2 (8-oz.) packages cream cheese
    ¼ cup California Dry Sherry
    2 tablespoons finely chopped stuffed green olives

Mash drained anchovies. Soften cheese and blend into fish. Beat in Sherry until mixture is smooth. Add olives. Cover and chill several hours to blend flavors. To serve, pile into bowl and place bowl in cracked ice, if desired. Garnish spread with strips of anchovy and pimiento and top with a stuffed green olive. Or, sprinkle with finely chopped green onion or sieved hard-cooked egg.

To accompany this spread: **California Dry Sherry** *or* **Rosé Lemonade,** *page 15*

Savory Mushrooms Hors d'Oeuvre

(10 to 15 servings)

If you haven't tried these very good mushrooms frozen in butter sauce, now is the time. Easy and quick for a special tidbit, the mushrooms are simply heated in their own sauce with the addition of California Dry Sherry and soy sauce. Serve them warm, of course, with your before-dinner glass of wine.

    2 (6-oz.) packages whole mushrooms frozen in butter sauce
    ¼ cup California Dry Sherry
    1 teaspoon soy sauce

Remove frozen mushrooms from pouches, place in saucepan, cover and place over high heat for 5 minutes. Remove cover from pan, reduce heat and add wine and soy sauce. Continue cooking, tossing mushrooms lightly with fork until liquid is absorbed and mushrooms are golden brown.

To accompany this hors d'oeuvre: **California Champagne, Dry Sherry** *or* **Dry** *or* **Sweet Vermouth**

Mock Paté De Foie Gras: This is somewhat like the famous spread, and certainly very smooth and good to eat, spread on crisp crackers or rounds of toast. It's good as a dipping mixture, if you thin it slightly with California Sherry. Remove casing from ½ pound liverwurst; place in bowl with contents 1 (3-oz.) package cream cheese and mash with fork; add 1 tablespoon mayonnaise, ¼ cup Sherry, a dash of onion salt and a dash of cayenne; beat until well blended.

SOUPS

Today's soup story is a very simple one of opening cans and pack-aged dry mixes for a quick preparation of steaming hot goodness and nourishment. In this way we can prepare in a few minutes soups that at one time took hours to make. Because most of them require the addition of some liquid to dilute them, it is easy to enhance them with wine. In many homes—and a few specialty restaurants—a shaker of Sherry is brought to the table to allow each person to add additional flavor. No matter which wine has previously been added during the cooking or heating, a few drops of Sherry provide a pleasant accent.

Rosy Shrimp Chowder
(5 servings)

A rather elegant chowder is this one with its care-fully selected vegetable flavors and light seasonings all blended together with California Rhine Wine or other white table wine. The bouillon cube may be omitted if desired.

       2 tablespoons butter or margarine
    ¼ cup each chopped onion, green pepper
    ½ cup chopped celery
       1 (1-lb.) can whole peeled tomatoes
    ½ teaspoon salt
    ⅛ teaspoon each pepper, garlic powder, crushed oregano
       1 chicken bouillon cube, crushed
    1½ cups water
       1 cup California Rhine wine or other white table wine
       1 (4-oz.) can deveined shrimp

Melt butter or margarine in saucepan; add onion, green pepper and celery and cook until just soft, but not brown. Add tomatoes, salt and seasonings, bouillon cube and water. Bring to boil, then cover pan, lower heat and simmer soup gently for about 20 minutes. Add wine and undrained shrimp; simmer 10 minutes longer before serving.

To accompany this soup: **California Dry Sauterne, Chablis** *or* **Rosé**

Fisherman's Wharf Special
(6 servings)

This soup is designed as the main attraction for a luncheon, or as a quick put-together for those com-ing in from the cold. Serve it with bread sticks or sturdy thick slices of buttered and heated sour dough French bread. A word about the curry—the strength of this spice varies, so try a small amount and add according to your wishes.

    ½ cup California Dry Sherry
       1 cup each crabmeat and shrimp
       1 (11½-oz.) can condensed pea soup
       1 (10½-oz.) can condensed tomato soup
    ¼ teaspoon curry powder
    1½ cups rich milk
       2 tablespoons very finely chopped parsley

Pour wine over crab and shrimp in bowl; let stand while heating soups. In saucepan combine pea and tomato soups; sprinkle with curry powder. Place over low heat and gradually stir in rich milk; con-tinue stirring until smooth. Add fish; check season-ings, especially for curry and salt content, then let stand for a few minutes for flavors to blend. Serve with a light sprinkling of very fine parsley.

To accompany this soup: **California Dry Sherry** *or* **Chablis**

Potato Soup with Sauterne
(5 to 6 servings)

No one would dream you could come up with a creamy potato soup like this in a minimum amount of time. Instant potato flakes is the answer in part, plus California Sauterne and a judicious blending of seasonings from your spice cabinet. Designed to be served quite cold, this soup is delicious too when piping hot.

  1½ cups water
   2 chicken bouillon cubes
  ½ teaspoon salt
  ⅛ teaspoon each garlic and onion powders, pepper
  ½ cup cold milk
  ½ (5⅝-oz.) package (1⅓ cups) instant whipped potatoes
   1 cup California Dry Sauterne or
     other dry white table wine
  1½ cups heavy cream
   2 tablespoons butter
   3 tablespoons finely chopped green onion

In a saucepan heat to boiling, water, bouillon cubes and seasonings. Stir in milk and instant potato flakes, stirring until smooth. Blend in Sauterne, cream and butter. Simmer gently for about 15 minutes to blend flavors. Remove from heat, cool, then chill thoroughly. Serve topped with chopped green onion. If desired, soup may be thinned with a little cream or rich milk.

To accompany this soup: **California Sauterne**

Cheese and Bacon Soup
(4 servings)

Here is a very simple soup, golden in color, easy to prepare and made noteworthy by a few quick additions such as white table wine, seasonings and bits of bacon.

   1 (10¾-oz.) can condensed Cheddar cheese soup
  ½ cup water
  ½ cup California Dry Sauterne, Chablis
     or other white table wine
  ¼ cup finely chopped green pepper
  ¼ cup finely chopped onion
  ⅛ teaspoon dried dill
   2 slices bacon

In saucepan, combine cheese soup with water and wine, stirring until smooth. Add green pepper, onion and dill. Cover and simmer over low heat 10 to 15 minutes until pepper is tender. Meanwhile, sauté bacon until crisp; drain well and crumble. Serve soup piping hot, topped with bacon.

To accompany this soup: **California Dry Sherry, Dry Sauterne, Chablis** *or* **Johannisberger Riesling**

Spanish Green Pea Soup
(3 servings)

Be grateful to those geniuses who created canned soups. Think of all that flavor condensed in a can. Here green pea soup takes on a special air with a simple addition of bacon bits and a welcome amount of California Dry Sherry. Black bean soup may be used this way too.

   1 (11½-oz.) can condensed green pea or black bean soup
   1 soup can water
   3 slices bacon
   2 tablespoons California Dry Sherry
  ½ cup hot, cooked rice

Empty soup into saucepan; gradually add water, stirring until smooth; heat. Cook bacon until crisp; remove. Add bacon fat to soup; mix well. Just before serving, stir in Sherry. Toss crumbled bacon with rice. Ladle soup into bowls and put a mound of bacon-rice mixture in each.

To accompany this soup: **California Dry Sherry, Dry Sauterne** *or* **Chablis**

California Green Pea Soup
(4 servings)

Often in this world of cookery we find that a little experimenting with a regular method of preparation leads to something downright delicious. Take pea soup, for instance, by adding a little California white table wine and some bits of cooked ham we have a "Class A" gourmet product.

  ½ cup finely chopped ham or luncheon meat
   2 tablespoons butter or margarine
  ½ cup California Dry Sauterne, Chablis
     or other white table wine
   1 (11½-oz.) can condensed green pea soup
   1 soup can milk

Sauté ham or luncheon meat in butter just until lightly browned. Add wine, soup and milk, stirring until mixture is blended. Simmer slowly, about 5 minutes; serve immediately.

To accompany this soup: **California Dry Sauterne, Chablis** *or* **Grey Riesling**

Potage Boula

(6 servings)

This delicately colored pea soup is full of bold garden-fresh flavor. Use the amount of California Dry Sherry you like best in the soup. Add the small amount first, then add more to suit your taste.

    2 (8½-oz.) or 1 (17-oz.) cans small early peas
      Drained liquid from peas
    1 (13-oz.) can consomme
    2 tablespoons butter or margarine
    2 to 4 tablespoons California Dry Sherry
      Heavy cream, whipped

Puree peas in blender or with fine strainer. In saucepan combine puree with drained liquid from peas, consomme and butter; heat to boiling point. Stir in Sherry and serve at once topped with spoonful of whipped cream.

To accompany this soup: **California Dry Sherry, Dry Sauterne** *or* **Semillon**

Onion Soup Sauterne

(4 to 5 servings)

This creamy onion soup is delightfully different. It's especially nice to make if you have an electric blender to whirl it to smoothness.

    1 (No. 2) can whole white onions, undrained
    1 (10½-oz.) can condensed cream of celery soup
    1 (10½-oz.) can condensed cream of chicken soup
    1 cup rich milk or evaporated milk
    ½ cup California Sauterne or other white table wine
    2 tablespoons grated American cheese
    2 tablespoons minced parsley

In saucepan combine onions, soups and milk. Place over heat and bring to boil, stirring occasionally; cover pan and simmer gently for 10 minutes. Cool slightly and whirl in blender or force through sieve or food mill. Add Sauterne, cheese and parsley; heat thoroughly and pour into heated soup bowls or cups and garnish with croutons.

To accompany this soup: **California Dry Sherry, Dry Sauterne,** *or* **Pinot Chardonnay**

Quick Minestrone with Wine

(6 servings)

There's such substantial nourishment in this delicious main-dish soup that you will want to keep a good supply of the makings for regular appearances. While the soup is heating, make toasty pieces of French bread, sprinkled with cheese, and provide a tossed green salad. Dinner is then ready to be served.

    1 (11½-oz.) can condensed bean soup
    1 (10½-oz.) can condensed vegetable-beef soup
    1 (No. 303) can solid pack tomatoes
    ¾ cup California Burgundy or Claret or
      other red table wine
    ½ cup water
    ¼ teaspoon dried basil
      Salt to taste

Combine all ingredients in saucepan and bring to boil slowly, over gentle heat. Cover pan and simmer, stirring occasionally, for about 15 minutes. Pour into heated soup bowls and serve with a little grated Parmesan cheese drifted over the top.

To accompany this soup: **California Burgundy** *or* **Claret**

Hearty Cold Chicken Soup

(6 servings)

Although no special cookery skill is needed to put this soup together, it does take a little time to assemble the ingredients and carry on the cooking over boiling water. This method is used to protect the delicate texture and flavor of the soup ingredients. Made ahead of time, the soup profits by refrigeration. Serve it icy cold with hot biscuits to make a fine summertime meal.

    1⅓ cups instant nonfat dry milk
    3½ cups water
    2 tablespoons instant tapioca
    2 chicken bouillon cubes
    ½ cup finely chopped celery
    1 tablespoon sweet pepper flakes
    ½ teaspoon minced onion
    2 tablespoons finely chopped carrot
    ¼ teaspoon curry powder
      Freshly ground pepper
    2 drops bitters
    2 cups coarsely cut cooked chicken
    1 (4-oz.) can sliced mushrooms, drained
    ¼ cup California Dry Sherry

In top of double boiler, combine nonfat dry milk and water; stir until blended. Add tapioca, bouillon cubes, vegetables and seasonings; cook over boiling water until vegetables are tender. Add chicken and mushrooms; heat thoroughly. Remove from heat; cool. Stir in Sherry. Refrigerate until icy cold.

To accompany this soup: **California Dry Sauterne** *or* **Chablis**

Corn and Seafood Chowder

(4 to 5 servings)

Rugged individualists who demand their chowder in the pure form, made from the kettle up, will probably succumb to this delightful from-the-can short-cut. Heat it with California Sauterne and see. The chowder may be enriched with cooked vegetables such as canned mixed vegetables, carrots, green beans or peas.

1 (1-lb. 1-oz.) can yellow cream style corn
1 (10½-oz.) can condensed cream of potato soup
1 (7½-oz.) can minced or chopped clams
1 (10-oz.) can whole oysters
½ cup California Dry Sauterne or other white table wine
2 cups milk
Salt and pepper

Combine all ingredients in a large kettle. Heat slowly, stirring now and then to simmering. Chowder can be thinned with a little additional wine or milk. Serve hot in generous bowls.

To accompany this soup: **California Sauterne, Chablis** *or* **Rhine Wine**

City Kitchen Chowder

(4 to 6 servings)

Created to be enjoyed just as much in suburbia as in the city is this full meal chowder. It is guaranteed to satisfy the appetite of the hungry and delight the gourmet in his search for perfection. If the soup seems a little thick, thin it with either additional wine or cream.

1 (10½-oz.) can condensed tomato soup
1 (10½-oz.) can condensed cream of mushroom soup
½ cup California Chablis, Sauterne or other white table wine
½ cup milk or cream
1 (7½-oz.) can minced clams
1 (10-oz.) can whole oysters
1 tablespoon toasted instant minced onion
Frozen chives or parsley sprigs

Blend soups with wine and milk or cream until smooth. Add undrained clams and oysters and onion. Heat slowly until piping hot. Garnish with frozen chives or parsley sprigs; serve with oyster crackers.

To accompany this soup: **California Dry Sauterne, Chablis** *or* **Rhine Wine**

Chicken Mushroom Soup Supreme

(4 to 5 servings)

Disarmingly simple to make, this soup turns out to be quite impressive for almost any luncheon or dinner. For a gourmet touch, float two or three button mushrooms on top of each serving as a garnish.

1 (10½-oz.) can condensed mushroom soup
1 (10½-oz.) can condensed chicken soup with rice
1 cup rich milk or evaporated milk
⅓ cup California Rhine, Sauterne, Chablis or other white table wine
2 tablespoons minced parsley
Celery salt and pepper to taste

Combine soups, milk and wine; heat to boiling, stirring to blend well. Add parsley and seasonings. Pour into heated soup bowls or cups.

To accompany this soup: **California Dry Sherry, Chablis** *or the same white table wine used in the soup*

Sunday Night Shrimp-Crab Soup

(4 to 6 servings)

For an intimate Sunday night supper you can't do much better than a carefully prepared soup, served perhaps from a lovely old tureen and accompanied by some special crackers or small hard rolls. To garnish the soup, cut cream cheese into ½-inch cubes, then coat with very finely chopped parsley.

1 (10-oz.) can frozen shrimp soup
1 (10½-oz.) can condensed mushroom soup
1 cup instant nonfat dry milk
1¼ cups water
1 cup chopped fresh, frozen or canned crabmeat
¼ cup California Dry Sherry

In medium saucepan combine frozen shrimp soup and mushroom soup. Blend instant nonfat dry milk with water until smooth, then add to soups. Remove and discard any boney tissue from crabmeat, then add. Heat thoroughly and just before serving stir in Sherry.

To accompany this soup: **California Chablis** *or* **Riesling**

Chicken Curry Soup: Follow recipe for Sunday Night Shrimp-Crab Soup using 1 (10½-oz.) can condensed cream of chicken soup instead of the frozen shrimp soup. Add 1 cup chopped cooked chicken instead of crabmeat. Season with ½ to 1 teaspoon curry powder (try a small amount first, then taste), and add the Sherry just before serving.

To accompany this soup: **California Dry Sherry** *or a white table wine such as* **Dry Sauterne, Chablis** *or* **Riesling**

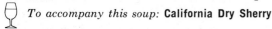

Sherried Avocado Consomme
(5 to 6 servings)

Give brightness to the first course of a luncheon with this consomme, lightly touched with California Sherry and bearing finely diced avocado floating on its surface.

    2 (10½-oz.) cans condensed consomme
    1⅓ cups water
    ¼ cup California Sherry
    2 tablespoons chopped parsley
    Salt and pepper to taste
    1 medium avocado, peeled and diced very fine

Heat consomme and water to boiling point; add wine and parsley; taste and adjust seasoning with salt and pepper. Remove from heat and add diced avocado. Pour at once into heated bouillon cups.

To accompany this soup: **California Dry Sherry**

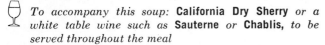

Quick Clam Bisque
(4 servings)

Use this quick bisque to fill out a meal that may not seem quite enough for hearty fare. Or perhaps use it in warm weather for the one hot dish with a full meal salad.

    1 (7-oz.) can minced clams
    2 tablespoons butter or margarine
    1 (10½-oz.) can condensed cream of chicken soup
    1 cup light cream
    ¼ cup California Sauterne or other white table wine
    2 tablespoons finely chopped parsley

Combine undrained clams, butter, soup, cream and wine. Heat, stirring, until smooth and piping hot. Serve garnished with parsley.

To accompany this soup: **California Dry Sherry** *or a white table wine such as* **Sauterne** *or* **Chablis**, *to be served throughout the meal*

Sherried Clam Soup
(4 servings)

Use this clam soup in thin cups for a luncheon with salad, or serve it in sturdy bowls for fireside nourishment in a ski lodge. In saucepan stir together contents 1 (10½-oz.) can condensed celery soup, 1 soup can milk and 1 (7-oz.) can minced clams, undrained. Bring to gentle boil, then remove from heat. Just before serving, add ½ cup California Medium or Dry Sherry. Garnish with freeze-dried chives or garlic croutons, if desired.

Mushroom-Asparagus Soup
(3 to 4 servings)

Combinations of good canned soups are almost endless and always pleasing to the taste; especially when sparked as this one is, with California Dry Sauterne. In saucepan combine contents 1 (10½-oz.) can condensed mushroom soup, 1 (10½-oz.) can condensed asparagus soup, 1⅓ cups rich milk, ½ cup California Sauterne or other white table wine and 3 tablespoons grated Parmesan cheese. Heat just to simmering; pour into heated soup bowls or cups and sprinkle with paprika.

Borsch Burgundy
(5 to 6 servings)

This is a hot beet soup, made robust with California Burgundy or Claret. Drain 1 (No. 2) can beets, reserving liquid; chop beets very fine. In saucepan combine chopped beets and liquid, 2 (10½-oz.) cans condensed consomme, ½ cup California Burgundy or Claret, 1 tablespoon lemon juice and 1 tablespoon grated onion; heat to simmering. Add salt to taste. Pour into heated bowls or cups. Top each serving with a generous spoonful of dairy sour cream and sprinkle with finely chopped dill pickle.

Sherried Black Bean Onion Soup
(3 to 4 servings)

The title explains the combination of the soup, but it can't give you any idea of its wonderful flavor. It tastes as if it has been simmering on the back of the range for hours. For the onion soup use homemade, canned or one prepared from a dehydrated mix.

    1 (10½-oz.) can condensed black bean soup
    1½ cups onion soup
    ⅓ cup California Dry Sherry

In a saucepan combine all ingredients, stirring to blend well. Place over heat and bring to simmering. Taste and add salt if needed. Serve very hot in heated soup bowls or cups. Garnish each serving with a thin slice of hard-cooked egg and a thin slice of lemon.

To accompany this soup: **California Dry Sherry, Sauterne** *or* **Traminer**

Bayou Seafood Gumbo
(6 to 8 servings)

We would be the first to agree that the method of making this gumbo is entirely unorthodox; it's too easy. But it does make a delicious soup that tastes like the genuine article, and that's what counts. The small amount of California Dry Sherry added at the very last points up the flavor.

- ⅓ cup chopped onion
- 2 tablespoons butter or margarine
- 2 (5-oz.) cans shrimp
- 1 (10½-oz.) can condensed tomato soup
- 2 (10½-oz.) cans condensed Manhattan clam chowder
- 1½ cups canned clam juice or chicken broth
- 1 (7-oz.) can crab meat
- 1 (1-lb.) can cut okra
- ¼ cup California Dry Sherry
- 3 to 4 cups hot, cooked rice

In large saucepan sauté onion in butter until tender. Drain and rinse shrimp in cold water. Add shrimp, tomato soup, clam chowder, clam juice and crab meat to onion. Heat almost to boiling. Add okra with the liquid from it; bring to boil. Reduce heat and simmer gently 10 minutes. Add Sherry just before serving. To serve, mound ½ cup rice in center of each flat soup plate. Pour gumbo around rice.

To accompany this gumbo: **California Dry Sauterne** *or* **Chablis**

Consomme with Sherry
(4 servings)

It's a pleasant custom, when serving broth or any other soup to have a bottle of California Sherry on the table, so that each person may add an extra portion to suit his taste. In saucepan, heat 2¼ cups consomme (use diluted canned consomme or chicken broth or bouillon cubes with water) to boiling point. Put about ½ tablespoon Sherry into each soup bowl or cup; pour in hot broth and serve at once.

Sherried Cheese Soup
(4 servings)

California Dry Sherry blends its good flavor with cheese soup to make this highly nourishing fare. Blend ¼ cup Sherry, contents 1 (11½-oz.) can Cheddar cheese soup and 1 cup thin cream in saucepan. Heat slowly, stirring now and then. Meanwhile, stir together lightly, ½ cup dairy sour cream, ⅛ teaspoon celery seed and 1 tablespoon finely chopped parsley. When ready to serve, portion soup into heated cups and float a spoonful of the cream on each serving.

MEATS

 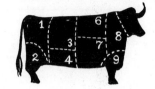 

Historians speculate that wine cookery began centuries ago, because meats were poor to start with and rapidly became less good if they were allowed to stand even a short time before cooking and eating. What originated with necessity has been continued over the years for the sake of enjoyment. Nowadays, the better the meat, the more likely it is that a good cook will choose it to make a wine-flavored specialty. As the meat moves from the kitchen to the dining room, so does the wine. The wine beverage suggestions in this chapter are both traditional and innovative. It is logical that a bottle of table wine, opened before dinner to flavor the food, will be served also as the mealtime beverage. But the wine choices for both the recipe and the beverage are flexible, a matter of personal preference. The suggestions listed after each recipe may point the way to new and interesting wine and food combinations.

Santa Clara Pot Roast
(6 to 8 servings)

The red wine, California Burgundy, works magic with a packaged onion soup mix, making a simple pot roast into a dinner special. It's very easy to do with little or no attention from the cook.

- ½ cup California Burgundy or other red table wine
- ½ package onion soup mix
- 1 3½- to 4-pound boneless beef brisket
  Large square heavy duty foil

Measure wine into cup; stir in soup mix. Place meat in center of foil and set in shallow roasting pan. Pour wine mixture over meat, then wrap foil around it to make a tight package. Place in slow oven (325°) for an hour per pound of meat (3½ to 4 hours). To serve, transfer meat to heated platter; pour meat juices into pan and thicken for gravy or serve as is. Slice brisket across the grain in thin portions.

To accompany this pot roast: **California Charbono, Burgundy** *or* **Claret**

Chili Burgundies
(4 servings)

Deliciously filling are these hamburgers, topped with a generous portion of chili beans and simmered briefly in California Burgundy. A whole meal, when served on toasted hamburger buns with a tossed green salad and accompanied by wine.

- 1 pound ground beef
- 1 tablespoon shortening
- 2 (15-oz.) cans chili con carne with beans
- ⅔ cup California Burgundy or other red table wine
- 2 hamburger buns, halved, toasted and buttered

Shape beef into 4 flat patties the same size as the hamburger buns; brown well on both sides in shortening. Heat chili con carne to boiling; stir in Burgundy. Pour chili mixture over browned meat patties; cover and simmer for 5 minutes. To serve, place a bun half on each plate; top with meat; pour chili mixture over all.

To accompany these hamburgers: **California Burgundy** *or* **Barbera**

Delicious and Easy Pot Roast
(8 to 10 servings)

No watching is needed for this simple and easy-to-make oven main dish. The inexperienced cook will love it for the confidence it is bound to give her in creating tender meat and excellent sauce or gravy.

> 4-pound pot roast, boned and rolled
> 1 small clove garlic, crushed
> 1 teaspoon salt
> Freshly ground pepper
> ¼ cup California Burgundy or other red table wine
> New potatoes
> Small tender carrots

Rub the pot roast with garlic, salt and pepper. Set in center of large sheet heavy duty foil; place in shallow baking pan. Slide under broiler and brown meat turning to brown on all sides. Remove from broiler; pour on Burgundy. Close foil to make a tight package; bake in moderate oven (350°) 2½ to 3 hours. About 1¼ hours before the pot roast is finished, place well scrubbed new potatoes and scraped carrots on heavy duty foil. Brush them well with melted butter or margarine and season to taste; close package and place in oven beside meat. Bake 1 to 1¼ hours longer. Open one end of foil and carefully pour juices into a saucepan. Skim off and discard fat. Thicken juices if desired, adding a little more seasoning to taste. Place roast on heated platter and border with vegetables. Serve sauce separately.

To accompany this dish: **California Burgundy** *or* **Gamay**

Savory Swiss Steak
(4 servings)

California red table wine and a packaged soup mix make it easy to give this traditional favorite a zesty, new flavor.

> 2 pounds beef chuck, bottom round or rump
> cut for Swiss steak (about 1 inch thick)
> 2 tablespoons oil
> 1 (1⅜-oz.) package dry onion soup mix
> 1 (8-oz.) can tomato sauce
> ¾ cup California Burgundy, Claret or
> other red table wine

In a heavy skillet brown meat in oil. Blend onion soup mix, tomato sauce and wine, and pour over browned meat. Cover and simmer until tender, about one hour.

To accompany this meat: **California Barbera** *or* **Claret**

Marinated Roast Beef
(6 to 8 servings)

This specialty of the kitchen has a big bold flavor—just right to serve generously with parslied noodles.

> ¾ cup chopped celery tips and leaves
> ⅔ cup chopped onions
> ½ cup chopped green pepper
> 2 envelopes garlic salad dressing mix
> 1 cup California Burgundy or other red table wine
> ½ cup salad oil
> ⅓ cup wine vinegar
> 1 tablespoon Worcestershire sauce
> 1 4-pound top round steak

To make marinade, combine all ingredients but meat and mix well. Pour over meat and allow to marinate in refrigerator 12 to 24 hours, turning meat occasionally. Place roast on rack in pan and pour on marinade. Roast in moderate oven (325°) 1½ to 2 hours, or until done, basting occasionally. If desired, serve with Barbecue Sauce.

For 6-pound blade bone chuck roast, allow 2 to 2½ hours for cooking. Even a 12-pound roast may be marinated in this quantity of marinade when placed in a large shallow pan.

To accompany this roast beef: **California Burgundy** *or* **Pinot Noir**

Jiffy Beef Bourguigonne
(6 servings)

When you have drop-in company and they stay for dinner, the best chef in the world couldn't make this high-style beef stew any faster than you can in your own kitchen; provided of course you have been forehanded enough to keep a well-stocked emergency shelf. California Burgundy gives a distinctive flavor to this dish.

> 4 ounces uncooked noodles
> 1 (4-oz.) can mushrooms
> ½ cup California Burgundy
> 2 (1-lb.) cans beef stew
> 1 (3½-oz.) can French fried onions
> ¼ teaspoon thyme
> ¼ teaspoon pepper
> ½ bay leaf

Cook noodles following package directions. Pour liquid from mushrooms; combine with beef stew, wine and remaining ingredients, except noodles. Simmer about 10 minutes to blend flavors. Remove bay leaf. Serve beef stew surrounded by hot drained noodles.

To accompany this beef stew: **California Burgundy**

Barbecued Chuck Roast

(5 to 6 servings)

½ cup California Burgundy or other red table wine
½ cup salad oil
  Juice of 1 lemon
1 tablespoon soy sauce
2 tablespoons Worcestershire sauce
¼ teaspoon dry mustard
2 small cloves garlic, crushed
1 4- to 5-pound chuck roast

Combine all ingredients for the marinade and pour over chuck roast; cover and place in refrigerator 12 to 24 hours. Turn several times. Remove meat from refrigerator about an hour before barbecuing. When coals are ready, place roast on grill and cook slowly, about 20 to 25 minutes on each side. Brush frequently with remaining marinade. Carve in thin slices across the grain of the meat.

To accompany this barbecued roast: **California Burgundy** *or* **Pinot Noir**

Pepper Steaks with Sherried Sauce

(4 servings)

If you like the sharp bite of good black pepper, try these quick-cooking minute steaks. Pepper may be pressed into hamburger patties too.

4 minute steaks, cut from beef round
2 teaspoons cracked black pepper
  Salt
¼ cup coarsely chopped suet
¼ cup California Dry Sherry
½ cup water
½ (⅞-oz.) package quick brown gravy mix

Lay minute steaks on waxed paper; sprinkle each with about ¼ teaspoon of the black pepper; press down with flat side of heavy knife or spatula; turn steaks over and pepper second side. Salt lightly.

In a heavy skillet brown chopped suet bits; pour off all but about 1 tablespoon of the accumulated fat; take out suet bits and hold in reserve. Brown meat quickly on both sides; remove to hot serving platter. Return browned suet bits to pan; add Sherry, water and gravy mix, stirring well to blend. Bring to boil and let cook about 5 minutes. Pour over steaks and serve.

To accompany these pepper steaks: **California Pinot Noir** *or* **Burgundy**

Gourmet Corned Beef

(10 servings)

The long cooking time for corned beef is important; so why not simmer the meat in California Medium Sauterne, water and some interesting seasonings the evening before, then put on the finishing touches the next day. Serve the corned beef sliced cold, or reheat in the cooking liquid, or pat a coating of brown sugar and mustard over the surface and brown it in the oven, like ham. Baste with ¼ cup or more Sauterne.

1 4- to 5-pound corned beef brisket or rump
2½ quarts water
2 cups California Medium Sauterne or other white table wine
½ cup finely chopped onion
⅛ teaspoon garlic powder
1 teaspoon dried dill
2 stalks celery
2 bay leaves
1 small orange, sliced
1 stick cinnamon
3 whole cloves
2 or 3 drops red pepper sauce

Cover corned beef completely with cold water; bring to boil and simmer ½ hour. Discard this cooking water. Add the 2½ quarts water, Sauterne and all remaining ingredients. Cover and simmer until meat is tender, about 3 hours. Allow beef to cool in liquid if not to be served hot.

To accompany this corned beef: **California Burgundy** *or* **Zinfandel**

Green Pepper Hamburgers

(6 servings)

Lots and lots of bright green pepper strips in an interesting wine and soy sauce make plain meat patties into something to make the family sit up and take notice of at the dinner table. Serve them with crisp Chinese noodles.

2 pounds ground beef
¼ cup oil
¼ cup California Dry Sherry
⅓ cup water
¼ cup soy sauce
1 tablespoon cornstarch
2 teaspoons sugar
4 medium green peppers, cut in strips

Shape ground beef into 6 oval patties. In a large skillet heat oil. Brown meat patties lightly on both sides. Combine Sherry, water, soy sauce, cornstarch and sugar; pour over meat. Add green peppers. Cover and simmer for 10–15 minutes, or until meat is done.

To accompany this dish: **California Gamay** *or* **Cabernet**

Savory Soup Stew
(6 servings)

For a family supper dish, or an informal pot-luck invitation, serve this hearty and flavorful stew.

        6 beef shanks (about 3½ pounds)
          Seasoned salt, dried dill, paprika
        2 or 3 tablespoons oil or drippings
     1½ cups water
        1 cup California Sauterne or other white table wine
       ⅓ cup finely chopped onion
        3 carrots, peeled and sliced
        3 stalks celery, sliced
        3 medium tomatoes, quartered
          Shredded Parmesan cheese

Season beef shanks well with salt, dill and paprika. Brown well in heated oil or drippings in deep kettle or Dutch oven. Add water, Sauterne and onion; cover and simmer about 1½ hours or until meat is almost tender. Add carrots and celery and continue cooking about 25 minutes; add tomatoes and cook 5 minutes longer. When beef and vegetables are tender, serve with surrounding liquid and Parmesan cheese.

To accompany this meat: **California Rosé, Mellow Red Vino Rosso** *or* **Sauterne**

Simple Swiss Steak
(5 to 6 servings)

This is a main meat dish that can be put together with ease and dispatch. The California Sauterne combines with the mushroom soup to make a cooking sauce that has a gourmet touch. Serve it with a light sprinkling of very finely chopped parsley.

        1 1½- to 2-pound thick top round steak
     1½ teaspoons salt
        1 medium onion
        1 tablespoon oil
        1 cup California Medium Sauterne or
          other white table wine
        1 (10½-oz.) can condensed cream of mushroom soup

Cut steak in serving size pieces and sprinkle with salt. Chop onion. Brown steak in oil slowly on both sides. Add onion and cook until transparent. Pour on Sauterne, cover and bake in moderate oven (350°) 1 hour. Add mushroom soup and continue cooking about 1 hour longer. Serve with fluffy white or brown rice.

To accompany this meat: **California Barbera, Burgundy** *or* **Sauterne**

California Beef Stew
(6 servings)

Be proud to serve this most attractive beef stew as a company dish. Make it a day ahead, then just before serving time, heat the stew and add ¼ cup more California Zinfandel. Turn it into a casserole or baker. Place mashed or duchess potatoes around the edge and set it under the broiler for a few minutes to brown evenly. When you make the stew, pay attention to the vegetables; they should look good as well as taste good.

        2 pounds stewing beef, cut in 1½-inch cubes
        1 tablespoon seasoned salt
       ½ teaspoon seasoned pepper
        1 bay leaf
        2 cups water
        1 cup California Zinfandel or other red table wine
        6 carrots, cut in 2-inch lengths
       12 small boiling onions, pierced with fork
        3 medium zucchini, cut in quarters
        2 large tomatoes, quartered
        2 tablespoons flour
       ¼ cup water

Brown beef cubes in small amount of shortening in heavy skillet or Dutch oven; sprinkle with seasoned salt and pepper. Add bay leaf, water and wine. Bring to a boil, reduce heat, cover tightly and simmer about 1 hour 15 minutes. Add carrots. About ten minutes later add onions and zucchini. Continue simmering until meat and vegetables are tender, about 20 minutes. Add tomatoes and thickening paste of flour and water. Combine carefully but thoroughly. Bring to a boil, reduce heat and simmer 2 to 3 minutes. Serve immediately.

To accompany this stew: **California Zinfandel** *or* **Chianti**

Claret Cranberry Jelly
(6 medium glasses)

California Claret has been used here for a special wine jelly, but there is no reason why California Pinot Noir couldn't be used too for a different flavor. These jellies are especially good with game and meats, and they are good with cheeses too.

     3½ cups sugar
        1 cup bottled cranberry juice cocktail
        1 cup California Claret
       ½ bottle fruit pectin

Measure all ingredients, except fruit pectin, into top of double boiler; mix well. Place over rapidly boiling water and stir until sugar is dissolved. Remove from heat. At once stir in fruit pectin and mix well. Skim off foam with metal spoon. Pour quickly into glasses. Cover at once with thin layer hot paraffin.

Beef Burgundy Flambé
(6 servings)

Richly flavored with carefully selected ingredients, this meat dish becomes most spectacular when it bursts into bright flames at the table. The California Brandy used is heated in the top of a small double boiler over hot water before it is poured onto the surface of the meat and lighted.

            2 slices bacon, cut up
            2 pounds sirloin tip steak, cut in bite-sized strips
            2 tablespoons flour
            1 teaspoon seasoned salt
            1 cup California Burgundy or other red table wine
            1 cup water
            1 package beef stew seasoning mix
           12 small boiling onions, ends pierced
           ¼ pound fresh mushrooms, sliced
           16 cherry tomatoes, stems removed
           ¼ cup California Brandy

In a heavy skillet fry bacon until crisp; add meat strips that have been coated with flour and seasoned salt; brown carefully. Pour in Burgundy and water; sprinkle on beef stew seasoning mix; stir. Cover pan tightly and simmer gently for about 45 minutes. Add onions and cook for 40 minutes longer, then add mushrooms and cherry tomatoes; simmer 5 minutes. Remove meat to shallow serving dish; pour heated California Brandy over top. Set aflame at table. Stir gently and serve immediately.

To accompany this dish: **California Burgundy** *or* **Pinot Noir**

Epicurean Beef Casserole
(6 servings)

For one of those days when you wish dinner would take care of itself, look to this casserole. Combine the beef chunks with California Burgundy and other ingredients and put it in the oven, then you are free until time to serve it with a large green salad and perhaps a fruit dessert.

            2 pounds beef chuck or
               stewing beef, cut in 2-inch chunks
            1 cup California Burgundy or other red table wine
            2 (10½-oz.) cans condensed consomme
           1½ teaspoons salt
           ¼ teaspoon pepper
            2 medium onions, sliced
           ½ cup fine dry bread crumbs
           ½ cup flour

Combine beef, wine, consomme, salt, pepper and onion in casserole. Mix crumbs with flour and stir into meat. Cover and bake in a slow oven (300°) about 3 hours, or until beef is tender.

To accompany this casserole: **California Burgundy** *or* **Claret**

Teriyaki Steaks
(6 servings)

Steak becomes tender and delicious when it is marinated in a special sauce like this one with California Sauterne. Cut the steak into individual servings before you add the marinade. The steak can be broiled this way, or cut into 1-inch strips and threaded on metal or wooden skewers before broiling.

            2 pounds top sirloin or sirloin tip steak,
               cut ½-inch thick or 6 rib-eye steaks
           ½ cup California Sauterne or other white table wine
            2 teaspoons powdered ginger or
               2 tablespoons chopped fresh ginger
            1 clove garlic, minced
            1 small onion, chopped
           ½ cup soy sauce
            1 fresh pineapple, cut in lengthwise wedges

Cut steak as desired. Combine Sauterne with ginger, garlic, onion and soy sauce; pour over meat and let stand, covered, in refrigerator overnight, or 6 to 8 hours at room temperature. Turn occasionally. Brush pineapple wedges with meat marinade and place them on broiler pan with meat. Broil about 5 minutes on each side. Good on barbecue grill too. Serve steaks with mounds of fluffy white rice and pineapple garnish.

To accompany this steak: **California Sauterne**, **Gamay** *or* **Zinfandel**

London Broil
(4 servings)

           ¼ cup California Dry Sherry
           ¼ cup salad oil
               Juice of 1 lemon
           ¼ cup soy sauce
            1 small clove garlic, minced
            1 flank steak, not scored

Prepare marinade by combining Sherry, oil, lemon juice, soy sauce, garlic and seasonings to taste. Pour over flank steak and refrigerate overnight. Turn several times. Before broiling, let meat stand at room temperature for at least an hour. With sharp knife slash edges of steak to prevent curling, and broil about 3 inches from the heat 5 to 6 minutes; turn and broil other side for 5 more minutes.

To accompany this steak: **California Burgundy** *or* **Cabernet Sauvignon**

Estofado de Vaco Espanola
(Spanish Beef Stew)
(4 servings)

Now in Spain good cooks start their stew making with beef, wine, and a careful balance of seasonings. Don't let the list of ingredients frighten you. Once assembled and in the pot, practically all you have to do is serve. You may want to double the recipe, for this stew really gains in flavor when reheated.

        3 slices bacon, diced
        1 pound beef chuck, cut in small cubes
        2 small cloves garlic, crushed
        1 large onion, sliced
       ¼ teaspoon each sage, marjoram
        1 small bay leaf, crumbled
       ½ teaspoon each paprika, curry powder
        3 medium tomatoes, peeled and diced
        2 tablespoons wine vinegar
       ¾ cup beef broth or bouillon
       ½ cup California Chablis or other white table wine
        1 teaspoon salt
       ⅓ cup sliced, pimiento-stuffed olives
        2 tablespoons chopped parsley
        4 medium potatoes, pared and quartered

Sauté bacon, garlic and onion in large heavy saucepan 5 minutes. Remove from pan. Put beef in pan and cook over low heat until browned on all sides. Return bacon, garlic and onion to pan; add seasonings, tomatoes, vinegar, broth, wine and salt. Cover tightly and cook over low heat 1 hour, stirring occasionally. Add remaining ingredients and continue cooking 40 minutes longer, stirring occasionally.

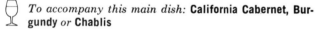 *To accompany this main dish:* **California Cabernet, Burgundy** *or* **Chablis**

Wine in Stew: Use California Burgundy wine not only as a mealtime beverage but as a cooking ingredient. Its full body and fine flavor make beef stew a superb dish. About 1 cup Burgundy wine added as part of the liquid is a good proportion for the average stew.

Cranberry Apple Wine Sherbet: To make an attractive meat accompaniment, one that is tart and refreshing, try this smooth and sassy one. In electric blender combine 1 (1-pound) can jellied cranberry sauce, 1 apple, peeled and sliced, and 1 cup California Port. Blend at high speed until smooth. Pour into refrigerator tray and freeze until firm.

Steak Colbert with Rice
(4 servings)

With all ingredients at hand these meat strips in a savory sauce can be prepared in record time. If a slightly thicker sauce is preferred, don't hesitate to stir in a small portion of cornstarch mixed with wine. Cook a few minutes more to clear.

    1½ pounds sirloin steak, cut in strips ⅛ inch thick
        3 tablespoons butter or margarine
        1 teaspoon salt
       ¼ teaspoon pepper
       ½ cup California Burgundy or other red table wine
        1 (10½-oz.) can beef bouillon
        1 (4-oz.) can mushroom stems and pieces, undrained
        1 (5-oz.) can water chestnuts, drained and sliced
        3 cups hot cooked rice

In a heavy pan sauté steak strips in butter until brown; season with salt and pepper. Add wine, bouillon, mushrooms including liquid, and water chestnuts. Cover and simmer until liquid is reduced to half and meat is tender, about 20 minutes. Serve over beds of hot fluffy rice.

To accompany this dish: **California Burgundy, Zinfandel** *or* **Claret**

Easy Stroganoff
(4 to 6 servings)

This is one of those dependable company or family meat dishes, prepared with little or no effort, and always received with great enthusiasm. The California Burgundy in the cooking sauce not only flavors but tenderizes the meat. Be sure to add the sour cream at the very last, and do not over heat it, as you want to keep a nice smooth sauce.

    1½ pounds top round steak, cut into narrow strips
       ¼ cup all-purpose flour
       ½ teaspoon salt
       ⅛ teaspoon pepper
       ¼ cup shortening, melted
        1 cup beef broth or bouillon
       ¼ cup chopped onion
        2 (2½-oz.) cans sliced mushrooms, undrained
        1 teaspoon Worcestershire sauce
       ½ cup California Burgundy or other red table wine
        1 cup dairy sour cream
           Hot buttered rice

Coat steak strips well in flour seasoned with salt and pepper. Brown in heated shortening in large heavy frying pan. Stir in Burgundy, broth, chopped onion, sliced mushrooms, and Worcestershire sauce. Simmer over low heat about 30 minutes or until meat is tender and sauce has thickened. Remove from heat; blend in sour cream. Heat thoroughly; do not boil. Season lightly with salt and pepper. Serve over buttered rice.

To accompany this dish: **California Burgundy** *or* **Rosé**

California Beef Balls
(6 servings)

Large generous beef balls are these, simmered in a creamy rich sauce carefully flavored with California Sauterne. To make them look more impressive, serve them in a rice ring. Add finely chopped parsley to hot fluffy rice; press lightly into a ring mold, then turn out on serving plate.

        1 pound ground chuck
        ¼ cup fine dry bread crumbs
        ⅔ cup chopped onion
        1 teaspoon salt
          Dash of pepper
        ⅔ cup evaporated milk
        ¼ cup butter or margarine
     1½ cups thinly sliced celery
        1 cup sliced green onions
        ½ pound fresh mushrooms, sliced
     1½ cups boiling water
        1 beef bouillon cube
        ½ cup California Medium Sauterne
        ½ teaspoon each thyme, marjoram
        ¼ cup all-purpose flour

Combine ground beef, crumbs, onion, salt, pepper and evaporated milk, mixing lightly, but well; shape into 12 meat balls. In large skillet heat butter or margarine, add meat balls and brown on all sides, then take from pan while making sauce. Add celery and onion to pan and cook until onion looks transparent; add mushrooms, boiling water (in which bouillon cube has been dissolved), Sauterne, thyme and marjoram. Combine flour with a little water to make smooth paste, then stir into liquid; heat to boiling, stirring constantly to smooth. Add meat balls, cover and simmer about 30 minutes.

To accompany this meat: **California Burgundy** *or* **Zinfandel**

Burgundy Hashburgers
(4 servings)

Ordinary corned beef hash can be transformed into a house special by simply using a little California Burgundy and a few ingredients at hand.

        1 (1-lb.) can corned beef hash
        4 slices onion
        ½ cup California Burgundy or other red table wine
        1 cup tomato catsup
        2 hamburger buns, split, toasted, buttered

Cut hash in 4 slices. Place in shallow baking dish; top each slice with onion. Mix wine, catsup; pour over hash. Bake uncovered, in moderate oven, (375°) about 30 minutes, basting occasionally. Serve on half of bun.

To accompany these hashburgers: **California Burgundy** *or* **Zinfandel**

Buffet Meat Balls
(8 servings)

For a party, make the meat balls and sauce the day before, refrigerate everything and simply heat it up in a chafing dish or electric skillet. Waiting makes the flavor even better.

        2 slices bread, trimmed
        ½ cup milk
        1 egg, beaten
        1 cup finely minced onion
        ½ teaspoon each nutmeg, paprika
     1½ teaspoons salt
          Dash pepper
        1 pound ground beef
        ½ pound each ground veal, pork
        ½ cup California Burgundy or other red table wine
        2 tablespoons butter or margarine

Sauce:

        2 tablespoons catsup
        3 tablespoons flour
        1 cup milk
        1 cup dairy sour cream
        ¼ cup California Burgundy or other red table wine
        1 tablespoon sugar
        ¼ cup finely minced parsley

Crumble bread into mixing bowl; add milk and egg allowing crumbs to soften, then beat until smooth. Add seasonings, meats and California Burgundy, mixing only to blend well. Form into 1-inch balls; brown in heated butter or margarine in heavy pan or electric skillet. Remove from pan and set aside while making sauce.
Sauce: Measure catsup into pan; add flour and blend. Add 1 cup milk and stir until smooth and thickened. Blend in sour cream, then return balls to pan and let simmer for 15 minutes. Add remaining Burgundy, sugar and parsley. Adjust seasonings. It's very good served on hot buttered rice or noodles.

To accompany these meat balls: **California Burgundy** *or* **Rosé**

Sherried Stroganoff

(4 servings)

- 1 pound well-trimmed tender beef steak
- 3 cups sliced fresh mushrooms
- 3 green onions, thinly sliced
- 6 tablespoons butter or margarine
- ¼ teaspoon powdered thyme
- ¾ cup California Dry Sherry
- 1 tablespoon cornstarch
- ¾ cup canned consomme
- 1 teaspoon salt
- 1 cup dairy sour cream
  Parsley, chopped very fine

Cut steak into thin diagonal strips. Sauté mushrooms and onions in about 3 tablespoons of the butter or margarine. Add thyme and Sherry; simmer until liquid is reduced to ¼ cup. Blend cornstarch into consomme; stir into mushrooms and cook, stirring constantly until mixture boils and thickens. Keep warm. Brown steak strips in remaining butter or margarine; sprinkle with salt. Just before serving, add browned steak and sour cream to sauce, then heat carefully, but do not boil. Sprinkle with chopped parsley.

To accompany this dish: **California Dry Sauterne, Dry Semillon** *or* **Rosé**

Wild West Beef Kabobs

(4 servings)

The secret of the seemingly effortless preparation of these kabobs lies in the work done ahead of time. First prepare the marinade with California Cream Sherry and seasonings and cover the meat squares. Then assemble the vegetables and keep them in the refrigerator until time to assemble everything.

- 1½ pounds sirloin steak, cut thick
- ¾ cup California Cream Sherry
- ¼ cup soy sauce
- ½ cup salad oil
- ¾ teaspoon powdered ginger
- ⅛ teaspoon powdered garlic
- 2 tablespoons instant minced onion
- 1 teaspoon salt
- ¼ teaspoon freshly ground pepper
  Vegetables for skewers: 8 small cooked onions, 2 green peppers, cut in squares, 8 plum tomatoes and 8 fresh mushroom caps

Make marinade by combining Sherry with soy sauce, oil, ginger, garlic, onion, salt and pepper. Pour over beef squares and let stand for at least 2 hours. Alternate beef squares, onions and green peppers on skewers. Broil, turning to brown sides (takes about 10 minutes), brushing with marinade during cooking. A few minutes before serving, put tomato and mushroom cap on end of skewer and complete broiling.

To accompany this beef: **California Claret** *or* **Cabernet**

Parmesan Meat Balls

(5 to 6 servings)

California Sauterne and Parmesan cheese work their wonders on this meat combination.

- 1 pound ground round or chuck
- ½ cup soft bread crumbs
- ½ cup Parmesan grated cheese
- 1 tablespoon minced onions
- 1 egg, slightly beaten
- ½ cup milk
- 1 teaspoon monosodium glutamate
- 2 tablespoons oil or margarine
- ¼ cup flour
- ½ cup Medium Sauterne
- 1 cup beef bouillon
- 1 (4-oz.) can sliced mushrooms, undrained or
- ½ pound fresh mushrooms
- 1½ teaspoons salt
- ¼ teaspoon pepper

Combine beef with crumbs, cheese, egg, milk, minced onion, monosodium glutamate, salt and pepper. Handle gently and form into balls; brown in hot oil. When browned on all sides, remove meat balls from pan and set aside. Blend flour into remaining drippings, then add wine, bouillon and mushrooms with their liquid. (If fresh mushrooms are used, add ¼ cup of water.) When all is blended, add seasonings to taste and return meat balls to sauce. Cover and simmer for 30 minutes.

To accompany this dish: **California Charbono** *or* **Chianti**

Beef Casserole with Bulgur

(4 to 6 servings)

- 2 tablespoons butter or margarine
- 1 large onion, chopped
- 1 cup sliced fresh mushrooms
- 1½ cups sliced celery
- ½ cup chopped green pepper
- 1 pound ground beef chuck
- ¾ cup California Dry Sauterne
- 1 (10½-oz.) can condensed cream of mushroom soup
- 1 (10½-oz.) can condensed consomme
- 1 cup bulgur (cracked processed wheat)

In heavy skillet melt butter and sauté onion until limp, but not brown; add mushrooms, celery and green pepper and cook briefly. Remove vegetables and hold in reserve. Brown meat quickly in pan; return vegetables to pan. Add wine and stir lightly. Combine with remainder ingredients and turn into lightly greased 1½-quart casserole. Bake in moderate oven (350°) about 1 hour. Serve with fresh fruit or molded fruit salad.

To accompany this casserole: **California Rosé** *or* **Burgundy**

Sherried Cheeseburgers

(4 servings)

1 (1⅜-oz.) package cheese sauce mix
½ cup California Sherry
½ cup milk
1 pound ground beef
1 teaspoon salt
¼ teaspoon pepper
1 tablespoon minced onion
1 tablespoon bacon drippings or other fat
4 hamburger buns, split, toasted and buttered
4 tomato slices
Pickles or olives

Empty cheese sauce mix into small saucepan. Slowly stir in Sherry and milk. Heat just to boiling, stirring constantly. Let stand over hot water until ready to serve. Mix meat, salt, pepper and onion lightly but thoroughly; shape into 4 patties the size of hamburger bun; sauté in drippings to the desired degree of doneness.

To serve, place hamburger bun half on plate; top with meat patty and tomato slice; pour some hot sauce over all. Serve other half of bun as accompaniment, along with pickles and radishes.

To accompany these cheeseburgers: **California Pinot Noir, Barbera** *or* **Claret**

Special of the Kitchen

(4 to 6 servings)

When time is short and appetites large, turn to this hearty meat combination. Although there are many versions of it, you will find this one really special because it includes California Dry Sherry. Serve it with toasted buttered buns or mashed potatoes made from prepared potato flakes.

1 small onion, chopped
2 tablespoons butter or margarine
1 pound ground beef chuck
   Salt and pepper
¼ cup California Dry Sherry or dry white table wine
1 cup chopped fresh spinach, pressed down in cup
4 eggs, beaten

In heavy skillet cook onion in melted butter until limp but not brown; remove from pan. Brown meat quickly; season with salt and pepper. Pour in Sherry; return onions to pan, add spinach and stir well. Let cook about 5 minutes. Lower heat and stir in beaten eggs; cook briefly, turning frequently, just long enough for eggs to set. Serve at once.

To accompany this dish: **California Burgundy** *or* **Gamay**

Rancher's Beef Short Ribs

(5 to 6 servings)

It's really not much trouble to prepare this favorite. After soaking in a California Riesling-flavored marinade, the ribs are ready for the barbecue.

3 pounds beef short ribs
   Sprig of parsley
1 large onion
2 cloves garlic
3 stalks celery
1 bay leaf
2 teaspoons salt

Place shortribs, vegetables and seasonings in large saucepan; barely cover with water and simmer gently about 1½ hours or until tender. Remove short ribs and cover with spicy baste to marinate overnight in refrigerator. When barbecue coals are ready, place meat on skewers or in wire broiler. Barbecue until well browned, basting continuously with marinade.

Spicy Baste: Combine ½ cup California Riesling, ¼ cup brown sugar (or juice from sweet pickles), 1 tablespoon wine vinegar, 1 teaspoon soy sauce, and ¼ teaspoon each garlic salt and dry mustard.

To accompany these short ribs: **California Claret** *or* **Cabernet Sauvignon**

Pot Roast Superior

(8 servings)

This homey pot roast has an absolutely delicious liquid formed around it after the cooking period.

1 3½- to 4½-pound pot roast
1 small clove garlic
6 small onions, peeled
½ pound large fresh mushrooms or
1 small can mushrooms, drained
1 teaspoon salt
¼ teaspoon pepper
⅛ teaspoon dried dill
   Sprig of parsley
⅓ cup California Burgundy or other red table wine

Tear off enough heavy duty foil to completely wrap roast and allow space for vegetables. Place meat in center of foil with shallow pan underneath, and rub meat with cut surface of garlic. Fold foil up around meat pan-fashion and place under broiler turning once or twice until all sides are browned fairly well; brown vegetables too. Pour Burgundy over meat. Crush a tiny bit of the garlic in the salt and add with freshly ground pepper, dill and parsley. Close the foil, sealing all edges with a tight double fold to form tight package and place in oven. Bake in slow oven (300°) 3 to 3½ hours. Remove from foil, arrange on serving platter, and prepare sauce or gravy.

To accompany this dish: **California Burgundy** *or* **Cabernet**

California Beef Sukiyaki

(4 to 5 servings)

The technique of making sukiyaki is not hard to manage once it is understood. All the ingredients for the dish are prepared and arranged at hand to be divided and cooked in two parts. The first part is cooked quickly and served, with the second one to follow. This seems a sensible way to assure hot, freshly cooked food, and it takes very little time.

- ¼ cup California Chablis
- ⅓ cup soy sauce
- ¼ cup water
- 1 tablespoon sugar
- ¼ cup oil
- 1½ pounds beef (round, sirloin, rib or tenderloin), sliced very thin
- 1 bunch green onions, with tops, cut in 2-inch lengths
- ½ pound fresh mushrooms, sliced lengthwise
- 1 pound fresh spinach or chard (cut large leaves)
- 1 bunch watercress, cut in 3-inch lengths

Combine Chablis with soy sauce, water and sugar; set aside. Place oil in heavy frying pan or electric skillet, and when very hot, add half of the beef. Pour half of the wine and soy sauce mixture over the meat. Place half remaining ingredients on top of beef slices. Cook lightly *only* until meat changes color. Cook briefly, then with tongs or chop sticks transfer beef to top of vegetables. Do not stir, but turn vegetables frequently. Cook over moderate heat until vegetables are just tender, about 5 minutes. Serve portions on heated plates and start cooking second serving using remainder of ingredients.

To accompany this dish: **California Cabernet** *or* **Burgundy**

Veal-Noodle Casserole with Wine: Cut one pound veal steak in small (about ¾-inch) cubes. Slice 1 medium-sized onion. Sauté veal and onion in 3 tablespoons fat until meat loses its red color. Add ¾ cup California Rhine, Sauterne, or other white table wine, ¾ cup canned consomme or bouillon-cube broth, 1 can condensed mushroom soup, 1 (4-oz.) can sliced mushrooms (including liquid), 1 teaspoon Worcestershire sauce and salt and pepper to taste. Mix well and bring to a boil, then add ½ pound fine noodles; cook and stir for about 5 minutes, or until noodles are limp and well mixed with the remaining ingredients. Pour mixture into a greased casserole; cover and bake in a moderate oven (350°) 1 hour. Serve Parmesan cheese as an accompaniment.

Baked Veal Chops

(5 servings)

It's a happy circumstance that onion soup blends so well with California Sauterne. Fortunate guests asked to dine on these veal chops will think you spent hours making the sauce.

- 5 thick veal chops
  Salt and pepper
  Flour
- 2 tablespoons shortening
- ⅓ cup California Sauterne or other white table wine
- 1 (10½-oz.) can condensed onion soup
- 2 tablespoons tomato paste or catsup

Season chops and dredge with flour. Brown slowly, on both sides, in heated shortening. Combine Sauterne, soup and tomato paste; pour over chops. Cover and bake in moderately hot oven (375°) until tender, about 45 to 50 minutes. Serve with the sauce.

To accompany this dish: **California Dry Sauterne** *or* **Rosé**

Veal in White Wine Sauce

(4 to 5 servings)

Veal cooks to perfection when teamed with a white table wine. We used Chablis here to work its magic in producing this extremely good stew. Add the undrained mushrooms toward the end of the cooking period, then they hold their shape yet yield their full flavor.

- 2 pounds lean veal stew meat, cut in small pieces
- 1½ teaspoons salt
- ½ teaspoon pepper
- ⅓ cup chopped parsley
- 1 clove garlic, chopped very fine
- ¾ cup California Chablis or other white table wine
- 1 (10½-oz.) can bouillon or consomme
- 1¼ cups water
- 1 (4-oz.) can mushrooms, undrained
- 1 (8-oz.) can pitted ripe olives, small size

In a heavy skillet, or electric pan, brown veal in a small amount of olive oil. Drain off excess fat. Season veal with salt and pepper; add chopped parsley and garlic and cook a few minutes. Pour in wine, bouillon, and water, cover pan and simmer meat for about an hour. Then add mushrooms and olives. Continue simmering for 15 minutes longer, or until meat is tender. When ready to serve, thicken liquid with a little flour blended with water to make a paste, but keep the sauce on the thin side. Serve over noodles with a green vegetable on the plate, and a fresh fruit salad.

To accompany this dish: **California Chablis** *or* **Pinot Chardonnay**

Stuffed Veal Birds in Sour Cream Gravy
(6 to 8 servings)

½ cup diced celery
¼ cup chopped onion
½ cup butter or margarine
2 cups soft bread cubes
¾ teaspoon salt
⅛ teaspoon sage
    Dash pepper
1 tablespoon chopped parsley
¼ cup milk
8 (4- to 5-oz. each) boneless veal cutlets
⅓ cup all-purpose flour
½ cup California Sauterne
1 cup dairy sour cream
1 (4-oz.) can mushrooms, drained

Sauté celery and onion in ¼ cup of the butter until onion is tender; combine with bread cubes, ¼ teaspoon of the salt, sage, pepper, parsley and milk; toss lightly. Divide dressing evenly between cutlets, placing dressing in center of each cutlet. Roll meat around dressing, and fasten with wooden picks or skewers. Roll meat in flour, saving leftover flour. Brown meat in remaining ¼ cup butter, turning as necessary to brown on all sides. Add California Sauterne; cover tightly; cook slowly until meat is tender, about 45 minutes. Remove meat to serving platter and keep warm. Blend together leftover flour and sour cream. Stir into drippings; add mushrooms and remaining ½ teaspoon salt. Cook, stirring constantly, until gravy is heated and thickened. Serve with veal birds.

To accompany this dish: **California Sauterne** *or* **Rosé**

Braised Veal Chops with Mushroom Sauce: Dust 4 veal shoulder chops with flour seasoned with salt and pepper. Heat 3 tablespoons bacon drippings in a large, heavy skillet; add chops and brown slowly on both sides. Add 1 thinly sliced onion and 1 cup California Sauterne or Rhine Wine; cover tightly and simmer gently for 45 minutes to 1 hour, or until chops are tender. Stir in 1 can condensed mushroom soup; heat thoroughly before serving. Buttered noodles, sprinkled liberally with grated Parmesan cheese, are an excellent accompaniment.

Roman Veal Rolls
(8 servings)

Neatly rolled bundles of veal, ham and Swiss cheese cooked ever so gently in an inspired wine sauce.

4 (about 1½ lbs.) veal round steaks
8 slices boneless boiled ham
8 slices process Swiss cheese
1 (10½-oz.) can condensed cream of mushroom soup
½ cup evaporated milk
¼ cup California Medium Sauterne
¼ teaspoon Tabasco

Cut veal steaks in half and remove bone. Stack a slice each of ham, veal and cheese. Roll up tightly, ham on outside, and fasten securely with wooden picks. Repeat, making 8 rolls. Place in greased 13 x 9 x 2-inch baking pan. Cover with aluminum foil, and bake in moderate oven (350°) near center about 1 hour and 20 minutes, or until rolls are tender. Take from oven and drain off drippings. In mixing bowl combine soup, evaporated milk, wine and Tabasco; blend until smooth; pour sauce over rolls and re-cover. Continue baking about 20 minutes more, or until sauce is well heated. Sprinkle about ¼ teaspoon parsley flakes over top before serving.

To accompany this dish: **California Dry Sauterne** *or* **Rosé**

Veal and Pimiento
(6 servings)

1½ pounds veal steak, cut in julienne strips
    about 1½ inches long
4 tablespoons butter or margarine
½ cup California Medium Sherry
1 teaspoon basil
1 (4-oz.) can sliced mushrooms
1 cup thinly sliced onion
2 (7-oz.) can pimientos, sliced in strips
2 (8-oz.) cans tomato sauce
1 cup water
2 teaspoons salt
¼ teaspoon pepper

Sauté veal in heavy skillet in 2 tablespoons butter until brown on each side. Add wine and basil; simmer 30 minutes. Sauté mushrooms and onions in remaining butter until tender; add pimientos and tomato sauce. Stir into veal; add water and seasonings; simmer until meat is tender, about 25 minutes longer. Serve over Onion Rice.

Onion Rice: In saucepan combine contents 1 (1⅜-oz.) onion soup mix, 3 cups water, 1½ cups uncooked rice and 1 tablespoon butter or margarine; bring to boil, stir once, then cover and simmer 15 minutes until rice is tender. Remove from heat, add ⅓ cup grated Parmesan cheese and fluff lightly with fork.

To accompany this meat: **California Rosé**

Veal and Rice Buffet
(6 servings)

This chilled veal dish may not be quick to make, but it is undeniably gourmet fare, one you will be proud to present. Count on it then as a party or special occasion meat, one to be prepared well in advance. The rice may be served hot with the chilled veal, or both may be heated as the menu dictates.

    1 (2-oz.) can anchovies
    2 pounds boned rolled veal
    2 sprigs parsley
    1 each small onion, bay leaf, stalk celery, carrot
    1 teaspoon salt
    1 cup California Riesling or other white table wine
    1 cup water
    ½ cup mayonnaise
    1 (3½-oz.) can tuna, drained
    2 tablespoons lemon juice
    ¼ cup capers
    2 cups quick cooking rice

Insert 4 of the anchovy fillets into folds of rolled veal roast. Place in heavy pan with parsley, onion, bay leaf, celery, carrot, salt, wine and water. Cover tightly and bring to a boil; then skim off top surface. Cover again and cook gently over low heat, about 1½ hours or until tender. Thinly slice meat; arrange on serving platter with slices overlapping. (Reserve veal stock in pan.)

Place mayonnaise, tuna, remaining anchovy fillets, lemon juice, 2 tablespoons capers, and 2 tablespoons veal stock in blender; whirl until creamy, adding more stock if necessary to achieve the consistency of heavy cream. Pour over veal slices. Sprinkle with remaining capers. Chill thoroughly.

Meanwhile, measure remaining veal stock and add water to make 2 cups. Bring to a boil. Stir in rice. Cover, remove from heat, and let stand 5 minutes. Chill thoroughly. Serve with chilled veal.

To accompany this dish: **California Riesling** or **Rosé**

Veal Chops and Rice Chablis: Dust 4 veal shoulder chops with flour seasoned with salt and pepper. Heat 3 tablespoons bacon drippings in a large, heavy skillet; add chops and brown slowly on both sides. Add 1 tablespoon minced onion and 1 cup California Chablis, Sauterne or other white table wine; cover and simmer for 20 minutes. Add 1 (2-oz.) can mushroom stems and pieces (including liquid) and 1 cup hot, well-seasoned chicken stock (canned or bouillon-cube broth may be used) sprinkle in 1 cup uncooked rice; cover and simmer 30 minutes longer, or until chops are tender and rice has absorbed all the liquid. Arrange chops and rice on a platter or dinner plates; sprinkle with grated Parmesan cheese.

Veal Marengo
(12 servings)

It's a pretty smart trick when making casseroles to double the recipe and end up with two: one to serve immediately and one to freeze for another time. This recipe has been designed for two casseroles, 3 quarts each and not necessarily the same shape.

    1 4-pound veal shoulder
    3 tablespoons olive oil
    1 clove garlic, minced
    1 pound fresh mushrooms, sliced
   20 small white onions, peeled
    3 tablespoons flour
   2½ teaspoons salt
    ½ teaspoon freshly ground pepper
    2 cups canned tomato sauce
    1 cup California Dry Sauterne
    2 cups fresh or canned chicken broth
      Bouquet Garni (celery, parsley, thyme, bay leaf)

Cut the veal in 1½-inch cubes. Heat olive oil in large skillet with garlic and brown veal, placing just enough in skillet at a time to cover bottom. Divide veal into 2 casseroles. Add a little additional oil to skillet, if necessary; then brown mushrooms and onions quickly and arrange over meat. Add flour and seasonings, stirring them into remaining oil. Stir in tomato sauce (or 4 fresh tomatoes, peeled, seeded and chopped), wine and broth. Cook stirring constantly until thickened and smooth. Pour over veal mixture. Add to each casserole a small herb bouquet consisting of a 3-inch celery stalk with leaves, 2 sprigs parsley, a small bay leaf and a sprig of fresh thyme. Tie together with stem of parsley. Cover casseroles (use foil if casseroles lack covers). Bake in slow oven (325°) 1¼ hours. Remove herb bouquets. Serve one casserole; cool and freeze the second.

To accompany this veal: **California Dry Sauterne** or **Rosé**

Veal Sauterne
(4 to 6 servings)

Veal is especially good prepared this way with California Sauterne or other white table wine. Try it for a buffet supper dish sometime, and do look for those green noodles for they add such a spritely note to the serving platter. Of course well buttered egg noodles, or rice may be used instead.

- 1 1½-pound veal steak, cut ¼ inch thick
- 1 teaspoon salt
- ½ teaspoon pepper
- ⅔ cup sifted flour
- 6 tablespoons butter or margarine
- ½ cup chopped onion
- 1 (4-oz.) can sliced mushrooms, undrained
- ⅔ cup California Dry Sauterne
- 1 (13-oz.) can evaporated milk
- 1 (12-oz.) package green noodles
- 3 tablespoons butter or margarine
- ¼ cup chopped fresh parsley

Cut veal steak into 1½-inch squares; dredge in seasoned flour; save remaining flour mix. In large skillet heat 6 tablespoons butter or margarine and cook onion until transparent; add veal and drained mushrooms (save liquid) cooking until lightly browned. Pour in Sauterne and mushroom liquid, cover pan and reduce heat to simmering about 40 to 45 minutes or until veal is tender. Remove from heat and blend in reserved seasoned flour; gradually stir in evaporated milk. Cook over low heat, stirring occasionally, until thickened, about 10 minutes. Taste and adjust seasonings. Meanwhile, add green noodles to 4 quarts boiling water to which 2 tablespoons salt has been added; cook according to package directions. Stir parsley into cooked veal mixture and serve over buttered green noodles.

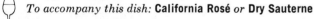 *To accompany this dish:* **California Rosé** *or* **Dry Sauterne**

Breaded veal is a delightful dish when the meat is dipped in egg and grated Parmesan cheese, browned in butter, then covered and simmered in California white table wine until fork-tender. Serve glasses of the same wine along with the entree.

Veal Francisco
(6 servings)

There's all kinds of good things in this meat dish, including California Chablis, mushrooms and cheese. Somehow they blend in a light-hearted way to enhance the veal. It's easy to prepare too, once you have assembled the ingredients.

- 1½ pounds veal, sliced about ⅓ inch thick
- ¼ cup oil
- ¼ cup onion, chopped
- 1 clove garlic, minced
- 1 tablespoon finely chopped parsley
- 1 teaspoon crumbled rosemary
- 1½ teaspoons salt
- ¼ teaspoon pepper
- 1 (No. 303) can peas
- ¼ cup California Chablis or other white table wine
- 1½ cups sliced fresh mushrooms
- 4-6 slices Monterey Jack or Mozzarella cheese
- 1 tablespoon cornstarch

Brown meat on both sides in oil. Add onions and garlic. Cook slowly until onion is tender. Sprinkle meat with parsley, rosemary, salt and pepper. Pour in ½ cup liquid from peas and add wine. Cover and simmer until meat is tender, about 20 minutes. Add mushrooms to meat and cook about 5 minutes. Pour drained peas over mushrooms. Top meat with sliced cheese. Cover and heat until peas are hot and cheese is melted. Remove to a warm serving dish. Mix cornstarch with 2 tablespoons wine and thicken sauce to desired consistency. When serving, spoon peas around meat.

To accompany this dish: **California Chablis** *or* **Pinot Blanc**

Shish Kebab Sauterne

(6 servings)

3 pounds lean, boned lamb shoulder,
   cut in 2-inch pieces
1 cup finely cut onion
1 tablespoon cumin seed
2 tablespoons brown sugar
½ teaspoon each rosemary, celery seed, pepper
1 cup California Sauterne
¼ cup olive oil
3 tablespoons California white wine vinegar
1 teaspoon salt

In a bowl, toss lamb with other ingredients to mix thoroughly. Cover and refrigerate several hours or overnight, stirring occasionally. Fasten lamb pieces on skewers, place on rack in shallow pan and broil slowly about 35 minutes. Baste with marinade and turn once. Add wine as desired to drippings and serve as sauce. Or broil over glowing charcoal until well browned, basting often with marinade.

To accompany this Shish Kebab: **California Claret** *or* **Rosé**

Lamb and Prunes Armenian

(4 to 6 servings)

Give lamb a touch of the exotic by cooking it with California Burgundy and prunes. The inexpensive cut of meat used in this fashion with a few vegetables may be coaxed into making a whole meal. The prunes will hold their shape better if they are not pitted.

2 pounds breast of lamb, cut in serving-size pieces
2 teaspoons seasoned salt
¼ teaspoon pepper
2 small cloves garlic, sliced
1 (6-oz.) can tomato paste
¼ teaspoon thyme
1 cup California Burgundy or other red table wine
2 onions, sliced
3 carrots, sliced
1 cup dried prunes

Brown lamb in some of the fat trimmings. Discard excess fat and season meat with salt and pepper. Add garlic, tomato paste, thyme and Burgundy. Cover pan and simmer 45 minutes. Then add onions, carrots, prunes and 1 cup water to meat. Cover and simmer 45 minutes longer or until vegetables are tender. At the last, if needed, add about 2 tablespoons or more wine. Serve with hot cooked rice quickly made (the precooked kind) from a package.

To accompany this dish: **California Burgundy, Barbera** *or* **Gamay**

Braised Leg of Lamb

(6 to 8 servings)

In this recipe leg of lamb is prepared in old world style. That is, the meat is browned first, then cooked with wine, herbs and vegetables. But instead of using a covered pan or roaster, heavy aluminum foil is put to work, wrapped confidently around the lamb to keep in all the succulent flavors and juices. Easy to handle too, as proved by the procedure here.

1 6-pound leg of lamb
1 clove garlic
1 teaspoon salt
¼ teaspoon each pepper, rosemary
1 tablespoon olive oil
1 tablespoon honey
1 carrot, sliced
1 onion, quartered
½ cup California Burgundy
   Small new potatoes and whole carrots, cooked

Place lamb on a large sheet of heavy duty foil with a shallow pan underneath. Cup foil close to meat. Crush garlic into salt, add pepper, rosemary, olive oil and honey; rub this mixture over the meat. Surround with carrot and onion. Place in hot oven (450°) to brown lamb (this takes about 30 minutes). Reduce heat to moderate (375°). Pull pan from oven and pour wine over meat. Fold foil loosely over top of lamb, then close on both ends, turning up so that juice cannot escape. Return lamb to oven and roast for about 1½ hours. Then, open foil and fold it back. Using a bulb type baster or spoon, remove the fat from drippings; take out vegetables. Add small cooked new potatoes and tiny cooked carrots. Baste lamb and vegetables with juice. Return to oven to glaze vegetables. Remove to heated platter and serve.

To accompany this dish: **California Rosé** *or* **Johannisberger Riesling**

For barbecuing marinate one-inch cubes of lamb shoulder in a blend of California Sherry, instant minced onion, salt, pepper and oregano in a glass or porcelain container. Cover and refrigerate overnight. Skewer meat and cook over charcoal.

Savory Lamb Shoulder Chops
(6 servings)

Add some dry white wine, such as California Sauterne to an inexpensive cut of meat like lamb shoulder chops. After a session in the oven there's an elegant dish to present at the table. Be sure to skim off excess fat from the pan liquid before thickening the sauce so there will be no hint of grease.

> 6 shoulder lamb chops, 1 inch thick
> ½ cup chicken broth
> ½ cup California Dry Sauterne or
>   other white table wine
> 1 medium onion, sliced
> ¼ cup chopped parsley
> 1 tablespoon cornstarch
> 2 tablespoons California Dry Sauterne or
>   other white table wine

In a large skillet brown chops slowly and well on both sides; drain off drippings and add broth, ½ cup Sauterne, onion and parsley. Cover skillet tightly and simmer 45 minutes or until lamb is tender. Remove chops to heated platter. Skim off excess fat from pan liquid, blend cornstarch with the 2 tablespoons wine and stir into liquid; cook, stirring constantly until sauce boils and thickens. Pour over chops and garnish with parsley.

 *To accompany this dish:* **California Sauterne** *or* **Cabernet**

Sesame Lamb Rack
(4 to 6 servings)

The combination of honey with California Chablis makes an ideal baste for lamb, not too sweet, but helpful in attaining a nice brown color and good flavor. The crushed sesame seeds are unusual, and add that gourmet touch. If necessary, add a few tablespoons of water to the pan during the last part of the roasting as the rich drippings begin to thicken and stick.

> 1 (3-lb.) rack of lamb
> ½ cup honey
> ½ cup California Chablis or other white table wine
> 2 tablespoons sesame seed, crushed
> 1 tablespoon soy sauce
> 1 small clove garlic, crushed
> ¼ teaspoon powdered ginger

Place lamb on rack in shallow roasting pan. Roast in slow oven (325°) ½ hour. Combine remaining ingredients in saucepan; simmer 10 minutes; stirring now and then. Remove from heat and use to baste lamb during cooking. Roast 1 hour longer or until meat thermometer registers 175° for medium done.

To accompany this dish: **California Medium Sauterne** *or* **Chablis**

Lamb Chops in Potato Cheese Sauce
(6 servings)

This special potato cheese sauce tastes as though hours had been spent in its preparation. However, the answer is found easily in packaged foods and the help of California Chablis to blend it all into one fine dress-up for broiled lamb chops.

> 12 rib or loin lamb chops
> 1 envelope instant whipped potatoes
> 2 (14½-oz.) cans evaporated milk
> 2 (6-oz.) packages Guyere cheese slices, shredded
> 1 tablespoon salt
> 1 teaspoon white pepper
> 1 cup California Chablis

Broil lamb chops. In saucepan, prepare 4 servings of instant whipped potatoes according to package directions. Set aside. Heat, but do not boil, evaporated milk in a large saucepan. Add cheese, salt, pepper and prepared potatoes. Cook, stirring constantly, until cheese melts and sauce is well blended. Stir in wine. Cook an additional five minutes, stirring occasionally. Serve piping hot over broiled lamb chops.

To accompany this dish: **California Burgundy** *or* **Dry Sauterne**

Lamb Shanks Canterbury
(6 servings)

The richly flavored liquid in which these lamb shanks are first marinated and then simmered is most unusual. Anise seed (try it first in the 2 tablespoon amount) is tied in a small bag to keep it from floating around in the sauce.

> ½ cup California Dry Sherry
> 1 cup soy sauce
> ¼ cup brown sugar, firmly packed
> 2 to 4 tablespoons anise seed, tied in cheesecloth
> 6 lamb shanks
> 2 tablespoons oil
> 2¼ cups water
> ¼ cup cornstarch
>   Hot cooked noodles or rice

Combine Sherry, soy sauce, sugar, and anise; pour over lamb and marinate overnight. Remove lamb from marinade. Brown on all sides in hot oil in large skillet; drain off drippings. Add marinade with spice bag; bring to a boil and simmer 10 minutes. Add 2 cups of the water; cover and simmer 1 hour or until lamb is tender; remove shanks and keep warm; remove anise. Mix cornstarch with remaining ¼ cup water and stir into liquid; cook over low heat, stirring constantly until sauce thickens. Serve lamb and sauce on noodles.

To accompany this dish: **California Dry Sauterne** *or* **Chianti**

Lamb Shanks in Wine
(4 servings)

Red table wine (we used California Burgundy) is a delightful companion to the browned lamb shanks in this cozy, need-no-attention casserole, flavoring and tenderizing all during the cooking process. The herbs are tied in a cheesecloth bag before they are placed with the meat, making it easy to retrieve them before the dish is brought to the table.

     1 tablespoon salt
    ½ teaspoon pepper
     4 lamb shanks, knuckle bone removed
     2 tablespoons oil
     2 carrots, cut into strips
    1½ cups diced celery
     2 teaspoons chopped parsley
     1 teaspoon rosemary leaves
     2 bay leaves
     2 tablespoons grated onion
    ½ teaspoon mashed garlic
     1 cup California Burgundy or other red table wine

Combine salt and pepper and rub into lamb shanks. Heat oil in a large skillet over medium heat. Add seasoned meat. Cook slowly until meat is browned, turning frequently. Transfer shanks to large casserole. Add carrot strips and celery. Place parsley, rosemary and bay leaves on a square of double cheesecloth. Pull up corners and tie securely. Place bag of herbs in casserole with meat. Combine onion, garlic and red wine with drippings in skillet; pour over meat in casserole. Cover; bake in moderate oven (350°) until meat is tender, or about 1½ hours. Remove bag of herbs before serving.

♆ *To accompany this dish:* **California Burgundy, Zinfandel or Vino Rosso**

Minted Wine Jelly
(5 medium glasses)

Make this bright jelly for yourself and share some with a friend. This quick and easy jelly makes a delightful gift. Generally thought of as an accompaniment to roast lamb, it is just as companionable with poultry and beef.

     2 cups California White Port
       Green food coloring
     3 cups sugar
    ½ bottle fruit pectin
    10 to 12 drops mint extract

Measure wine into top part of double boiler. Add food coloring to desired shade; add sugar and mix well. Place over rapidly boiling water and stir until sugar is dissolved. Remove from heat; stir in fruit pectin and mint extract. Skim off foam with metal spoon; pour quickly into glasses. Cover at once with thin layer hot paraffin.

Flaming Raisin Sauce
(1⅓ cups)

Keep this meat sauce on hand to use on ham in almost any form—broiled or baked ham slices, ham loaf or canned ham. Add brandy to sauce and light it just before serving.

    ¼ cup brown sugar
     1 tablespoon grated orange or lemon peel
     1 teaspoon arrowroot
    ½ cup seedless raisins, whole or chopped lightly
     1 cup water
    ⅓ cup California Brandy

In saucepan or chafing dish combine brown sugar, orange peel, arrowroot, raisins and water; cook over medium heat, stirring constantly until sauce clears and thickens slightly, about 3 minutes.

When ready to use sauce, reheat. Warm Brandy briefly in double-boiler, then light carefully and pour over raisin sauce. Spoon sauce gently while Brandy burns. Serve at once over meat.

♆ *To accompany Ham with Raisin Sauce:* **California Rosé**

Wine Marinated Barbecued Lamb
(6 to 8 servings)

Have the butcher bone and roll the leg of lamb for this special barbecue treatment. California Port and olive oil form the basis of the marinade, and help to flavor and tenderize the meat. The vegetables used in the marinade are served as a salad or relish at the end of the cooking period.

     1 cup California Port
     1 medium green pepper, diced
     2 medium tomatoes, diced
     1 medium onion, sliced
    ½ cup finely chopped parsley
     2 or 3 small cloves garlic, minced
     1 tablespoon salt
     1 teaspoon pepper
    ⅛ teaspoon each marjoram, dry mustard,
       red pepper sauce
     1 cup water
    ½ cup olive oil
     1 6-pound boned leg or shoulder of lamb, rolled and tied

In large shallow pan, mix together Port, vegetables, seasonings, water and oil. Place lamb in pan, cover and refrigerate 1 day in marinade, turning meat occasionally. Remove lamb from marinade. Drain, reserving both marinade and vegetables. Place lamb on spit; cook in rotisserie or on outdoor grill 2½ hours or until meat thermometer registers 175° to 180° (depending on desired degree of doneness). Brush lamb frequently with marinade while cooking. Serve lamb with marinated vegetables.

♆ *To accompany this dish:* **California Burgundy, Cabernet Sauvignon or Barbera**

Butterfly Leg of Lamb
(8 to 12 servings)

Something quite different for the barbecue is this highly seasoned leg of lamb. First the meat is treated with a marinade of California Chablis, dressing mix (all the seasonings collected in a package for you) and oil, then cooked over hot coals. It could be broiled in the oven too, allowing 15 to 20 minutes longer for medium done. Use a meat thermometer if you have doubts.

    1 5- to 6-pound leg of lamb
    1 package Italian dressing mix
    2 tablespoons water
    ½ cup California Chablis
    ½ cup oil
       Seasoned salt

Have lamb boned and cut open butterfly fashion. Place dressing mix in screw-top, pint size jar. Add water and shake well. Add wine and oil. Shake again, about 30 seconds. Pour over lamb in shallow pan and marinate overnight. Sprinkle generously with seasoned salt before broiling. Place lamb, fat side up, on grill over hot coals. Broil 40–50 minutes, turning every 10 minutes and basting with remaining marinade. Remove from grill and cut across the grain into thick slices. Serve immediately.

To accompany this dish: **California Grey Riesling** *or* **Rhine Wine**

Artichoke and Ham Casserole
(8 servings)

Casserole buffs will approve this truly elegant repast, one in which all ingredients are readily identified, yet their flavors are subtly blended into one fine whole. Yellow corn bread squares and a green salad tossed with sliced orange wheels and sharp dressing go well with this dish.

    2 packages frozen artichoke hearts
    2 cups diced cooked ham
    2 (10½-oz.) cans condensed cream of mushroom soup
    1 tablespoon minced onion
    ¼ cup California Medium Sherry
    ¼ teaspoon garlic salt
    ⅛ teaspoon pepper to taste
    8 hard-cooked eggs, quartered
    4 slices Cheddar cheese

Cook artichoke hearts as directed on package; drain. Combine ingredients; except cheese, in 3-quart casserole. Top with slices of cheese; bake in moderate oven (350°) 40 minutes.

To accompany this casserole: **California Rosé**

Holiday Ham
(10 to 14 servings)

Count on ham as one of your most dependable meats; it's good for all special occasions as well as for family fare. Glorify it then with California Sauterne and cling peaches. The basting sauce made of wine and peach syrup gives a slight glaze to the ham, and the heated fruit slices make a sunny ring around the ham platter.

    ½ (about 6 lbs.) cook-before-eating ham
    1 (1-lb. 13-oz.) can cling peach slices
    ¼ cup brown sugar, lightly packed
    3 tablespoons garlic wine vinegar
    2 tablespoons finely chopped onion
    2 tablespoons cornstarch
    1 tablespoon prepared mustard
    ½ cup California Sauterne
       Parsley sprigs

Place ham cut-side down on rack in shallow open pan. If you wish, insert meat thermometer through fat side in center of thickest part of ham. Bake in slow (325°) oven about 3½ hours or until thermometer registers 160°. Meanwhile, drain peaches, saving syrup. Blend brown sugar, vinegar, onion, cornstarch and mustard; mix in peach syrup and wine. Cook, stirring, until thickened. About 30 minutes before baking is completed, remove ham from oven; mix 1 tablespoon drippings from pan into syrup mixture. Cut rind away from ham; score fat. Stud with cloves. Place ham scored-side up in pan. Finish baking, brushing occasionally with syrup mixture. Transfer to serving platter; garnish with 8 to 10 peach slices and parsley. Add remaining peaches to syrup mixture in saucepan; heat. Serve in sauce-boat with ham.

To accompany this ham: **California Rosé** *or* **Medium Sauterne**

Sherry Walnut Ham
(18 to 22 servings)

An unusual, but certainly easy method of making good ham even better. Treat canned ham with this sweet and crunchy coating made with California Dry Sherry and chopped nutmeats.

  1 (5-lb.) canned ham
  1 cup brown sugar, firmly packed
  2 teaspoons dry mustard
  ¼ cup California Dry Sherry
  ¾ cup chopped walnuts

Heat ham in slow oven (325°) about 2 hours, according to directions given on can label. About half hour before ham is done, take from oven and spread with mixture of brown sugar, dry mustard, Sherry and chopped walnuts. Return to oven and continue baking for 30 minutes more; spoon drippings from pan over topping.

To accompany this ham: **California Rosé**

Sauterne Pork Chop Bake
(4 servings)

California Sauterne and apple jelly work their wonders in the preparation of these pork chops. They are delightfully good to eat and easy to fix for an oven dinner.

  4 medium pork chops
    Flour
    Oil or shortening
  1 teaspoon salt
  ¼ teaspoon pepper
  ¾ cup California Sauterne or other white table wine
  ¼ cup apple jelly

Coat chops with flour; brown in small amount of oil. Place in casserole and then season. Combine wine and jelly. Pour over chops. Cover and bake in moderate oven (350°) 1 hour.

To accompany these chops: **California Sauterne, Chenin Blanc** *or* **Rosé**

Glaze for Baked Ham: There will be a brown and beautiful glaze on your ham if you give it a treatment of wine and brown sugar. Pour 1 cup California Medium or Cream Sherry over ham before baking. The last half hour, score ham surface and stud with cloves, sprinkle lightly with brown sugar and baste with an additional cup of wine. When the ham is glazed, remove from pan, skim fat from the pan juices and serve sauce with ham.

Wine Glazed Ham
(4 servings)

It takes only a small portion of California Cream Sherry or Muscatel with preserves to make an interesting meat dish out of a slice of ham or can of luncheon meat. Good with this are whole kernel corn, cabbage slaw with a tart dressing.

  1 (1-inch) slice ham or 1 (12-oz.) can luncheon meat
  8 cloves
  ½ cup apricot-pineapple preserves
  ¼ cup California Cream Sherry or Muscatel

Stud meat with cloves and spread with preserves. Pour on wine. Bake in moderate oven (350°) about 45 minutes or until lightly browned. Baste often.

To accompany this ham: **California Rosé** *or* **Chenin Blanc**

A delicious glaze for baked ham or corned pork combines ½ cup California Sauterne or Chablis with 1 cup pineapple-apricot jam. For a sweet-sour variation, add 2 or 3 tablespoons wine vinegar.

Spareribs Pacifica
(5 to 6 servings)

Exotic yet easy to prepare are these spareribs. Select the ribs with an eye toward lean meat, and trim off any excess fat before the spareribs are arranged in the baking pan.

  3½ pounds lean pork spareribs, cut in pieces for serving
    Salt and pepper
  1 tablespoon cornstarch
  ¼ cup brown sugar, firmly packed
  1 (9-oz.) can crushed pineapple, undrained
  ½ cup California wine vinegar
  ⅓ cup California Medium Sherry
  2 tablespoons soy sauce
  5 or 6 servings cooked sweet potatoes

Sprinkle spareribs with salt and pepper. Arrange meaty side up in single layer in shallow baking pan. Mix cornstarch and sugar in saucepan; stir in pineapple, vinegar, wine and soy sauce; stir over medium heat until mixture boils and thickens. Pour sauce over spareribs. Bake in moderate oven (350°) 1 hour, basting and turning occasionally. Arrange sweet potatoes around spareribs. Continue baking 30 minutes more, basting occasionally.

To accompany these spareribs: **California Rosé** *or* **Grey Riesling**

Jelly and Wine for Pork Chops: Create extra-delicious pork chops by topping them, after browning, with a little quince, apple or currant jelly. Season as usual, then pour on ½ cup California Sherry for 6 chops. Cover tightly and simmer over low heat until meat is fork tender.

French Pork Birds
(6 servings)

Somehow it's comforting to know that although this pork dish is undeniably homey, it is still good enough for any company that might drop in. The California Sauterne used in the sauce gives the pork that extra something. Scatter chopped chives, fresh or frozen over all.

    6 lean pork shoulder steaks, ¼ inch thick
    1 teaspoon salt
    ¼ teaspoon pepper
    ¼ teaspoon ground marjoram or sage
    2 slices bacon, diced
    1¼ cups (½-inch) toasted bread cubes
    ½ cup finely chopped carrots
    ¼ cup finely chopped onion
    1 egg, beaten
    ¼ cup hot bouillon
    ½ teaspoon salt
    ¼ teaspoon pepper
    ¼ cup flour
    1 cup California Medium Sauterne

Sprinkle pork steaks with salt, pepper and marjoram. Fry bacon until crisp, then turn into bowl (reserving about 2 tablespoons drippings in which to brown meat) and add toasted bread cubes, carrots, onion, beaten egg, bouillon, salt and pepper; mix well. Spread stuffing on pork steaks, roll meat up and tie with string; roll each in flour and brown birds in drippings. Place pork birds in 1½-quart casserole and add Sauterne. Cover and bake in moderate oven (350°) for 1½ hours. (If desired, small carrots and onions may be placed in the casserole about 45 minutes before the meat is done.) To serve, remove strings and arrange pork birds on platter, then pour some sauce from the casserole over them. Thicken sauce if it seems a little thin.

To accompany this dish: **California Medium** *or* **Dry Sauterne** *or* **Rosé**

Wine Glazed Corned Pork
(8 to 10 servings)

This special glazed meat is handsome enough for your most important entertaining occasion. The pork cooks to an attractive pink, the glaze sparkles and the peaches add a sunny glow as they decorate the serving platter. Since it does take time to simmer the pork for the initial cooking, it's a good plan to do this the day before.

    1 7-pound leg corned pork, boned and tied
        Wine-Nectar Glaze
    1 or 2 (1-lb. 13-oz.) cans cling peach halves

Cover meat with cold water; bring to boil and skim. Cover and cook slowly until tender, about 2½ to 3½ hours. Cool meat in cooking liquid. Remove any fat from meat; place in shallow roasting pan. Spoon on some of the Wine Nectar Glaze and bake in moderate oven (375°) until hot and richly glazed, about 45 minutes. Baste meat frequently while cooking with remaining Wine Nectar Glaze.

During the last 15 minutes of baking, arrange drained cling peach halves in bottom of pan; spoon glaze on peaches and heat well. To serve, arrange Corned Pork on platter and surround with peach halves and green beans.

Wine Nectar Glaze

    3 tablespoons brown sugar
    ½ teaspoon dry mustard
    2 tablespoons wine vinegar
    ¾ cup apricot whole fruit nectar
    ¾ cup California Medium Sauterne
    1½ teaspoons instant minced onion
    2 teaspoons cornstarch

Combine all ingredients; bring to a boil before spooning over meat.

To accompany this dish: **California Chablis** *or* **Pinot Blanc**

Bake pork chops in a wine-mushroom sauce for company dinner. Brown chops in heavy skillet, season and top with green pepper rings. Mix Sauterne or other California white table wine with undiluted mushroom soup and pour around meat. Cover and bake until tender. Serve with cooked rice or noodles and glasses of chilled California table wine.

Pork Chops with Piquant Sauce
(4 servings)

Pork chops were never dressed up any better than in this remarkable sauce. Products from your kitchen shelves unite easily and quickly to make it. And there's just a small amount of both California Sherry and Sauterne to blend everything well.

> 2 tablespoons unsalted or sweet butter
> 4 lean, loin pork chops
> 2 tablespoons instant minced onions, freshened as directed on package
> 1 tablespoon flour
> Dash black pepper
> 1 chicken bouillon cube, dissolved in ½ cup hot water
> ⅓ cup California Dry Sauterne
> 2 teaspoons wine vinegar
> 1 sour pickle, cut into ⅛-inch slices
> 1 tablespoon California Medium Sherry

In skillet, melt butter over medium heat; sauté pork chops until golden brown, about 25 minutes. Add well-drained onions and continue heating until onions are golden brown. Remove chops from skillet. Sprinkle flour into juices in skillet and stir until brown. Stir in bouillon gradually, keeping mixture smooth. Add Sauterne, vinegar and pickle slices; simmer 1 minute. Return chops to skillet and simmer in sauce 10 minutes. Stir in Sherry 2 to 3 minutes before serving. Serve hot.

To accompany this dish: **California Rosé** *or* **Dry Sauterne**

For the main dish of a backyard supper, cut frankfurters into 1-inch thick diagonal slices. Add some canned bouillon, California Rosé or Sauterne, a little finely chopped green onion; cover and simmer until frankfurters are plump and hot. Spoon over crusty toasted French bread. Bring on a bowl of mixed greens and vegetable salad, a chilled bottle of Rosé or Sauterne and the picnic is off to a good start.

On busy days serve this meal-in-a-skillet. For four, brown 4 pork chops, and drain off excess fat. Add 8 prunes, 4 sweet potatoes, peeled and halved, a little chopped onion and about ½ cup California Sauterne. Cover closely, and bake in moderate oven 45 minutes, or until meat and sweet potatoes are tender.

pOULTRY

Wines of every type complement chicken, as the recipes in this section illustrate. There's a high proportion of white table wines, both in the recipes and suggested as the accompanying beverage, reflecting the preference of many wine enthusiasts for this combination. A seasoning of Sherry is another trend evident in this collection of poultry recipes.

Della Robia Chicken
(6 servings)

The inspiration for garnishing a roast chicken or turkey with a ring of wine-spiced fruits comes from the Della Robia plaques and platters of Italy.

- 1 (5-lb.) roasting chicken
  Salt and Pepper
- ¼ cup melted butter or shortening

Season chicken, inside and out, with salt and pepper. Place in pan, brush on melted shortening. Bake in hot oven (450°) for 15 minutes, just until chicken begins to take on color. Reduce heat to moderate (350°) and roast, uncovered, ½ hour. Spoon one quarter of Wine Baste (below) over chicken and continue roasting for about one hour longer, basting frequently with additional Wine Baste.

Wine Baste   (Makes about 2 cups)

- 1 cup California Rosé or Chablis or
  other white table wine
- ¼ cup wine vinegar
- ⅔ cup cooking oil
- 1 teaspoon dry mustard
- 1 tablespoon seasoned salt
- 1 teaspoon seasoned pepper
- ½ teaspoon finely crumbled dried rosemary or oregano
- ¼ cup honey or brown sugar
- 2 teaspoons grated onion
- 1 small clove garlic, finely crushed

Combine all ingredients; heat to blend flavors, bring only to boiling. Cool. Brush over chicken frequently during roasting or grilling.

 To accompany Della Robia Chicken: **California Rosé**

Basic Syrup for Quick Spiced Fruits
(Makes about 3½ cups)

To follow the Della Robia plan for garnishing a roast chicken or turkey, use several different kinds of fruit to give an attractive form and color to the edible decoration.

- 2 cups syrup from canned fruits
- 1 cup California Rosé or Chablis or
  other white table wine
- ½ cup wine vinegar
- 3 sticks cinnamon
- 1 teaspoon whole cloves
- ½ cup brown sugar (packed)
- ⅛ teaspoon salt

Combine all ingredients in a saucepan. Bring to a boil, lower heat and simmer 10 minutes. Cool slightly. Pour over drained canned fruit. Use one fruit or a selection such as peaches, pears, pineapple, kadota figs, etc. Cover and chill overnight. Sufficient syrup to spice 1 to 1½ quarts fruit.

Note: The following are three more variations.

Curry: Add ½ teaspoon curry powder to basic syrup.

Mint: Add 2 sprigs bruised fresh mint to basic syrup. For light flavor, remove mint before pouring syrup on fruits. For heavier flavor, allow mint to chill with fruits.

Citrus: Remove rind from 1 small orange and 1 small lemon in one piece *or*, cut into large strips. Add to basic syrup along with ½ cup orange juice.

NOTE: Della Robia Chicken illustrated on cover.

Chicken Breasts in Sour Cream
(4 servings)

    4 small chicken breasts
    2 teaspoons salt
    1 teaspoon pepper
 ¼ cup butter, and 2 tablespoons butter
 ½ cup California Dry Sauterne or other white table wine
 ⅓ cup finely chopped onion
    1 cup dairy sour cream
 ¼ cup sliced pitted ripe olives
 ¼ cup chopped fresh chives

Remove skin from chicken breasts; sprinkle chicken with salt and pepper. Melt ¼ cup butter in skillet. Add chicken and sauté carefully until golden, turning occasionally. Pour wine over chicken, cover and steam until tender, 20 to 25 minutes. Remove chicken breasts to heated serving platter and place in warm oven. Add 2 tablespoons butter and onions to skillet; sauté until soft, then stir in sour cream and olives. Heat gently but do not boil. Add chives and pour over chicken. Serve with rice or small new potatoes and peas.

To accompany this chicken dish: **California Rhine Wine** *or* **Dry Sauterne**

Chicken Curry in a Hurry
(4 servings)

In preparing this curry be sure to take into account the varied strength of curry powders and family preference. Start with a small amount of curry and gradually increase it to the desired proportion.

    2 (5-oz.) cans boned chicken
    1 (10½-oz.) can condensed cream of chicken soup
    1 teaspoon curry powder
 ¼ cup California Sauterne or other white table wine
    3 cups hot steamed rice

Cut chicken into pieces. In skillet combine chicken with soup, curry powder and wine. Heat gently until well blended and hot. Serve over hot steamed rice. Offer a choice of condiments to sprinkle over curry, such as coconut, orange sections, chutney, chopped salted peanuts or crisp, crumbled bacon. Condiments may be in small bowls on one tray or in compartments of one large plate.

To accompany this Chicken Curry: **California Sauterne** *or* **Sauvignon Blanc**

Barbecued Chicken Legs
(4 to 6 servings)

There are some fine seasonings used to perfect this special baste for barbecuing the dark meat of chicken. They have all been carefully selected to blend together for just this purpose. Young turkey may be used too. The barbecuing may also be done in your kitchen broiler.

    8 chicken legs, both joints
    1 (6-oz.) can tomato paste
 ½ cup tomato catsup
 ¼ cup brown sugar, firmly packed
 ½ cup California Dry or Medium Sauterne
    1 tablespoon each vinegar, soy sauce, prepared mustard, onion juice
    2 teaspoons all-purpose seasoning
    1 teaspoon barbecue spice
      Dash garlic powder or garlic salt
 ¼ teaspoon each monosodium glutamate, black pepper
 ¼ cup melted butter or margarine

Dry chicken legs well. In saucepan, combine all remaining ingredients, mixing well; place over low heat and bring to boil; simmer about 5 minutes. Adjust grill 5 to 6 inches from hot coals. Brush chicken legs with baste and place skin side down on grill; brown on both sides, then begin basting with sauce. Continue cooking, basting and turning legs frequently, about 45 minutes or until done. Serve with a little of the heated baste. Accompany with corn on the cob or a good potato salad, made with white wine dressing, and a generous tray of assorted relishes.

To accompany this chicken: **California Dry** *or* **Medium Sauterne** *or* **Rosé**

Crunchy Creamed Chicken
(6 servings)

Here's a treatment of creamed chicken that is a little different. It can be made in a hurry from foods you have on hand, and the corn chips prove to be a crunchy, flavorful accompaniment.

    6 tablespoons butter or margarine
 ½ cup all-purpose flour
    1 teaspoon salt
    1 (10½-oz.) can condensed chicken broth
 1⅔ cups milk
    1 cup diced cooked mushrooms (optional)
    2 cups diced cooked chicken
 ¼ cup California Dry Sherry
    2 cups corn chips

In saucepan melt butter and blend in flour and salt; add broth and milk gradually. Cook about 8 minutes, stirring constantly. Add mushrooms and chicken; heat thoroughly, then add Sherry. Serve on corn chips.

To accompany this dish: **California Rhine Wine** *or* **Sylvaner**

Stuffed Chicken Bigarade

(4 servings)

If you are searching for an unusual way to cook chicken, try this method. The chicken isn't really stuffed, but placed on top of the seasoned bread cubes. Then a special sauce, made with California Dry Sherry and citrus peels and juices, is poured over all.

```
2 teaspoons grated lemon peel
1 teaspoon grated orange peel
⅓ cup orange juice
2 tablespoons lemon juice
½ cup brown sugar, firmly packed
¼ cup California Dry Sherry
1½ quarts (½-inch) soft bread cubes
⅔ cup chopped parsley
1 teaspoon salt
1 (3-lb.) frying chicken, quartered
```

In small saucepan place 1 teaspoon of the lemon peel, all of the orange peel, orange and lemon juices and brown sugar; bring to boil and simmer 20 minutes. Remove from heat and add Sherry. Combine soft bread cubes, parsley, salt and remaining lemon peel. Place bread mixture in bottom of lightly greased (9-inch) square baking dish. Top with chicken. Pour half of the sauce over chicken and bake in moderate oven (350°) 45 minutes. Pour remaining sauce over chicken and cook for an additional 30 minutes.

To accompany this chicken: **California Medium Sauterne** *or* **Pinot Blanc**

Mahogany Chicken

(6 servings)

You'll have to try this unorthodox method of cooking beautifully browned chicken to be convinced. The secret is in using California Cream Sherry, which is sweet enough to help brown and glaze the chicken, and a high temperature not usually associated with chicken cookery.

```
6 large pieces frying chicken
  Salt and pepper
½ cup butter
1 cup California Cream Sherry
```

Season chicken with salt and pepper; sprinkle, if desired, lightly with your favorite herb. Place chicken pieces close together and skin-side down in baking pan. Slice butter over chicken; pour on Cream Sherry. Bake in hot oven (425°) 15 minutes. Turn chicken pieces, skin-side up. Continue baking until tender, 40 to 45 minutes longer.

To accompany this chicken: **California Traminer** *or* **Chablis**

Artichokes and Chicken a la Crème

(4 servings)

```
3 tablespoons butter or margarine
1½ cups thinly sliced onions
2 large chicken breasts, each cut in half
¾ teaspoon salt
¼ teaspoon each white pepper, curry powder
4 medium artichokes
2 tablespoons lemon juice
¾ cup California Riesling or other white table wine
3 cups heavy cream
  Fresh parsley sprigs
```

In large skillet or Dutch oven, melt butter and stir in onions. Cover and cook over low heat 5 minutes or until onions are tender but not browned. Add chicken to skillet and turn to coat with butter. Cover and cook over low heat for 10 minutes. Sprinkle with seasonings.

Meanwhile wash artichokes; cut off stems and remove bottom leaves. Quarter artichokes and remove chokes (thistle portion); rub cut edges with lemon juice. Add to chicken in skillet. Pour in wine; boil rapidly until liquid has almost evaporated. Pour in 2¾ cups of the cream which has been brought to a boil. Cover and simmer gently 35 to 45 minutes or until chicken and artichokes are tender. Transfer chicken and artichokes to platter and keep warm. Remove skillet from heat; stir in 1 tablespoon lemon juice. Gradually beat remaining ¼ cup cream into sauce. Pour over chicken and artichokes. Garnish with parsley and serve with rice.

To accompany this chicken dish: **California Riesling** *or* **Chablis**

Burgundy Pear Poultry Garnish: Use these simple-to-make but attractive bright red pear halves as a garnish for the turkey platter or with chicken and dumplings. Spoon contents 1 (1-lb. 13-oz.) can pear halves into deep bowl; drop 2 lemon slices on top. Measure syrup from pears and add enough water to make 1½ cups; pour into small saucepan. Add ½ cup California Burgundy and ½ teaspoon red food coloring. Heat to boiling, then pour over pears. Cool; refrigerate several hours or overnight until pears are well flavored with the wine and absorb the color.

Chicken Livers Sauté

(4 servings)

¼ cup butter or margarine
1 pound chicken livers, fresh or frozen, cut up
3 tablespoons flour
1 cup canned consomme or bouillon-cube broth
½ cup California Dry Sherry
  Salt and pepper
1 (3-oz.) can sliced, broiled mushrooms, drained
2 tablespoons chopped parsley

Heat butter in skillet; add livers and sauté quickly until well browned, turning frequently; remove from pan to warm plate and add flour to pan drippings and blend well; add consomme and Sherry; cook, stirring constantly, until mixture is thickened and smooth; season. Add livers, mushrooms and parsley to sauce. Heat and serve on toast or with rice.

To accompany this dish: **California Dry Sauterne** *or* **Pinot Chardonnay**

Chicken Tetrazzini

(6 servings)

Canned boned chicken will come to your rescue when you need something to serve in a hurry. You might even want to use dehydrated onion and green pepper to save chopping time. With this casserole set out a generous bowl filled with green salad, tossed with a sharp dressing and sections of little mandarin oranges, or wedges of peeled ripe tomato.

4 ounces spaghetti, broken
1 (10½-oz.) can condensed cream of chicken soup
1 (4-oz.) can sliced mushrooms
1 small onion, chopped
¼ cup diced pimiento
¼ cup diced green pepper
1¾ cups grated sharp Cheddar cheese
2 (5-oz.) cans boned chicken, cut up
¼ cup California Sauterne or other white table wine

Cook spaghetti following package directions; drain. Mix soup, mushrooms and liquid, chopped onion, pimiento, green pepper and 1¼ cups of the cheese. Add spaghetti, chicken and broth and Sauterne; toss lightly until mixed. Put in casserole and sprinkle with remaining cheese. Cover; bake in moderate oven (375°) 15 minutes; uncover and continue baking an additional 30 minutes.

To accompany this casserole: **California Dry Sauterne, Semillon** *or* **Sylvaner**

Chicken and Mushrooms

(4 servings)

Keep this method of chicken cookery in mind for the next time you want to have a head start with your dinner preparations.

8 pieces frying chicken (breasts, thighs, legs)
6 tablespoons butter or margarine
½ pound fresh mushrooms
  Salt, pepper
1 tablespoon chopped parsley
1 teaspoon rosemary
½ cup California Dry Sherry or Sauterne

In heavy skillet, brown chicken lightly in butter or margarine. Have ready 4 large pieces of foil wrap and place 2 pieces of chicken in center of each. In the same skillet give the lightest touch of brown to the mushrooms; divide among the four servings. Sprinkle each serving with salt, pepper, parsley and rosemary. Add 2 tablespoons of wine to each. Bring ends of foil wrap together over chicken and seal in double fold; seal opposite ends to make tight package. Place packages in shallow pan and bake in moderate oven (375°) 1 hour. If serving very informally, open packages and crimp foil back around edges before placing on plate. Otherwise, transfer contents of package onto serving plate to accompany steamed rice or cooked noodles with parsley.

To accompany this chicken dish: **California Dry Sauterne** *or* **Sauvignon Blanc**

Golden Gate Chicken on Rice

(6 servings)

1 tablespoon butter or margarine
2 tablespoons flour
1 cup chicken broth
3 cups cooked chicken, in large pieces
¼ cup diced cooked ham
1 teaspoon salt
⅛ teaspoon pepper
2 tablespoons chopped pimiento
1 egg, slightly beaten
1 cup dairy sour cream
¼ cup California Dry Sauterne or other white table wine
½ cup diced Swiss cheese
3 cups hot fluffy rice

In saucepan melt butter, blend in flour; add broth and cook, stirring constantly until thick and smooth. Add chicken, ham, salt, pepper, and pimiento; heat thoroughly. Stir together beaten egg, sour cream and wine, then add to sauce; add cheese and cook only until cheese melts. Serve over hot rice.

To accompany this dish: **California Dry Sauterne, Sauvignon Blanc** *or* **Rosé**

Chicken and Lobster with Sherry
(6 servings)

This rich combination of chicken and lobster is a good selection for your next company dinner. Keep it hot in a chafing dish and provide light fluffy rice to serve it on. Blanched slivered almonds and preserved kumquats are an elegant garnish. Instead of plain rice you might like a cooked saffron-flavored rice to make it even more attractive.

    ¼ cup butter or margarine
    ¼ cup finely minced onion
    ¼ cup all-purpose flour
    1¼ cups milk
    ½ cup light cream
    2 chicken bouillon cubes
    1½ cups cubed, cooked chicken
    ¾ cup cubed, canned lobster
    ½ cup sliced canned mushrooms
    ½ cup California Medium Sherry
      Salt and pepper to taste
    1 egg yolk, slightly beaten

In saucepan melt butter, add onion and cook until transparent but not brown. Blend in flour then add milk, cream and bouillon cubes, stirring constantly; cook until smooth and thickened. Add chicken, lobster and mushrooms; heat to serving temperature. Add wine, salt and pepper to taste, and egg yolk. Cook over low heat, stirring gently until sauce is thickened.

To accompany this dish: **California Rhine Wine** *or* **Pinot Chardonnay**

Chicken Marengo with Sauterne
(4 servings)

This version is highly seasoned and a little richer. It may be served with rice or with hot noodles tossed with very finely chopped parsley.

    1 (2½-lb.) broiler-fryer, cut up
    1 teaspoon seasoned salt
    1 package spaghetti sauce mix
    ½ cup fine dry bread crumbs
    ¼ cup salad oil
    ½ cup California Dry Sauterne
    3 fresh tomatoes, peeled and quartered
    2 cups sliced fresh mushrooms

Sprinkle chicken pieces with seasoned salt. Blend dry spaghetti sauce mix with crumbs; coat chicken pieces. In heavy skillet sauté chicken carefully in heated oil. Add wine, tomatoes, mushrooms and remaining crumb mixture. Cover and simmer over low heat, about 45 minutes or until chicken is tender.

To accompany this chicken: **California Chablis** *or* **Dry Sauterne**

NOTE: A Chicken Marengo with Sherry included in this book, results in an excitingly different flavor.

Italian Chicken in Foil
(8 servings)

    1 onion, chopped
    1 stalk celery with leaves, chopped
    2 broiler chickens, quartered
    3 tablespoons olive oil
    1 (8½-oz.) can garbanzo beans or chick peas
    1 teaspoon salt
      Freshly ground black pepper
    ½ teaspoon oregano
    1 (8-oz.) can tomato sauce
    ½ cup California Burgundy

Place large sheet of heavy duty foil wrap on shallow pan. Add onion and celery and then the chicken, cut side up. Brush chicken with olive oil. Brown lightly under broiler, turning chicken once and again brushing with oil. Add garbanzo beans and seasonings. Blend together tomato sauce and wine; pour over chicken. Close foil to make a tight package. Return to oven and bake in moderate oven (350°) about 1½ hours. Serve from the foil with crusty Italian bread and tossed green salad.

To accompany this chicken: **California Rosé** *or* **Vino Rosso**

Sherried Supper Special
(4 to 6 servings)

This recipe should appeal to all good cooks. The young and inexperienced can handle the details fearlessly, while the experienced ruler of the kitchen will be delighted at the speed with which it can be put together.

    1 package noodles romanoff
    1 (10½-oz.) can condensed cream of mushroom soup
    2 (5-oz.) cans boned chicken, drained, or
      2 cups cooked chicken, coarsely diced
    1 (10-oz.) package frozen chopped broccoli,
      thawed and well drained
    ½ cup pitted ripe olives, cut into wedges
    ¼ cup California Dry Sherry

Prepare noodles romanoff as directed on package except increase milk to ¾ cup. Stir in remaining ingredients; pour into 2-quart casserole. Cover and bake in moderate oven (350°) 25 to 30 minutes or until broccoli is tender.

To accompany this chicken dish: **California Dry Sauterne, Chablis** *or* **Riesling**

Breast of Chicken Eugénie

(6 servings)

All the delicious flavor and juices of the chicken will be held in when the chicken is cooked in foil wrap.

- 2 center slices ready-to-eat ham, cut ¼ inch thick
- ¼ cup butter or margarine
- 3 whole chicken breasts, each cut in half
- 1 (10½-oz.) can condensed cream of chicken soup, undiluted
- 2 stalks celery, chopped
- 1 teaspoon minced onion
- ½ cup California Medium Sauterne or other white table wine
- ½ cup light cream

Cut ham into 6 servings; sauté until lightly browned in butter. Place each portion of ham in center of large square of foil wrap. In the same skillet sauté chicken breasts lightly; place one on each portion of ham. In saucepan heat soup, celery, onion, wine and cream. Spoon equal portions onto each serving, about ½ cup each. Bring edges of foil wrap over chicken, sealing first in double fold, then sealing each end to make a tight package. Place packages on shallow baking sheet; bake in moderate oven (350°) 1¼ hours.

To accompany this dish: **California Sauterne, Riesling** *or* **White Pinot**

Chicken Marengo with Sherry

(4 servings)

There are many versions of this famous chicken dish, reported to have been named after one of Napoleon's battles, when for the victory celebration a fortunate chef created it.

- 1 (3½-lb.) frying chicken, cut in serving pieces
- 2 tablespoon all-purpose flour
- ½ teaspoon each salt, pepper
- 2 tablespoons olive or salad oil
- 1 (8-oz.) can tomato sauce
- 1 cup stock or bouillon
- ½ cup California Dry Sherry
- 1 cup sliced mushrooms
- ½ cup sliced pimiento-stuffed olives

Coat chicken pieces well with combined flour, salt and pepper; sauté in heated oil until lightly browned. Add remaining ingredients; cover pan and cook over low heat about 50 to 60 minutes, or until chicken is tender, lifting chicken pieces occasionally. Serve with hot fluffy rice.

To accompany this chicken: **California Johannisberger Riesling** *or* **Rosé**

NOTE: Chicken Marengo with Sauterne included in this book, provides an interesting variation in flavor.

Sauce for Chicken: Keep this super-rich sauce suggestion handy for leftover chicken, or a hurry-up seafood or tuna dish. Blend ¼ cup California Sherry into undiluted canned cream of celery soup. Add a teaspoon instant minced onion and ½ cup mayonnaise. Fold in chicken or seafood and heat thoroughly. Serve in avocado half shells or over toast squares.

Chicken with Avocado

(4 to 6 servings)

If you want to prepare chicken in a very new way—something quite unusual—consider this combination with avocado and California Dry Sherry. The seasoning is somewhat detailed, but that's what makes the simmering sauce so good. Select avocados that are ripe, but not too soft to hold their shape when they are diced and cooked for that brief minute.

- 1 (about 2½ lbs.) frying chicken, cut up
- 2 tablespoons flour
- 1 teaspoon salt
- ¼ teaspoon pepper
- 3 tablespoons cooking oil
- 1 medium onion, minced
- 1 clove garlic, minced
- 1 small green pepper, chopped
- 2 pieces celery, chopped
- ⅛ teaspoon each ground comino, paprika
- ½ cup California Dry Sherry
- ½ cup chicken broth
- 1 whole pimiento, chopped
- ¼ cup sliced blanched almonds
- 2 firm avocados, peeled and diced

Coat chicken pieces in mixture of flour, salt and pepper. In heavy skillet, brown chicken carefully in heated oil. Add onion, garlic, green pepper and celery; cover and let simmer about 5 minutes. Add comino, paprika, chicken broth and wine; cover again and let simmer about 30 to 35 minutes or until chicken is tender. Add pimiento, almonds and avocado, distributing them carefully to avoid breaking the chicken pieces; let simmer a minute or so more. Taste and check salt content, adding a little more if necessary. Serve with steamed rice and fresh broccoli or asparagus.

To accompany this chicken dish: **California Medium Sauterne** *or* **Chablis**

Broiled Chicken: Easy "chicken broil" makes use of your oven. Shake 4 broiler halves in seasoned flour and arrange breast side down in shallow pan. Add ½ cup each California Sauterne or other white table wine and chicken broth, cover and bake in a moderate oven (350°) 45 minutes. Turn breast side up. Sprinkle lightly with your favorite herb, drizzle on 2 tablespoons melted butter, and salt lightly. Turn on broiler until chicken is crisp and richly browned. Serve with the rich pan sauce.

Poultry Salad: The next time you make chicken or turkey salad, try marinating the meat for about an hour in a California white dinner wine such as Sauterne or Chablis. It adds considerable flavor. Afterward, the wine can be used for seasoning such dishes as canned cream soups, or the cream sauce for hot cooked vegetables.

Chicken and Riesling
(4 servings)

Carefully made, this chicken recipe will produce elegant results. The chicken must be nicely browned and the vegetables cut evenly. Avoid over-cooking or handling so that each piece retains its shape in the very good sauce. The blazing of the chicken with brandy is optional, although it does add to the flavor of the dish. Warm the brandy in top of small double boiler over hot water, pour over the chicken and light. Spoon it up and over the pieces, and when the flames burn out, add the seasonings and proceed.

    1 (2½- to 3-lb.) frying chicken, cut in quarters
    ½ cup all-purpose flour
    ¼ cup cooking oil
    8 small white onions
    4 carrots, cut in thirds, crosswise
    4 shallots or scallions, finely chopped
    ¼ cup California Brandy
    ¼ cup chopped parsley
    1 teaspoon salt
    ½ teaspoon pepper
    1 clove garlic
    ½ cup California Riesling or other white table wine
    ½ pound mushroom caps

Dust chicken well with flour. In large heavy skillet heat oil and brown chicken lightly. Remove chicken and keep warm. To skillet add onions, carrots, and shallots; brown very lightly. Return chicken pieces and blaze with warmed brandy. Season with parsley, salt, pepper and garlic. Add Riesling, cover pan and simmer 25 minutes. Add mushrooms and turn chicken pieces. Continue cooking gently until chicken is tender, about 20 minutes. Remove garlic. Serve chicken and its sauce with baked potatoes.

To accompany this chicken: **California Riesling or Chablis**

Mission San Jose Chicken
(8 servings)

The eight servings indicate that this could be a handsome company dish. Serve the chicken breasts on a bed of rice, spooning generous portions of the Sherry sauce over all.

    4 large boned chicken breasts, each cut in half
    ½ teaspoon seasoned pepper
    1 teaspoon salt
    2 tablespoons melted butter or margarine
    3 slices bacon, diced
    1 cup chopped onion
    1 (4-oz.) can sliced mushrooms, undrained
    2 tablespoons butter or margarine
    3 tablespoons all-purpose flour
    2¾ cups chicken broth
    12 stuffed olives, sliced
    ½ cup California Dry Sherry
    4 cups cooked rice

Sprinkle chicken breasts with salt and pepper; brush with butter. Place in baking pan, cover and bake in a very hot oven (450°) 20 minutes; remove cover and continue cooking 20 minutes longer or until golden brown. Meanwhile prepare Sherry sauce: Sauté bacon and chopped onion until onion is tender; add sliced mushrooms, with liquid, and butter. Blend in flour; add broth gradually, stirring constantly to smooth. Add olives and Sherry, then simmer sauce over low heat 25 to 30 minutes.

To accompany this chicken dish: **California Chablis or Chenin Blanc**

Company Chicken: Here's the easiest way possible to make "company chicken." Arrange halved chickens (allowing one half per serving) in baking pan. Dot with butter, sprinkle with salt and dried herbs, and add about ½ cup California white table wine. Cover and bake in moderate oven about one hour, basting occasionally. Uncover and bake about 15 minutes longer, until tender and browned. Make gravy from the rich drippings to serve over almond-rice.

Spanish Padre Chicken
(4 servings)

Men will be enthusiastic about this bold treatment of chicken. There's a generous amount of seasoning that goes into this dish, but everything blends well with the California Chablis to make fine eating. Use the whole chicken, cut up, or select the pieces you like best.

                1 (3½-lb.) chicken, cut in pieces
                ⅓ cup all-purpose flour
                1 teaspoon each salt, black pepper
                ½ cup butter or margarine
                ½ cup California Chablis or other white table wine
                2 tablespoons instant minced onion
                ⅛ teaspoon ground nutmeg
                ½ teaspoon dry mustard
                2 teaspoons all-purpose seasoning
                1 tablespoon each celery flakes, sweet pepper flakes
                1 (4-oz.) can mushrooms
                1 (8-oz.) can tomato sauce
                1 cup water

Coat chicken pieces with mixture of flour, salt and pepper. Reserve leftover flour mixture. In heavy skillet, brown chicken in butter, then transfer to baking dish and pour wine over chicken. Blend reserved flour mixture into butter left in skillet; add remaining ingredients and simmer about 5 minutes; pour over chicken. Cover dish and bake in moderate oven (350°) 45 minutes or until tender. This is good to serve with hot cooked spaghetti.

To accompany this chicken: **California Chablis, Rosé, Gringolino** *or* **Vino Rosso**

Wine Baked Chicken Quarters
(4 servings)

This is a very simple and easy way to prepare small, tender broiler-fryer chickens. The white wine baste —we used California Medium Sauterne—should be spooned over the chicken several times during the baking.

                1 (2-lb.) broiler-fryer chicken, quartered
                1 teaspoon monosodium glutamate
                ¼ cup California Medium Sauterne
                1 tablespoon melted butter or margarine
                1 teaspoon salt
                ⅛ teaspoon pepper
                1 teaspoon minced tarragon

Dry chicken pieces well with paper toweling. Sprinkle with monosodium glutamate; place, skin side up, in shallow baking pan. Combine wine, butter, salt, pepper and tarragon. Spoon wine mixture evenly over chicken. Bake in moderate oven (375°) about 45 to 50 minutes, or until tender, basting every fifteen minutes with pan juices.

To accompany this chicken: **California Medium Sauterne** *or* **Rosé**

Sherried Turkey with Stuffing
(6 servings)

It's never any problem to use the larger slices of roast turkey that are left over, but the smaller pieces are something else again. Try using this turkey with well-seasoned bread cubes and California Sherry in a casserole.

                2 cups cubed cooked turkey
                3 cups (¼-inch) bread cubes
                ½ cup melted butter or margarine
                2 tablespoons finely chopped onion
                ½ teaspoon each poultry seasoning, salt
                ¼ teaspoon pepper
                2 tablespoons flour
                1½ cups turkey or chicken stock
                ½ cup California Dry Sherry

Combine turkey, bread cubes, 6 tablespoons of the butter, onion and seasonings; arrange in lightly greased 1-quart casserole. Melt remaining 2 tablespoons butter and blend in flour; add turkey stock and Sherry and cook, stirring constantly, until sauce boils and thickens. Pour over ingredients in casserole. Bake in moderate oven (350°) about 35 minutes.

To accompany this turkey dish: **California Dry Sauterne**

Chicken Chablis
(6 to 8 servings)

                1 (5-lb.) stewing chicken
                2 cups California Chablis or other
                  white table wine
                2 cups water
                3 teaspoons salt
                1½ cups canned tomato puree
                1 cup dairy sour cream
                ½ teaspoon finely chopped canned green chili
                1 (6½-oz.) bag corn chips
                ½ cup pitted ripe olives, whole or halved
                1 cup grated Cheddar cheese

Have chicken cut in serving pieces. Place in large kettle. Add wine, water, 2 teaspoons salt; cover and simmer until meat is fork tender, about 1½ hours. Cool chicken in broth, then remove and discard bones and skin. Keep chicken in large pieces when possible. Blend tomato puree, sour cream, chili powder, green chili and remaining 1 teaspoon salt together. Crush corn chips coarsely. Layer chicken, sauce, corn chips, olives and cheese in large casserole (about 1½ quart size). Bake in a moderate oven (350°) until hot and bubbly, 30 to 40 minutes.

To accompany this chicken: **California Chablis** *or* **Folle Blanche**

Turkey Nero Sandwiches
(6 servings)

These are generous sandwiches and most satisfying when appetites are hearty and too impatient to wait for a lengthy cooking period. All of the ingredients can be picked up at the nearest grocery and put together with speedy efficiency. These sandwiches are wonderful served with a California white table wine.

        1 (2-lb.) package giblet gravy and sliced turkey
        ½ cup California Chablis
        1 loaf brown-and-serve French bread
        3 tablespoons butter or margarine, softened
        ⅛ teaspoon crushed thyme
        1 (3½-oz.) can French-fried onion rings

Heat turkey according to package directions; carefully remove slices. Pour gravy into skillet, add wine and boil until reduced to almost half amount (about 1½ cups). Add sliced turkey. Meanwhile, split French bread and bake according to package directions. Combine butter and thyme, spread on bread, and cut each half into three pieces. Place heated slices of turkey on bread; spoon on gravy. Sprinkle slightly heated onion rings on top.

To accompany these sandwiches: **California Chablis** *or* **Dry Sauterne**

Grilled Young Turkey Halves
(4 to 5 servings)

When available, young turkey makes an interesting barbecue subject. To be sure that the meat is well flavored let the turkey pieces stay for several hours in the wine and herb marinade. Then use this same marinade as a helpful baste as the meat cooks.

        2 (4- to 5-lb.) young turkeys
        1 cup California Dry Sauterne or Sherry
        1 tablespoon seasoned herb mix
        1 teaspoon each salt, hickory-smoked salt
        2 tablespoons each tomato catsup, oil, brown sugar,
            garlic flavored red wine vinegar

Lay turkey halves in flat shallow pan. Combine all remaining ingredients. Pour over turkey, cover and marinate for several hours, turning turkey occasionally. When ready to cook, lift turkey from marinade and place breast side down over glowing coals on grill. Turkey should be about 9 inches from the heat. Grill 40 to 45 minutes, basting now and then with marinade; turn turkey halves. Make a hood of heavy duty quilted foil to cover turkey, lay loosely over meat on grill. Continue cooking until turkey is tender, about 30 to 40 minutes longer, or until drumstick twists easily in thigh joint.

To accompany this grilled turkey: **California Dry Sauterne** *or* **Dry Semillon**

Skewered Turkey
(6 to 8 servings)

Something different to broil over the barbecue coals, or under your range broiler if you wish, are these turkey squares. Purchase halves, quarters or cut-up turkey pieces. Remove the bones and skin, but try to keep the turkey in large pieces so they are easy to thread on skewers.

        5 to 6 pounds uncooked turkey
        1 cup California Dry or Medium Sauterne or
            other white table wine
        ⅓ cup soy sauce
        ½ cup finely chopped onion
        1 crushed clove garlic
        1 tablespoon fresh lemon juice
        ¼ cup oil

Cut turkey into 1½-inch chunks. Combine marinade ingredients and pour over meat; let stand 1 to 2 hours. Drain well; thread meat on skewers. Broil over charcoal, browning lightly on all sides. Do not overcook. Vegetables such as whole mushrooms, small whole tomatoes with green pepper squares between, and whole parboiled onions may be broiled at the same time, skewering each vegetable separately. Serve with mounds of rice, either on skewers or gently pulled from skewers and arranged on platter or serving plates.

To accompany this turkey: **California Dry Sauterne** *or* **Dry Sauvignon Blanc**

Gourmet Turkey Bits: To turn leftover turkey or ham into a gourmet supper dish, prepare your favorite macaroni and cheese recipe using California Sauterne for part of the liquid. Add bits of cooked meat, top with thin slices tomato and cover with buttered crumbs. Bake until hot and browned. Glasses of chilled Sauterne would be the perfect beverage with this elegant dish.

Turkey a la King: Use the last bits of a roast turkey in a wine-flavored turkey a la king. Add about ¼ cup or more of California Sauterne or Chablis to creamed turkey mixture. Spoon over toasted English muffins and top with sprinkling of grated cheese and slivered almonds.

Turkey Thermidor
(6 servings)

Any hostess in a quandary about what to serve at ladies' luncheon group might find the answer with this turkey dish. It's a little more elaborate than creamed turkey because the sauce is enriched with California Dry Sherry, egg yolks and cream. To accompany each individual serving, try a molded fruit salad or citrus salad made with orange wheels and fresh grapefruit sections with pineapple dressing.

    1 (4-oz.) can mushroom pieces and stems, drained
      (save liquid)
    6 tablespoons melted butter or margarine
    ¼ cup all-purpose flour
    ¼ teaspoon each salt, paprika
      Pinch ground thyme
      Dash cayenne pepper
    1½ cups light cream
    ¼ cup California Dry Sherry
    2 egg yolks, slightly beaten
    2 cups cubed (½-inch) cooked turkey roast
    ¼ cup grated Parmesan cheese
      Toast points

Cook mushrooms in butter until lightly browned; blend in flour and seasonings. Gradually add ⅓ cup mushroom liquid and cream, stirring constantly until thickened. Stir in Sherry. Slowly add portion of hot sauce to egg yolks, stirring constantly, then stir egg mixture into remaining sauce. Place over low heat and cook until thick. Add turkey. Pour over toast points in 6 individual au gratin dishes; sprinkle with cheese and paprika. Place under broiler to brown slightly.

To accompany this turkey dish: **California Chablis** *or* **Johannisberger Riesling**

Turkey on Rye: Cold cooked turkey slices make a pleasant supper sandwich when served with a chilled California table wine, such as Chablis or Rosé. Spread rye bread with softened cream cheese well seasoned with onion salt, a few drops of Tabasco and prepared mustard. Top with slices of turkey, tomato and avocado. Serve open faced with whole spiced peaches and ripe olives.

Glazed Turkey
(16 to 18 servings)

For a party or for a large family gathering this beautifully glazed turkey will do justice to your carefully planned menu. Roast the turkey with or without dressing, but keep basting it occasionally with the special wine and fruit juice baste.

    1 (15- to 18-lb.) turkey
    ¼ cup butter or margarine, melted
    3 tablespoons lemon juice
      Salt and pepper
    1 cup California Rosé
    ⅔ cup cranberry juice
    ⅓ cup pineapple juice
    ½ cup honey

Prepare turkey for roasting in your usual way. Combine melted butter and lemon juice; brush about half of it over turkey; sprinkle with salt and pepper. Place turkey in roasting pan and start roasting in moderate oven (350°). Combine Rosé with remainder of butter and other ingredients and when turkey begins to color, begin spooning on wine baste, 3 or 4 tablespoons at a time. Continue basting and roasting until turkey is glazed and tender, using wine baste and rich pan drippings. (Allow about 18 minutes to the pound.) Remove turkey to platter while making gravy. Skim excess fat from pan liquid; thicken liquid as desired with cornstarch mixed with water. Cook about 5 minutes. Pour into heated sauce bowl and serve with turkey.

To accompany this turkey: **California Rosé** *or* **Sauvignon Blanc**

Turkey with Wine Sauce: For a quick and easy way to roast turkey, start with one of the prepared (about 2½ lbs.) turkey roasts and follow the directions given on the package. When the roast is cooked, remove it from the foil roasting pan and add to the drippings: 1 tablespoon finely chopped onion, ¼ cup California Sauterne or other dry white table wine, ¼ cup tomato sauce, ⅓ cup water and ½ the contents of a gravy packet. Heat mixture to boiling point, stirring to blend well. Serve over slices of roast turkey.

Modesto Turkey with Waffles
(6 servings)

Chicken seasoned stock base found in the spice and herb department of any grocery makes a fine beginning for a rich Sherry-flavored sauce that is well adapted to the cooked turkey cubes. This Sunday-night-supper or quick-luncheon dish is easy to make and it's different because of the Herb Waffles.

```
¼ cup butter or margarine
½ cup all-purpose flour
 1 tablespoon chicken seasoned stock base
¼ teaspoon each white pepper, dry mustard
⅛ teaspoon nutmeg
2¾ cups milk
 2 to 4 tablespoons California Dry Sherry
 2 cups cubed cooked turkey
```

In saucepan melt butter and blend in flour, chicken base, pepper, mustard and nutmeg. Add milk gradually and cook over medium heat, stirring constantly until sauce thickens, about 8 minutes. Stir in Sherry and turkey; cook until turkey is well heated through. Serve over Herb Waffles. To make the Herb Waffles, add 1 teaspoon poultry seasoning to each cup of waffle mix.

To accompany this turkey dish: **California Dry Sauterne or Riesling**

Sacramento Skillet Duck
(6 servings)

You will need a very large skillet for cooking this wonderful company dish. If you find it more convenient, brown the duck quarters as directed, then place them in a large casserole or baking pan. Add the sauce, then cover the casserole and bake the duck in a moderate oven (350°) for the same length of time, or until meat is tender. Duck is very good served with white or brown rice.

```
⅓ cup all-purpose flour
1½ teaspoons salt
¼ teaspoon pepper
 3 ducks, quartered
⅓ cup butter or margarine
1¼ cups water
⅔ cup California Dry Sherry
⅓ cup orange juice
1½ tablespoons grated orange peel
```

Combine flour, salt and pepper; use to coat duck quarters well. Heat butter in large skillet and brown ducks on all sides. Combine remainder of ingredients and pour over ducks. Cover pan tightly, lower heat and simmer about 1½ hours or until tender. Before serving, skim off excess fat from pan sauce.

To accompany this duck: **California Pinot Noir or Sparkling Burgundy**

Turkey Timbales with Sherry Mushroom Sauce
(6 servings)

There is always some turkey left over from the big dinner, and this is a very easy and good way to serve both the turkey and the dressing with style. Canned sliced mushrooms may be added to the sauce if desired.

```
2 tablespoons California Medium Sherry
1 (10½-oz.) can condensed cream of mushroom soup
2 cups finely diced cooked turkey
2 cups baked stuffing
2 eggs, slightly beaten
```

Combine Sherry and soup for sauce. Combine turkey, stuffing and eggs with ½ cup of the sauce, mixing well. Place ½ cup of the turkey mixture into each of 6 well-greased custard cups; set in shallow pan of water and bake in moderate oven (350°) about 40 minutes or until firm. Unmold and serve with remainder of Sherry Mushroom sauce, heated.

To accompany this dish: **California Dry Sauterne**

Roast Wild Duck
(4 servings)

The hunter will be delighted to trust your culinary skills with his prize when you prepare the ducks like this, with California Burgundy. The seasoning is very easy too, if you use a package of French dressing salad mix.

```
2 (1-lb.) wild ducks
1 package French salad dressing mix
6 celery stalks and leaves
2 tablespoons melted butter or salad oil
⅓ cup diced onion (optional)
½ teaspoon coarsely ground black pepper
¼ cup diced orange
1 cup California Burgundy
```

Clean and wash ducks thoroughly; singe and wash again. Dry well. Rub inside and out with dry salad dressing mix. Stuff celery stalks into body cavities. Place ducks in roasting pan; brush with butter. Roast in hot oven (400°) about 10 minutes or until lightly browned, turning once. Pour off excess fat. Turn ducks breast side up and cover with onion, pepper, orange, and wine. Return to oven and roast 20 minutes longer for very rare; 40 minutes for medium; and 1 hour and 5 minutes for well-done. Remove celery stalks before serving.

To accompany this roast duck: **California Burgundy or Pinot Chardonnay**

Roast Duckling with Orange Sauce
(4 to 6 servings)

The sweet tartness of the Orange Sauce is excellent with the richness of the duckling roasted in a simple baste of California Port. At the end of the cooking period, remove the duckling pieces from the pan and keep warm while preparing the sauce. You may want to add some of the pan juices, carefully skimmed of fat, to the Orange Sauce.

```
 1 (5- to 6-lb.) duckling, cut for fricassee
   Salt
⅔ cup California Port
 1 tablespoon grated orange peel
 1 clove garlic, minced
 3 tablespoons cooking oil
 1 tablespoon cornstarch
1¼ cups fresh orange juice
 1 tablespoon honey
¼ teaspoon ground ginger
   Dash pepper
 1 cup fresh orange sections
```

With fork, puncture skin of duckling pieces; sprinkle with salt and place on rack in roasting pan; pour ½ cup of the Port over them. Roast in a slow oven (325°) basting and turning pieces occasionally, allowing about 25 minutes per pound. Keep warm while preparing sauce.

Orange Sauce: In saucepan, lightly sauté orange peel and garlic in cooking oil. Blend remaining Port with cornstarch, orange juice and honey; add slowly to saucepan, stirring constantly to smooth. Simmer sauce for a few minutes until clear, then stir in ginger, pepper and orange sections and heat well. Taste and add salt as necessary. Serve hot with roast duckling.

To accompany this roast duckling: **California Burgundy** *or* **Claret**

Baste for Cornish Hens: To keep Rock Cornish Game hens moist and flavorful while they cook, baste them with a mixture of equal parts California Sauterne and orange juice. Heat the baste before spooning over the birds so that the cooking won't be slowed down by cold liquid. The fruity flavor is very pleasant. Some of the same wine, well chilled, is a perfect beverage to serve with these little birds.

Pheasant in Sauce
(6 servings)

This is a very good way to cook both wild and domestic pheasant, and it may be used for chicken too. The cooking time may vary a little, so be sure to check for tenderness toward the end. You may want to add a little more wine too, increasing the amount of sauce. Some of the packaged processed wild rice is excellent served with this dish.

```
½ cup all-purpose flour
 1 teaspoon each salt, paprika
⅛ teaspoon each pepper, powdered sweet basil
 2 pheasants, cut into pieces
¼ cup shortening
 1 small clove garlic, crushed
½ cup water
½ teaspoon Worcestershire sauce
¼ cup chopped ripe olives
½ cup California Chablis or other white table wine
```

Combine flour, salt, paprika, pepper and basil; coat pheasant pieces well. Brown on all sides in shortening in large skillet. Add garlic, water and Worcestershire sauce. Cover pan tightly and simmer 45 minutes. Turn pheasant and add olives and wine. Recover pan and simmer 35 to 45 minutes longer or until tender. Add additional wine if necessary to increase amount of sauce.

To accompany this pheasant: **California Champagne** *or* **Chablis**

Cornish Hens with Herb Dressing
(4 servings)

```
 2 (1-lb., 6-oz.) Cornish hens
 1 cup California Dry Sauterne or other white table wine
 1 tablespoon salad oil
 1 (7-oz.) package herb stuffing mix
   Salt and pepper
 1 cup dairy sour cream
¼ cup melted butter or margarine
```

Defrost Cornish hens; remove giblets; cut each hen in half. Wipe dry, then marinate several hours in wine and oil. Crush 2 cups of the dressing mix into very fine crumbs. Drain hens well; sprinkle with salt and pepper; spread with sour cream. Coat thickly with fine dressing mix crumbs. Combine remaining dressing mix with wine and oil in which hens were marinated; add 2 tablespoons of the melted butter. Spread in shallow baking pan. Place coated hens over dressing mix; drizzle with remaining melted butter. Bake in a moderate oven (350°) about 1 hour or until tender.

To accompany this dish: **California Rosé** *or* **Dry Semillon**

fish and shellfish

Wine seems to accomplish an impossible feat with fish, complementing and accenting the delicate flavors of some varieties, and subduing the "too fishy" flavor of others. This two-way effect explains why those who like fish, enjoy it even more when it is cooked and served with wine. And those who have not been very fond of it in the past, suddenly find that it is delicious. Tradition suggests that a white table wine is the type most people prefer. Many of the recipes in this chapter are based on that combination. Red table wine as a seasoning for fish is often accompanied by tomato both for color and for flavor. Then, with a glass of red wine to accompany the dish, the results are very good indeed.

Seafood Nicholas
(6 servings)

Here a small amount of California Dry Sherry perfects the sauce for a very simple but good Sunday-night supper or luncheon dish. It's created from ingredients found on every modestly stocked pantry shelf. To give it a dramatic flair, the mixture is served in crisp pastry shells, and decorated with narrow curls of lemon peel and sprigs of parsley.

    1 (10½-oz.) can condensed cream of celery soup
    ½ cup mayonnaise
    ½ cup diced celery
    ½ cup sliced ripe olives
    ¼ cup chopped onion
    1 (7-oz.) can tuna
    2 tablespoons California Dry Sherry
    1 (5-oz.) can shrimp
    6 pastry shells, heated until crisp

In a saucepan combine soup, mayonnaise, celery, olives and onion. Place over heat, add Sherry and oil drained from tuna, stirring well to smooth. Add tuna broken into pieces and drained shrimp, combining gently. Continue cooking gently until well heated. Serve in pastry shells.

To accompany this dish: **California Dry Sauterne** *or* **Chablis**

Fish Fillets with Shrimp Sauce: Prepare fish fillets as in "Fish Poached in Wine" on page 66. After baking, open corner of foil and pour juices in saucepan and simmer to reduce quantity to about ¼ cup. Add contents 1 can frozen shrimp bisque (partially defrosted). Cook, stirring constantly, until smooth sauce is formed. Taste and check for additional seasoning. Pour sauce over fillets, sprinkle with cheese and brown.

To accompany this fish: **California Chablis** *or* **Pinot Chardonnay**

Sole with Mushroom Sauce
(3 servings)

Arrange 1 pound sole fillets in greased shallow baking dish; sprinkle with salt; pour over ½ cup California Sauterne or other white table wine. Bake in very hot oven (475°) about 10 minutes, or until fish is just tender. Remove from oven and pour off liquid into measuring cup. Combine ¼ cup of the liquid to contents 1 (10½-oz.) can condensed cream of mushroom soup; pour over fish; sprinkle with grated cheese and paprika. Broil until lightly browned and bubbling.

Fish Poached in White Wine
(4 to 5 servings)

For the best in texture and flavor with fish, use brief cooking and low temperature. This is the reason poaching (or simmering) the fish fillets in a flavorful liquid, such as white wine, is good.

    1½ pounds fish fillets or steaks
     1 small onion, minced
     2 sprigs parsley
     1 tablespoon butter or margarine
     ¾ cup California Chablis or other white table wine
       Salt and pepper
     ½ cup heavy cream
     ¼ cup grated Parmesan cheese

Place large sheet of heavy duty foil wrap on shallow baking pan. Sprinkle half of onion in center and arrange fish on it, overlapping fillets. If very thin fillets are used, roll them up jelly-roll fashion and fasten with picks. Sprinkle fish with remaining onion, add parsley sprigs and dot with butter. Pour wine over all; season with salt and pepper. Make cooking package by bringing long ends of foil up over fish and sealing with double fold; fold and turn up ends of foil to hold in juices. Bake in moderate oven (375°) 20 minutes. Gently pour out liquid in package into measuring cup. (There should be slightly more than 1 cupful.) Place package with fish on heat proof platter or serving dish; or remove fillets carefully from foil and arrange on platter.

Make sauce: In saucepan melt 3 tablespoons butter or margarine and blend in 3 tablespoons flour; cook and stir well, then add hot fish liquid gradually, stirring vigorously to smooth. Add cream, using just enough to make a sauce of medium consistency. Taste for seasoning content. You may want to add a few drops of lemon juice and salt. Open foil and crimp to form border. Pour sauce over fish; sprinkle with Parmesan cheese, then brown under broiler.

To accompany this fish: **California Chablis** *or* **Chenin Blanc**

Sole Bonne Femme: Follow "Fish Poached in White Wine" above. Just before seasoning, add ½ pound of fresh mushrooms which have been sautéd in about 3 tablespoons butter or margaine for a few minutes. Slice mushrooms if they are large. Spread over fillets. Use additional salt and pepper.

Garnish with Lemon Cups: Lemon cups are simple to make and provide a colorful garnish to the fish platter or individual serving of fish. Cut lemons crosswise, ream out juice carefully and scoop out the pulp lining. Cut a slice from the bottom so that the cups will stand upright. Scallop or notch edges as desired. Fill cups with tartar sauce sprinkled with very finely cut parsley; fruit sherbet or ice; pickle chips or relish.

Poached Halibut Florentine
(6 servings)

If you know you are going to be pressed for time when you want to serve this special fish dish, do part of the cooking ahead of time. Poach the halibut steaks in the California Sauterne and lemon juice, and prepare the sauce well in advance. With this forehanded preparation, it's easy to assemble the dish and heat it through, ready to bring to the table.

    1½ pounds halibut steak
     ½ cup California Medium Sauterne
     ½ cup lemon juice
     1 (10-oz.) package frozen chopped spinach
     ¼ cup finely chopped onion
     2 tablespoons butter or margarine
     3 tablespoons flour
     ¼ teaspoon salt
       Dash pepper
     1 cup undiluted evaporated milk
     4 egg yolks, beaten
     ½ cup shredded Cheddar cheese

Place halibut in shallow skillet; add wine and lemon juice, then enough water to just cover fish; cover pan partially, bring to boil and simmer gently about 5 to 7 minutes. (Be careful not to over-cook.) With wide server, remove fish to lightly buttered shallow baking dish or casserole. Boil down liquid to about ¾ cup. In another saucepan cook spinach and onions in ¼ cup water with ½ teaspoon salt according to package directions; drain. Push spinach to one side of pan, add butter, stirring to melt, then blend in flour, salt, and pepper; cook briefly. Pour in evaporated milk and the ¾ cup liquid from fish. Cook and stir over medium heat until sauce thickens and all ingredients are combined. Remove from heat and spoon a small portion into egg yolks; return to sauce pan and stir to blend well. Pour over poached halibut in baking dish. Top with shredded cheese. Bake in hot oven (400°) about 10 minutes until cheese is melted and dish is well heated. Serve at once.

To accompany this dish: **California Dry** *or* **Medium Sauterne** *or* **Traminer**

Fish and Tomato Bake
(6 servings)

1 (3- to 4-lb.) fish for baking
2 tablespoons lemon juice
  Salt and pepper
1 cup chopped onions
½ cup finely chopped parsley
2 small cloves garlic, minced
¼ cup cooking oil
½ cup California Dry Sauterne
1 cup tomato catsup
1 cup tomato juice

Rinse fish in cold water; dry well. Rub with lemon juice and sprinkle inside and out with salt and pepper; place in baking dish. In skillet sauté onions, parsley, and garlic in oil until onions are transparent, but not browned. Stir in Sauterne and remaining ingredients; simmer about 5 minutes, then pour over fish. Bake uncovered in moderate oven (350°), basting occasionally, allowing about 16 minutes per pound. Serve garnished with sliced lemon wheels and parsley.

To accompany this dish: **California Dry Sauterne** *or* **Chablis**

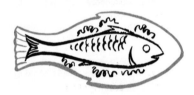

Fish Steaks in Burgundy Sauce
(4 servings)

Take a shortcut in making a good wine sauce for the fish steaks of your choice. California Burgundy is added to undiluted tomato soup along with a few seasonings and, in a very brief time, a really fine sauce is ready to pour over the fish arranged in the baking dish.

1 (10½-oz.) can condensed tomato soup
⅓ cup California Burgundy or other red table wine
1 cup shredded process pimiento cheese
2 tablespoons chopped parsley
1 tablespoon minced onion
4 fish steaks (halibut, swordfish, sea bass, salmon)

In saucepan combine soup, wine and cheese; stir over low heat until cheese melts. Add parsley and onion. Arrange fish steaks in shallow baking dish; pour hot wine sauce over them. Bake in moderate oven (375°) 25 to 30 minutes.

To accompany this fish: **California Chablis** *or* **Rosé**

Halibut with Shrimp Sauce
(6 to 8 servings)

The baked halibut fillets have their own built-in sauce when they are baked with a frozen cream soup and California Dry Sauterne. This is an easy and quick supper dish for family or company.

3 pounds halibut fillets
2 teaspoons seasoned salt
1 (10-oz.) can frozen cream of shrimp soup, thawed
¾ cup California Dry Sauterne or other dry white table wine
2 tablespoons minced parsley

Cut fish in serving-size pieces and arrange in a single layer in a buttered baking dish. Sprinkle with seasoned salt. Combine soup and wine; spoon over the fish. Bake in moderate oven (350°) 30 minutes. Sprinkle with minced parsley and serve.

To accompany this dish: **California Dry Sauterne** *or* **Sauvignon Blanc**

Cioppino
(4 servings)

Cioppino is always something of a production, but several convenience foods in this version shorten the traditional assembling and cooking process. The flavor is outstanding.

¼ cup olive oil
1 medium onion, finely chopped
2 cloves garlic, crushed
1 (1-lb. 12-oz.) can tomatoes
2 (8-oz.) cans tomato sauce
2 (1½-oz.) packages spaghetti-sauce-mix
1 teaspoon seasoned salt
¼ teaspoon seasoned pepper
2 cups water
1 cup California Dry Sauterne or other white table wine
1½ pounds white fish, such as halibut, cut in large chunks
1 pound raw shrimp or small prawns, shelled and deveined
4 (about 6-oz.) uncooked lobster tails, fins and soft undershell removed and cut in large chunks, shell and all
1 dozen well-washed clams

In large Dutch oven or kettle heat oil; add onion and garlic and sauté until tender. Add tomatoes, tomato sauce, spaghetti-sauce-mix, seasoned salt, seasoned pepper and water. Bring to boil, reduce heat, and simmer for 30 minutes, stirring occasionally. Add wine, fish, shrimp, lobster and clams. Cover and simmer about 15 minutes, stirring occasionally. Serve in large soup bowls with chunks of heated French bread.

To accompany this Cioppino: **California Pinot Chardonnay** *or other dry white table wine*

Baked Fish Fillets Piquant
(3 servings)

½ cup California Sauterne or other white table wine
¼ cup white wine vinegar
¼ cup water
1 teaspoon salt
1 pound fish fillets (sole, halibut or cod)
Fine dry bread crumbs
½ cup mayonnaise
½ cup dairy sour cream
2 tablespoons finely chopped green onion
Paprika

Combine wine, vinegar, water and salt; pour over fish fillets and marinate 1 to 2 hours. Drain fish thoroughly on paper toweling. Coat both sides of fillets with crumbs; arrange in single layer in lightly buttered shallow baking dish. Combine mayonnaise, sour cream and onion; spread evenly over fish. Cover with thin layer of crumbs and dust with paprika. Bake in a hot oven (425°) for 10 minutes, or until fish is done. Serve with lemon wedges.

To accompany this fish: **California Dry Sauterne** *or* **Chenin Blanc**

Salmon Mold Sauterne
(5 to 6 servings)

Soften contents 1 envelope unflavored gelatin in ¼ cup water; dissolve in 1 cup hot chicken broth. Add ½ cup California Dry Sauterne or other white table wine, 2 tablespoons grated onion, 2 tablespoons lemon juice. Season with salt and pepper to taste. Chill until mixture starts to thicken, then fold in contents 1 (1-pound) can salmon, drained and flaked. Pour into oiled fish-shaped mold (1-quart); chill until firm. Unmold on crisp lettuce and serve with mayonnaise.

Fish Sticks Piquant: For an excellent way to dress up fish sticks, follow the recipe for Baked Fish Fillet Piquant. Cut the marinating time to about 15 minutes and eliminate dipping in fine dry crumbs, as fish sticks are already coated. If fish sticks are quite thick, give them a few minutes longer in the oven.

Baked Fish With Chablis: To add interest to broiled or baked fish, heat ½ cup butter or margarine with ¼ cup California Chablis or other white table wine. Add 1 tablespoon each finely chopped parsley, green onion and pimiento, and a dash of wine vinegar. Spoon over fish when served.

Tuna Casserole
(4 to 5 servings)

The new feature of this dependable favorite is the addition of California Chablis and crisp chow mein noodles. With this casserole serve a colorful fruit salad.

1 (3-oz.) can chow mein noodles
1 (10½-oz.) can condensed cream of mushroom soup
1 (7-oz.) can tuna
¼ cup California Chablis or other white table wine
1 cup thinly sliced celery
1 tablespoon instant minced onion
Pepper

Set aside ½ cup noodles for topping. Blend all other ingredients and place in lightly greased casserole; sprinkle with reserved noodles. Bake in moderate oven (350°) about 30 to 40 minutes.

To accompany this casserole: **California Chablis** *or* **Dry Sauterne**

Southern Clam Casserole
(6 servings)

½ pound wide noodles
2 tablespoons butter or margarine
2 tablespoons salad oil
1 medium-sized onion, minced
1 clove garlic, minced
5 tablespoons flour
2 (7-oz.) cans minced clams
1 (No. 2) can stewed tomatoes
½ cup California Sauterne or other white table wine
1 cup grated Cheddar cheese
½ teaspoon Worcestershire sauce
Salt and pepper to taste

Cook noodles in boiling salted water until tender; drain. Heat butter and oil in a heavy skillet or saucepan; add onion and garlic; cook gently, stirring frequently, for 5 minutes. Blend in flour; add liquid drained from clams, tomatoes and wine; cook, stirring constantly, until mixture boils and thickens. Add ½ cup of the cheese; stir over low heat until melted. Season with Worcestershire sauce, salt and pepper. Add clams and noodles. Turn into a greased casserole; sprinkle with remaining ½ cup grated cheese. Bake in a moderately hot oven (375°) 25 minutes.

To accompany this dish: **California Sauterne, Rhine Wine** *or* **Chablis**

Poached Trout: Trout poached in wine is delicious either hot or cold. Use equal parts of California Sauterne and chicken or fish stock as the poaching liquid. A little chopped green onion, plus dill or rosemary and the usual salt and pepper are the only added seasonings needed. Accompany the trout with glasses of chilled white dinner wine for a gourmet meal.

Shrimp a la Newburg
(4 servings)

If time is limited, the Sherry-flavored sauce for this shrimp may be made in advance and refrigerated until just before serving time. Reheat the sauce in the top of a double boiler over hot water, adding the shrimp at the very last. Thin the sauce to desired consistency with a small portion of the Sherry marinade.

    ½ cup California Dry Sherry
    2 cups cooked and cleaned shrimp
    3 tablespoons butter or margarine
    2 tablespoons all-purpose flour
    ¾ cup light or heavy cream
      Yolks of 4 hard-cooked eggs
    1 teaspoon salt
    ¼ teaspoon dry mustard
      Dash of pepper
    2 tablespoons lemon juice
    4 cups hot cooked rice

Pour Sherry over shrimp. Cover and marinate several hours. Drain and reserve ¼ cup liquid. Combine butter and flour in top of double boiler. Add cream and cook, stirring constantly, until sauce thickens and smooths; do not boil. Press egg yolks through sieve into bowl. Rub to paste and stir, a little at a time, into hot sauce. Stir until smooth. Add ¼ cup Sherry marinade, salt, dry mustard, pepper, and lemon juice. When ready to serve, stir in shrimp. Some of the remaining marinade may be added for extra flavor and to thin sauce if necessary. Heat through. Serve over hot, cooked rice or individual rice rings.

Individual Rice Rings: Add 3 tablespoons butter or margarine to hot rice. Pack into 4 greased individual ring molds. Set in pan of hot water for about 1 minute, then invert on serving plates.

To accompany this shrimp dish: **California Dry or Medium Sauterne**

To pep up broiled or baked fish, heat ½ cup butter with ¼ cup California Chablis or Sauterne. Add 1 tablespoon each finely chopped parsley, green onion and pimiento and a dash of wine vinegar. Spoon over fish when served.

Last Minute Shrimp Newburg
(4 to 6 servings)

    1 (10-oz.) can frozen cream of shrimp soup, thawed
    ¼ cup evaporated milk
    1 (5-oz.) can deveined shrimp, well drained
    1 cup frozen peas, thawed
    1 cup shredded process American cheese
    2 tablespoons California Dry Sherry
    1 teaspoon Worcestershire sauce
    ¼ teaspoon Tabasco

In saucepan combine soup and evaporated milk; heat gently. Stir in shrimp, peas, cheese, Sherry, Worcestershire sauce and Tabasco. Continue to cook over medium heat, stirring occasionally, until steaming. Do not boil. Serve over hot rice.

To accompany this dish: **California Chablis or Sylvaner**

Barbecued Salmon Steaks, Vermouth
(Serves 6)

California Dry Vermouth makes an effective marinade for seafood because of the many herbs and spices that go into its production. Use a glass or enamelware dish for the marinating, so there'll be no chance of a metallic taste. While the salmon is on the grill, heat the seasoned wine mixture in which it is marinated, to use as a basting sauce.

    2 pounds salmon steaks or other fish steaks,
      fresh or frozen
    1 cup California Dry Vermouth
    ¾ cup melted fat or oil
    ⅓ cup lemon juice
    2 tablespoon chopped chives, fresh or freeze-dried
    2 teaspoons seasoned salt
    ½ teaspoon seasoned pepper

Thaw frozen steaks. Cut into serving-size portions and place in single layer in shallow baking dish. Combine remaining ingredients. Pour sauce over fish and let stand 4 hours, turning occasionally. Remove fish, reserving sauce for basting. Place fish in well-greased, hinged wire grills. Cook about 4 inches from moderately hot coals 8 minutes. Baste with sauce. Turn and cook 7 to 10 minutes longer or until fish flakes easily when tested with a fork.

To accompany this barbecued fish: **California Chablis or Cabernet**

Prawns Sarapico
(4 servings)

There will be a surprise package for each guest when you serve prawns this way. The prawns are cooked in individual squares of aluminum foil. Two kinds of cheese and pimientos with a generous portion of California Chablis form an interesting and quite good sauce. Serve the prawns with fluffy cooked rice.

> 1½ pounds fresh or frozen prawns, uncooked
> 2 (3-oz.) packages cream cheese
> 2 (3-oz.) packages bleu cheese
> 2 pimientos, chopped fine
> 8 thin slices lemon
> ½ cup California Chablis

Shell and clean prawns. Cream together cheeses and pimientos. Cut four squares of aluminum foil. On each square, mound an equal amount of cheese mixture. Flatten cheese mounds slightly with back of spoon. Divide raw prawns, placing equal amounts on each mound. Top each with two lemon slices. Bring edges of foil up to form a bag. Place bags on baking sheet. Just before sealing bags, pour 2 tablespoons Chablis in each. Bake in moderate oven (350°) 20 to 25 minutes or until prawns are done. Serve with fluffy cooked rice.

To accompany this dish: **California Chablis** *or* **Folle Blanche**

Pickled Shrimp
(5 to 6 servings)

California Dry or Medium Sauterne and a garlic-flavored wine vinegar plus a few seasonings make the marinade for these quick pickled shrimp. Use the shrimp for salads or serve as an afternoon or evening snack with crisp crackers, melba toast or heated bread sticks.

> ½ cup California Sauterne or other white table wine
> ¼ cup salad oil
> 2 tablespoons garlic-flavored wine vinegar
> ½ teaspoon seasoned salt
> ¼ teaspoon dried dill
> 2 drops Tabasco
> 3 cups large cooked shrimp, shelled

Shake in covered jar or beat together with rotary beater wine, oil, vinegar and seasonings. Pour over shrimp; stir to mix. Cover and refrigerate overnight. Drain and serve sprinkled with parsley or green onion, if desired.

To accompany this shrimp: **California Sylvaner** *or* **Dry Semillon**

Lobster Special
(8 servings)

The sauce for this creamy lobster dish is made basically from condensed mushroom soup just as it comes from the can and a generous amount of California Dry Sherry. It is served in a chive biscuit ring, one that is fashioned quickly from baking powder biscuits found in the grocery refrigerator case.

> 2 tablespoons chopped green pepper
> 2 tablespoons chopped pimiento
> ¼ cup butter or margarine
> 2 (10½-oz.) cans condensed cream of mushroom soup
> ⅔ cup milk
> ¼ cup slivered almonds
> 1 teaspoon salt
> ¼ cup California Dry Sherry
> ¼ teaspoon savory
> 2 (5½-oz.) cans lobster

Sauté green pepper and pimiento in butter until tender. Add soup, stirring until smooth. Add remaining ingredients to sauce and heat thoroughly, stirring occasionally. Serve in bowl set inside Flaky Chive Ring on serving plate.

NOTE: Instead of lobster you can use equal amounts of shrimp, crab or solid pack tuna.

Flaky Chive Ring:

> 2 cans refrigerated baking powder or buttermilk biscuits
> ¼ cup butter or margarine, melted
> 2 tablespoons chopped chives, fresh or freeze-dried
> 1 tablespoon finely chopped parsley

Dip each biscuit in butter, sprinkle lightly with chives and parsley. Stand on edge around sides of greased 8- or 9-inch layer pan. Bake in moderate oven (375°) 25 to 30 minutes, until golden brown.

To accompany this dish: **California Champagne** *or* **Chablis**

Scampi
(4 servings)

Shrimp prepared in this way may be used as a light main course, serving toast squares or rice with it. Or the shrimp are delightful as hot hors d'oeuvres when offered in a chafing dish. The amount in each 5-ounce can is about 1 cup, so if you wish to use frozen or fresh-cooked shelled shrimp in this recipe, you will need about 2 cups.

      2 (5-oz.) cans shrimp, drained
    ¼ cup butter or margarine
    ⅛ teaspoon garlic chips
      2 tablespoons parsley flakes
    ½ cup California Chablis or other white table wine

Melt butter or margarine in skillet or chafing dish. Add garlic, parsley and wine. Heat to simmering then add shrimp and cook over low heat until heated through, about 5 minutes.

To accompany this shrimp: **California Chablis** *or* **White Pinot**

Seafood en Coquille
(4 servings)

Some of the new ideas in food packaging are most helpful in the preparation of dishes once intricate enough to require hours of cooking time. Here we use peas frozen in butter sauce as the basis for an easy luncheon dish, delicious and rich, with a light touch of California Dry Sherry.

      1 (10-oz.) package little baby early peas
        frozen in butter sauce
      2 tablespoons all-purpose flour
      1 cup milk
      1 cup grated Cheddar cheese
      3 tablespoons California Dry Sherry
    ⅛ teaspoon white pepper
      2 (6½-oz.) cans crabmeat, drained and flaked
      1 (4½-oz.) can large shrimps, drained
      2 tablespoons butter or margarine, melted
    ⅓ cup fine bread crumbs
        Paprika

Slip pouch of peas into boiling water; bring water to second boil; continue cooking until butter sauce is melted. Open pouch; drain butter sauce into medium saucepan; stir in flour; gradually add milk. Place over medium heat; cook until thickened, stirring constantly. Add cheese; heat until melted. Stir in Sherry, pepper, crabmeat, shrimps and peas. Spoon into four large lightly greased baking shells; allow ¾ cup per serving. Combine butter and bread crumbs. Sprinkle around outside edge of baking shells. Bake in moderate oven (350°) 25 minutes. Dust with paprika before serving.

To accompany this dish: **California Dry Semillon, Johannisberger Riesling** *or* **Dry Sauterne**

Scallops in Wine Sauce
(6 servings)

Handle scallops with care, because they are quite delicate and require only the briefest of cooking. Cook them too long and they become tough. With this recipe you may prepare the sauce, add the scallops and refrigerate the mixture until close to serving time. Allow time for a brief and careful reheating and an interval under the broiler.

    ¾ cup California Dry Sauterne
    1½ pounds frozen scallops, thawed and drained
      3 tablespoons butter or margarine
      3 green onions, chopped
    ¾ cup canned drained mushrooms
      1 tablespoon chopped parsley
        Dash each of salt, pepper, marjoram, thyme
    1½ tablespoons flour
    ¾ cup undiluted evaporated milk
        Paprika, bread crumbs, butter

In medium saucepan heat wine; add scallops and simmer for about 3 minutes, or until done. Drain cooked scallops (saving liquid) and keep scallops warm. In another saucepan melt butter; add onions and cook until barely tender. Add mushrooms, parsley, salt, pepper, marjoram and thyme. Remove from heat; blend in flour gradually, keeping smooth. Slowly stir in evaporated milk and ½ cup liquid from scallops; heat to boiling, stirring constantly. (Sauce should be thick.) Add paprika and scallops; remove from heat. Fill individual baking dishes with mixture. Sprinkle with bread crumbs then dot with butter. Place under broiler until slightly browned. Serve immediately.

To accompany this dish: **California Johannisberger Riesling** *or* **Chablis**

Braised Prawns

(4 to 6 servings)

Prawns go well with a small amount of chopped cooked ham in this simple dish designed for a quick snack. With the addition of rice to serve it on, the braised prawns can be extended into a light luncheon or supper dish.

    1 pound uncooked prawns, shelled and deveined
    ¼ cup cooking oil
    1 (5-oz.) can sliced bamboo shoots
    ¾ cup stock
    ¼ cup California Dry Sherry
    1 teaspoon soy sauce
    1 teaspoon sugar
    ¼ cup finely chopped cooked ham
    1 tablespoon vinegar
    1 tablespoon cornstarch

Cut prawns in half lengthwise without cutting all the way through; press flat with wide knife. In large skillet, heat oil, add bamboo shoots and cook gently about 5 minutes. Add prawns, stock, wine, soy sauce and sugar, mixing well. Cook over medium heat 5 minutes; add ham and stir briefly. Spoon out into serving dish, leaving liquid in pan. Combine vinegar and cornstarch; gradually add to liquid stirring constantly until sauce thickens and clears. Pour over shrimp mixture. Serve with additional soy sauce or on hot cooked rice.

To accompany this dish: **California Rhine Wine** *or* **Grey Riesling**

Prawn Marinade: Marinate prawns in California Rosé or Sauterne for refreshing flavor. Add a generous sprinkle of dried dill, dash of cayenne and a shake of garlic or seasoned salt. Cover and refrigerate several hours before piling on crisp watercress for a change of greens.

Oyster Stew and White Wine

(4 to 6 servings)

White wine is very good in oyster stew. Heat 1½ cups milk with ½ cup light cream. Melt ¼ cup butter in skillet; add 1 pint oysters and their liquid. Cook just until edges of oysters start to curl. Add ¼ cup California Chablis or other white table wine, 1 teaspoon seasoned salt and a dash of white pepper. Combine with the heated milk and serve.

Tangy Seafood Sauce: Top seafood with a tangy sauce made by blending equal parts mayonnaise, tomato chili sauce and chopped pimientos. Accent with lemon juice or California white table wine to taste.

CHEESE, EGGS, PASTAS, AND RICE

The traditional listings of wine and food combinations usually classify dishes made with cheese and eggs as light main dishes, especially suitable for luncheons or suppers. And with them go the light wines — light in color and light in body. California's dry white wines are particularly well suited for use both in and with these recipes. Rosé is another excellent choice, and can usually be substituted for a white table wine in these recipes, unless the color is a factor. As an interesting variation, some of the lighter-bodied red table wines are a pleasant combination with dishes seasoned in bolder style.

Crusty Potato Cheese Casserole

(4 to 5 servings)

Count on this casserole for occasions when you need simple, but hearty fare. It's ideal for picnics, served with grilled frankfurters or steaks. Bake the casserole, and while it is still hot, wrap it in foil and sheets of newspaper to carry to the out-of-doors spot.

      2 (14½-oz.) cans small potatoes, sliced
      1 (10¾-oz.) can condensed Cheddar cheese soup,
          undiluted
      ¾ cup milk
      ⅓ cup California Dry Sauterne or other white table wine
      1 tablespoon each dried parsley flakes, green pepper
          Salt
          Crushed cereal flakes

Turn potatoes into casserole or baking pan. Blend soup with milk, then wine; stir in parsley and green pepper. Check and adjust salt content. Sprinkle with crushed cereal flakes. Bake in moderate oven (350°) about 30 minutes until well heated and lightly browned.

♓ *To accompany this dish:* **California Burgundy** *or* **Chianti**

Sausage Sampling Fondue

(About 1½ cups)

This is a good party idea for those who like to help themselves and try new foods. The fondue or dipping sauce is simple and easy to make with canned Cheddar cheese soup thinned with California Sauterne. Provide an assortment of small sausages to dip into the fondue.

      1 (10¾-oz.) can condensed Cheddar cheese soup,
          undiluted
      ¼ cup California Dry Sauterne or other white table wine
      1 package each of little wieners, smoked wieners,
          cheese wieners and beef franks

Heat soup and wine in saucepan or chafing dish, stirring until sauce is smooth. Keep warm over low heat in chafing dish. To heat sausages: In wide saucepan or skillet, heat water to boiling point, add sausages, cover pan, remove from heat and let steam for about 5 minutes. Arrange links on serving tray to accompany fondue. Dip heated sausages into fondue, using picks for serving.

♓ *To accompany this fondue:* **California Claret** *or* **Pinot Blanc**

Party Fondue
(4 to 6 servings)

Once this fondue is made, it should be kept hot over a candle warmer or some form of low heat. Each guest in turn spears a cube of French bread with a fondue fork or long pick and dips it into the fondue pot or chafing dish, twirling the fork to keep the cheese mixture on the bread.

    1 pound aged Swiss cheese
    1 clove garlic (optional)
    1 cup California Chablis, Rhine Wine or
      other white table wine
    2 teaspoons cornstarch
    1 tablespoon California Medium Sherry
      Dash each of nutmeg, white pepper
      Bite-sized cubes French bread

Shred cheese. If desired, cut garlic in half and rub inside of fondue pot, chafing dish or in top of double boiler; discard garlic. Pour in Chablis, add cheese and cook over low heat or boiling water, stirring constantly, until cheese is melted and mixture is smooth. Blend cornstarch with Sherry, then stir into cheese mixture; add nutmeg and pepper. Stir a few minutes longer until fondue thickens slightly. Serve at once with bread cubes.

To accompany this cheese fondue: **California Chablis or Rhine Wine**

Cheese Rarebit
(6 servings)

    1 pound (about 4 cups) shredded process
      Cheddar cheese
    1 cup undiluted evaporated milk
    1 teaspoon Worcestershire sauce
    ¼ teaspoon dry mustard
      Few grains cayenne
    ¼ cup California Dry Sherry
    12 Rusks or toasted bun halves
    ½ pound bacon strips, cooked until crisp

Mix in 2-quart saucepan cheese, evaporated milk, Worcestershire sauce, mustard and cayenne. Cook and stir over low heat until cheese melts. Remove from heat and carefully stir in Sherry. Serve over rusks and top each portion with bacon.

To accompany this cheese dish: **California Dry Sauterne or Claret**

Cheese and Wine Quiche
(5 to 6 servings)

This delicious entree, a custard base in a pastry shell, can be as varied as you have ingredients at hand. Serve it with a chilled California Chablis or Sauterne, accompanied by a green salad, and your brunch, luncheon, or supper menu is complete. Partially bake the pastry before adding the custard, as this helps to keep the bottom crust crisp. Instead of cheese and bacon, use 1 cup crab meat or shrimp; cut up bits of ham; mushrooms; black olives; cooked, chopped spinach or asparagus.

    1 9-inch unbaked pastry shell
    1 tablespoon freeze-dried chives
    4 strips bacon, cooked until crisp, broken into bits
    1 to 1½ cups grated Swiss or Cheddar cheese
    3 eggs, beaten
    1⅓ cups light cream
    ⅓ cup California Chablis or other white table wine
    ½ teaspoon salt
      Dash each nutmeg, white pepper

Place pastry shell in hot oven (425°) and partially bake, about 6 to 8 minutes. Remove from oven and cool until ready to use. Sprinkle chives, bacon bits and grated cheese over bottom of pastry shell. Combine remainder of ingredients and pour carefully into pastry. Bake on lowest shelf of hot oven (400°) 30 minutes until set in center. Allow to stand in warm place for about 10 minutes before cutting.

To accompany this dish: **California Chablis**

Pickled Eggs
(6 servings)

As you might guess, these pink eggs have a determined pickle flavor. They are very good to carry along as picnic fare or to serve as a relish on the barbecue menu. If you want a milder flavor, marinate small whole beets with the eggs. In saucepan simmer for about 10 minutes ½ cup California Rosé, ¾ cup each red wine vinegar and beet juice, 1 bay leaf, ¼ teaspoon allspice, 2 teaspoons seasoned salt and ½ teaspoon seasoned pepper. Pour into quart jar and add 6 hard-cooked eggs, shelled. Cover and refrigerate at least overnight. To serve, cut in halves or quarters.

Poached Eggs with Sherried Cream Sauce: Poached eggs topped with this cream sauce make breakfast exciting. Use 3 or 4 tablespoons California Dry Sherry in each 2 cups medium cream sauce. For extra flavor serve eggs on hot toast spread with deviled ham or liver paté.

Scrambled Eggs Chablis
(4 servings)

Have that confident feeling that you are never at a loss to produce something good to eat if you have eggs in the refrigerator. These scrambled eggs are a perfect example of dressing up a familiar food. We make them unusual with California Chablis or other white table wine, herbs and cheese. These eggs are also good served in individual baked tart shells. When the eggs are almost set, divide them into heated shells, sprinkle with grated cheese and put them into a moderate oven for a few minutes until the cheese melts.

      6 eggs
    ½ teaspoon salt
      2 tablespoons light cream
    ¼ cup California Chablis or other white table wine
    ⅛ teaspoon dried dill, rosemary or basil
      2 tablespoons butter
    ¼ cup coarsely crumbled bleu cheese
      1 tablespoon chopped chives, parsley or pimiento

Beat eggs slightly; add salt, cream, wine and seasoning. Melt butter in medium skillet, tilting pan so bottom and sides are covered. When hot enough to make drop of water sizzle, turn in egg mixture; reduce heat. Cook slowly, gently lifting eggs from bottom and sides as mixture sets so liquid can flow to bottom; do not overstir. Add cheese and chives while eggs are still creamy. Cook to desired moistness. Serve at once.

To accompany these scrambled eggs: **California Chablis** *or other white table wine*

Clam Spaghetti Sauce
(6 to 8 servings)

Ladle this unusual sauce over hot, cooked spaghetti tossed with Parmesan cheese. An 8-ounce package of spaghetti should do nicely with this amount of sauce. Cook it according to directions on the package and be as generous as you like with Parmesan cheese sprinkled over the top.

      2 small cloves garlic
      2 teaspoons cooking oil
      4 sprigs parsley, finely chopped
      2 (7-oz.) cans minced clams
    ⅓ cup tomato sauce
    ¼ cup California Medium Sherry
      Salt and pepper

Crush or mince garlic; cook in oil until softened, then add parsley and undrained clams. Stir in tomato sauce and Sherry. Simmer over low heat, about 10 minutes (do not boil). Season to taste with salt and pepper.

To accompany this spaghetti: **California Chianti** *or* **Burgundy**

Eggs in Sauterne Aspic
(8 servings)

These eggs in wine aspic, individually molded, may be used as the main part of a plate salad with fresh cooked asparagus tips or with lobster or crab salad. Arrange them around a green salad for buffet service, or use stuffed deviled eggs, garnished with tiny shrimp, in the aspic.

      1 envelope unflavored gelatin
      2 tablespoons cold water
      1 (10½-oz.) can condensed chicken consomme
    ⅓ cup California Sauterne
      2 teaspoons lemon juice
      Pimiento for garnish
      4 hard-cooked eggs

Soften gelatin in cold water. Heat consomme and dissolve gelatin in it. Stir in Sauterne and lemon juice. Cool until gelatin is slightly thickened. Place a tablespoon gelatin in each of 8 small molds. Center each mold with piece of pimiento cut with small decorative cutter. Chill a few minutes to hold pimiento in place. Cut eggs in halves crosswise. Place a half egg, cut side down, in each mold, and spoon in gelatin to cover egg. Chill until firm. Unmold just before serving.

To accompany this egg dish: **California Sauterne** *or* **Chablis**

Individual Tamale Pies
(8 servings)

    ½ cup chopped onion
      1 clove garlic, minced
    ¼ cup chopped green pepper
    ¼ cup shortening
      1 (No. 303) can cream-style corn
      1 (No. 2½) can tomatoes
      1 tablespoon each chili powder, salt
      2 cups uncooked yellow cornmeal
      1 cup tomato juice
      1 cup California Burgundy or Sauterne
    ⅔ cup grated Cheddar cheese

Cook onion, garlic and green pepper in shortening until soft; stir in corn, tomatoes, chili powder and salt. Simmer over low heat for about 15 minutes. Slowly stir in cornmeal, tomato juice and wine. Spoon mixture into individual baking dishes or large casserole. Top with cheese. Bake in moderate oven (350°) 25 to 30 minutes.

To accompany this casserole: **California Burgundy** *or* **Chianti**

Continental Lasagne
(6 to 8 servings)

This lasagna is a very rich company dish that is especially attractive if you use the green spinach-flavored noodles (you can use the plain lasagna too).

    ½ pound green lasagna noodles, spinach flavored
    2 pounds pork sausage
    2 cloves garlic, crushed
    ½ cup chopped onion
    1 teaspoon seasoned pepper
    1 (6-oz.) can tomato paste
    1 (4-oz.) can sliced mushrooms, undrained
    ¼ cup butter or margarine
    ¼ cup all-purpose flour
    1½ cups milk
    ½ cup California Chablis or other white table wine
    1 teaspoon seasoned salt
    ½ cup chopped parsley
    ½ pound ricotta cheese
    ½ cup Parmesan cheese

Cook lasagna in boiling salted water until almost tender; drain and rinse. Brown sausage, drain off fat and add garlic, onion, seasoned pepper, tomato paste and mushroom liquid; simmer 15 minutes. Meanwhile prepare sauce: In saucepan melt butter, blend in flour and gradually add milk, stirring constantly until sauce is smooth and thickened. Stir in wine, seasoned salt, parsley and mushrooms. Pour ½ cup of sauce into 12 x 8 x 2-inch baking dish. Cover sauce with strips of lasagna. Spread half of sausage mixture on lasagna and top with spoonfuls of ricotta cheese. Pour on half remaining sauce. Repeat layers once again ending with sauce; top with Parmesan cheese. Bake in moderate oven (350°) 20 minutes.

To accompany this casserole: **California Chianti** *or* **Rosé**

Summer Rice Mold: A delicious accompaniment for outdoor summer buffet suppers is a handsome rice mold topped with a rich Sherry sauce. Toss hot steamed rice with chopped parsley and pack lightly in a large buttered ring mold. To make Sherry sauce, thin cream of celery soup with a little California Sherry. Blend in shredded Swiss cheese and chopped pimiento and heat. Serve piping hot over the rice mold. Wonderful with baked ham, chicken or turkey.

Crabmeat and Spaghetti au Gratin
(5 to 6 servings)

Any luncheon group will pronounce this casserole as wonderful. Serve it with a carefully made green salad with sharp dressing. When you make the sauce for the dish, check the seasoning and adjust it to your taste.

    ½ pound broken spaghetti
    ¼ cup butter or margarine
    ¼ cup all-purpose flour
    1½ cups milk
    1 (4-oz.) can mushrooms, undrained
    1 cup grated process Cheddar cheese
    ⅓ cup California Dry Sherry
    2 tablespoons minced pimiento
    ½ teaspoon Worcestershire sauce
      Salt, celery salt, pepper
    1½ cups crabmeat, fresh or canned

Cook spaghetti according to package directions; drain. In saucepan melt butter and stir in flour; add milk and mushrooms (including liquid) and cook, stirring constantly, until sauce boils and thickens. Add ½ cup cheese; stir over low heat until melted. Remove from heat; add Sherry and seasonings to taste. Combine sauce with cooked spaghetti and crabmeat; turn into greased casserole; sprinkle with remaining cheese. Bake in moderate oven (350°) about 25 minutes, or until delicately browned.

To accompany this dish: **California Chablis** *or* **Riesling**

Sherried Orange Rice
(6 servings)

This rice is a fine example of gourmet cooking—a simple dish, carefully made and thoughtfully seasoned. Serve it with a pork roast or with chicken. The California Dry Sherry is best to use here because the raisins and oranges provide some sweetness.

    1 cup uncooked rice
    1 teaspoon salt
    ½ teaspoon thyme
    ½ cup minced onion
    ½ cup seedless raisins
    1 medium, unpeeled, thinly sliced orange, quartered
    1 (10½-oz.) can chicken broth
    6 tablespoons orange juice
    ⅓ cup California Dry Sherry

In greased, 2-quart casserole, combine rice, seasonings, onion, raisins, and orange slices. Bring chicken broth, orange juice and Sherry to a boil. Pour over rice mixture; stir once. Cover and bake in moderate oven (350°) about 45 minutes.

To accompany pork roast or chicken with this dish:
California Chablis *or* **Dry** *or* **Medium Sauterne**

Sauterne Rice

(4 to 5 servings)

Use California Sauterne or any of the white table wines to make this delicious, fluffy rice that is so good to serve with chicken or lamb dishes. In saucepan bring to boil 1 cup Sauterne, 1 cup water and 1 teaspoon seasoned salt; add 1 cup uncooked regular rice, cover and cook about 20 to 25 minutes until rice is tender and liquid is absorbed. Remove from heat and stir very lightly into rice ¼ cup chopped salted peanuts or pecans, ¼ cup butter or margarine and ½ teaspoon grated orange peel.

Buffet Rice: For buffet suppers, serve a handsome rice mold with a rich Sherry sauce. Toss hot steamed rice with chopped parsley and pack lightly into a large buttered ring mold. Make a Sherry sauce by thinning condensed cream of celery soup with California Medium Sherry to taste. Blend in shredded Swiss cheese and ripe olive wedges. Serve hot over rice—delicious with baked ham, turkey or chicken.

Wine Baked Pilaf

(4 to 5 servings)

This pilaf is made with bulgur, a processed cracked wheat, used in much the same way as brown rice. Bulgur has a chewy texture and nut-like flavor.

    1 small onion, chopped fine
    1 clove garlic, chopped fine
    3 tablespoons butter or margarine
    1 cup bulgur, or brown rice
    1 (10½-oz.) can condensed consomme
    1 cup California Chablis or other white table wine
    ½ teaspoon salt

Cook onion and garlic in butter until soft but not browned. Stir in bulgur and heat a few minutes; add remaining ingredients and bring to boil. Cover tightly (or transfer to casserole) and bake in moderate oven (350°) about 45 minutes to 1 hour, until liquid is absorbed and wheat is cooked. Stir now and then during the baking process. Serve with Cornish hens, lamb or beef.

To accompany Cornish hens or lamb with this rice: **California Riesling;** *to accompany beef:* **California Cabernet**

Liquid for Cooking Rice: Try using California Sauterne or Chablis for part of the liquid when cooking rice. Stir in some grated cheese, butter and chopped parsley when rice is tender, then serve with wild ducks, game meats and fish.

Skillet Parmesan Rice

(4 to 5 servings)

Now that brown rice has been processed, the cooking time has been shortened considerably with no loss of its good flavor. Cook it this way in a skillet, or if you have the oven heated to a moderate temperature for something else, cook the rice in a covered casserole about 25 to 30 minutes. It's wonderful to serve with baked ham, sliced hot tongue or prawns in the shell.

    ½ cup California Dry Sauterne
    1 cup chicken or beef broth
    2 tablespoons butter or margarine
    ½ teaspoon seasoned salt
    1 cup quick brown rice
    ½ cup shredded Parmesan cheese
    2 tablespoons frozen chopped chives or
      finely chopped parsley

Measure wine, broth, butter and salt into skillet with a tight-fitting cover. Bring to boil; stir in rice. Reduce heat to low. Cover pan tightly and cook about 15 minutes until rice has absorbed liquid and is tender. Remove cover and stir in cheese and chives. Serve at once.

To accompany dishes named above with this rice: **California Dry Sauterne, Chablis** *or other white table wine*

Curried Rice and Chicken Livers

(4 to 5 servings)

Unlike the classic curries which require many ingredients, intricate seasoning and long simmering, this curry calls for just three essentials: a package of curried rice mix, a package of frozen chicken livers and enough wine, either California Rosé or a white table wine, to blend their flavors.

    1 (6-oz.) package curried rice mix
    2 cups water
    ½ cup California Rosé or Chablis or
      other white table wine
    2 tablespoons butter
    1 (8-oz.) package frozen chicken livers
      Seasoned salt
      Paprika

Prepare curried rice according to package directions using 2 cups water and ½ cup wine as liquid. Meanwhile, melt butter. Add chicken livers and sauté over moderate heat until tender. Sprinkle lightly with seasoned salt and paprika. Add cooked livers and any rich pan juices to cooked rice. Toss lightly until well mixed and serve at once.

To accompany this dish: **California Rosé** *or* **Chablis**

Consomme Rice with Ham

(4 servings)

A main dish can be made in a hurry when you use quick-cooking rice, some of the canned foods on your pantry shelf and the rest of the cooked ham from a recent dinner. Best of all, it won't give the impression it's made from left-overs, for it will be beautifully flavored with California Sauterne and served from a chafing dish.

- 3 tablespoons butter or margarine
- 1 (5-oz.) package quick-cooking rice
- 1 (10½-oz.) can condensed consomme
- ½ cup California Dry Sauterne or other white table wine
- 1 (2-oz.) can mushrooms, undrained
- 4 tablespoons freeze-dried chives
- 1 cup finely diced cooked ham

Melt butter in saucepan, add rice and cook over low heat, stirring frequently until rice is golden brown. Add all other ingredients, bring to boil and simmer about 5 minutes. Remove from heat, place in chafing dish, cover and keep warm for 15 minutes. Fluff gently with fork before serving.

To accompany turkey or lamb with this rice: **California Dry Sauterne** *or* **Rhine Wine**

Saffron Rice

(6 servings)

A little saffron goes a long way in cookery, but it does add a distinctive flavor and a fascinating golden tint. Serve this saffron rice with chicken, lamb, curries or seafood dishes.

- ¼ cup butter or margarine
- 1 cup uncooked rice
- ½ teaspoon salt
  Pinch of saffron
- ½ cup California Dry Sauterne or other white table wine
- 1½ tablespoons chicken seasoned stock base
- 1½ cups water
- 1 tablespoon instant minced onion
- ¼ cup chopped fresh parsley
- ¼ cup grated Parmesan cheese

Melt butter in heavy skillet. Add rice and cook over medium heat, stirring constantly, until rice is lightly toasted. Turn heat low, add all remaining ingredients except parsley and cheese, mix well, and cover closely. Cook without stirring until liquid is absorbed, 20 to 30 minutes. Sprinkle with parsley and cheese; mix lightly and serve.

To accompany dishes named above with this rice: **California Dry Sauterne** *or other white table wine*

VEGETAbLES

Most vegetables respond well to wine cookery, or wine saucing, and thereby become more important in the menu than they might otherwise be. Only occasionally are they the deciding factor in choosing the wine to serve with the meal. Logically that is determined by the main dish. Therefore, wine choices are suggested in this chapter only when the recipe is likely to be the main dish of the meal, or so influential that it may tip the flavor balance towards red, or white, or a delicate pink table wine.

Vintner's Brussels Sprouts in White Wine
(6 to 8 servings)

Dry white wine does something very special to the flavor of Brussels sprouts. Here, wine butter touched with nutmeg is quite interesting and good with these diminutive cabbages. We have used frozen sprouts, but you might like to use the fresh vegetable, cooking the sprouts first about 10 minutes in boiling water. The grape garnish is very pretty but not really necessary.

    3 (10-oz.) packages frozen Brussels sprouts
    1/3 cup butter or margarine
    1/2 cup California Rhine Wine or
        other dry white table wine
    1/2 teaspoon salt
    1/8 teaspoon nutmeg
        White grapes (optional)

Cook Brussels sprouts according to package directions until almost tender, about 5 minutes. Drain. Melt butter in large skillet or chafing dish. Stir in wine, salt and nutmeg. Add sprouts and stir over low heat about 5 minutes. Garnish with grapes.

To accompany this dish: **California Rhine Wine** *or the wine that goes with the main dish*

Harvard Beets Burgundy
(4 to 5 servings)

Be grateful for beets, not only because they are bright and beautiful in themselves, but because they can be prepared ahead of time and because they actually improve on standing.

    1 (1-lb.) can julienne beets, or diced or sliced beets
    1/2 cup sugar
    1 tablespoon cornstarch
    1/8 teaspoon cloves
        Dash of salt
    1/2 cup California Burgundy, Claret or
        other red table wine
    1/4 cup wine vinegar
    2 tablespoons butter or margarine

Drain beets, reserving liquid. In saucepan mix sugar, cornstarch, cloves and salt. Gradually add wine, vinegar and 1/4 cup of the beet liquid, stirring until mixture is smooth. Place over medium heat and stir until sauce is thickened and clear. Add butter and drained beets. Remove from heat, cover and let stand 30 minutes or longer to blend flavors. Reheat before serving.

To accompany this vegetable: **California Burgundy** *or* **Claret**

California Wines and Beans

Beans are so delicious, so nourishing, and so easy to prepare, they deserve a place in every cook book. Add wine to them then and they become gourmet fare. Serve them in one of these interesting ways.

Ported Beans
(4 to 5 servings)

Double or triple this one and serve it on the patio when you have a hungry crowd at the barbecue. Carry it hot and well wrapped to a picnic.

    1 (1-lb. 12-oz.) can baked beans
    ⅓ cup California Port
    ½ cup grated sharp Cheddar cheese
    2 tablespoons chopped green onion

Combine all ingredients in small casserole. Bake in moderate oven (375°) 25 to 30 minutes.

Buffett Baked Beans
(8 servings)

This bean casserole is a little different, but very good for large or small occasions.

    4 slices bacon, cooked until crisp and crumbled
    1 large onion, chopped
    ⅓ cup California Medium Sherry
    1 tablespoon brown sugar
    1 teaspoon dry mustard
    1 teaspoon Worcestershire sauce
    2 (1-lb. 12-oz.) cans baked beans

In bacon drippings, sauté onion until golden. Add bacon, Sherry, sugar and seasonings; add baked beans. Turn into lightly greased casserole and bake in moderate oven (350°) about 45 minutes.

Sherried Picnic Beans
(4 servings)

Orange slices are placed on top of these beans, and California Sherry lends flavor too.

    1 (1-lb. 12-oz.) can baked beans
    ¼ cup California Dry or Medium Sherry
    2 tablespoons finely chopped onion
    1 teaspoon prepared mustard
    2 tablespoons brown sugar
    2 strips bacon, diced
    1 orange, sliced thin

Combine beans with Sherry, onion, mustard, sugar and bacon; turn into small casserole and top with orange slices. Bake in moderate oven (375°) 25 to 30 minutes.

Sherried Beans with Coffee
(4 servings)

Combine contents 1 (1-lb. 12-oz.) can baked beans with ⅓ cup California Dry or Medium Sherry, 2 tablespoons brown sugar, 1 tablespoon lemon juice, 1 teaspoon each instant coffee powder and dry mustard. Turn into individual bean pots or casseroles. Bake in moderate oven (350°) about 30 minutes.

To accompany these bean dishes: **California Burgundy** *or* **Claret**

Chili Garbanzos
(3 to 4 servings)

When you have to prepare something fast that will stick to the ribs, open cans of chili con carne and garbanzos. Don't forget to add some red table wine to make it good.

    1 (14- or 15-oz.) can garbanzos (chick peas)
    1 (1-lb.) can chili con carne without beans
    1 tablespoon flour
    ⅓ cup California Burgundy or Claret

Drain garbanzos; rinse with cold water and place in saucepan with chili con carne; heat to simmering. Combine flour and wine and stir into mixture and continue simmering, stirring frequently, for about 5 minutes. Serve in heated soup bowls or individual casseroles.

To accompany this dish: **California Burgundy** *or* **Claret**

Creamy Vegetables with Shrimp
(5 to 6 servings)

    2 (8-oz.) packages frozen mixed vegetables
        with onion sauce
    1 cup water
    ⅓ cup California Dry Sauterne, Chablis or
        other white table wine
    2 tablespoons butter
    1 (4½-oz.) can deveined shrimp
    1 (3-oz.) can chow mein noodles

Prepare vegetables according to package directions using 1 cup water and ⅓ cup wine. Add butter and drained shrimp. Heat, and when piping hot, turn into a serving dish and top with oven-crisped chow mein noodles.

To accompany this dish: **California Medium Sauterne** *or* **Chablis**

Fruited Yams with Sherry
(3 to 5 servings)

When you must prepare dinner with one eye on the clock, tuck this yam special on the same rack in the oven with a small canned ham or luncheon meat. Good served with cold sliced chicken or turkey too.

        6 thin orange slices
        6 thin lemon slices
        1 (1-lb.) can yams
    ¼ to ⅓ cup brown sugar, firmly packed
    ¼ cup California Medium Sherry
    2 to 3 tablespoons butter or margarine

Arrange orange slices in shallow baking dish; top with lemon slices. Drain yams and set one piece on top each lemon slice. Combine brown sugar and Sherry; pour over yams. Dot with butter. Bake uncovered in moderate oven (350°) about 20 minutes or until lightly browned and heated through.

To accompany this dish: **California Haut Sauterne** *or* **Rosé**

Baked Broccoli and Onions
(6 servings)

Although we prepared the sauce for this attractive vegetable from scratch as it were, there's no reason why you can't take a shortcut. Use undiluted chicken soup (one 10½-oz. can) instead of chicken stock. Heat and thin it with ½ cup California Sauterne or other white table wine. Proceed with the recipe as directed.

    2 (10-oz.) packages frozen broccoli,
        cooked according to directions on package
    1 (No. 303) can small white onions, drained
    ⅓ cup butter or margarine
    ⅓ cup flour
    1 cup milk
    ½ cup chicken stock
        (use canned or bouillon-cube broth)
    ½ cup California Medium Sauterne or
        other white table wine
        Salt and pepper to taste
    ⅓ cup shaved unblanched almonds
    ½ cup grated Cheddar cheese
        Paprika

In greased shallow baking dish arrange cooked broccoli; layer onions on top. *Make sauce:* In saucepan melt butter, stir in flour and add milk and chicken stock gradually, stirring constantly until mixture boils and thickens. Remove from heat, add wine and seasonings; pour over broccoli and onions. Scatter almonds on top, then sprinkle with cheese and paprika. Bake in moderate oven (375°) about 30 minutes or until just bubbly and delicately browned.

To accompany this vegetable: **California Dry Sauterne, Chablis** *or the wine that goes with the main dish*

Vegetable Supper Casserole
(4 to 5 servings)

Plan to serve this good vegetable combination some night when you have dinner on the patio. Or take it hot and bubbling to a pot luck supper. Depend on it too for a busy day, and have it ready and waiting to be heated while you prepare the rest of the meal.

    1 (10½-oz.) can condensed cream of chicken soup,
        undiluted
    ¼ teaspoon curry powder
    ¼ cup California Chablis, Dry Sauterne or
        other white table wine
    1 (1-lb.) can cut green beans
    1 (3½-oz.) can French fried onions
    ¼ cup shredded Parmesan cheese

In saucepan combine undiluted chicken soup with curry powder and wine; heat to boiling. Drain beans and layer with onions in lightly greased baking dish; cover with soup mixture. Top with cheese and bake in moderate oven (375°) 20 to 25 minutes or until heated through.

To accompany this vegetable dish: **California Chablis, Dry Sauterne** *or other white table wine*

Potato Parmesan
(6 to 8 servings)

Instant potatoes can be made to look and taste quite different from plain mashed potatoes, if they are dressed up with white wine and cheese. Serve as a meat accompaniment, or use to surround a planked steak or vegetable platter. Spoon the prepared potatoes into pastry bag with large star tube and pipe around edge of plank or platter, or make the border with small spoonfuls of potato.

    ½ cup California Dry Sauterne or other white table wine
    2 cups water
    1 teaspoon salt
    ¼ cup butter or margarine
    ½ cup milk
    2⅔ cups instant potato buds or
        3 cups instant potato flakes
    6 tablespoons Parmesan cheese
    2 egg yolks, lightly beaten

In saucepan combine Sauterne, water, salt and butter; heat to boiling. Remove from heat and add milk, then the instant potatoes, beating until smooth and creamy. Stir in 4 tablespoons of cheese and egg yolks. Mound individual servings of potato on lightly greased baking sheet or spoon into heat-proof serving dish; drizzle with butter and sprinkle with remaining cheese. Bake in very hot oven (450°) about 10 minutes or until lightly browned.

Creamed Onions and Peas
(6 to 8 servings)

Often the vegetable dish served at a buffet occasion is overlooked, not because it doesn't taste good, but because it has little visual appeal. Correct this situation with commonplace onions and peas served up in a glorified white wine sauce with a buttery crumb topping. Good for family meals too.

        3 tablespoons softened butter
        2 tablespoons flour
    1¼ teaspoons seasoned salt
    ⅛ teaspoon each dried dill, dry mustard
    1¼ cups light cream
    ⅓ cup California Sauterne, Chablis or
        other white table wine
        1 (10-oz.) package frozen peas
        2 (1-lb.) cans whole onions, drained

Blend butter, flour and seasonings together until smooth. In a saucepan heat cream to just below boiling, stir in butter paste; cook, stirring constantly until sauce boils and thickens. Add Sauterne and cook about 5 minutes longer. Remove from heat. Pour boiling water on peas, let stand 5 minutes; drain well and add to sauce; add onions. Heat, then turn into serving dish and sprinkle with Buttery Crumbs.

Buttery Crumbs: Heat 3 tablespoons butter in skillet; add 2 cups soft stale bread crumbs; sprinkle with ⅛ teaspoon powdered rosemary or thyme. Stir until crumbs are toasted and browned.

Glazed Onions
(6 to 8 servings)

These small onions respond so well to the wine and honey treatment that they come out of the baking dish shiny and delicately browned. You will be proud to serve them in a decorative ring around a beef roast or with the holiday turkey.

        2 (15½-oz.) cans whole small onions
    ¼ cup honey
    ½ cup California Dry Sherry
    ¼ cup butter or margarine
        Nutmeg

Drain onions and place in shallow baking dish. Combine honey and wine, then pour over onions. Dot with butter. Sprinkle with nutmeg. Bake in moderate oven (375°) until onions are hot and glazed, about 20 to 25 minutes.

Elegant Carrots
(4 servings)

These carrots are good enough to accompany your best lamb chops or small special steaks. Shred peeled carrots on coarse grater until you have 3 cups. Melt 2 tablespoons butter or margarine in saucepan; add carrots and ⅓ cup California Medium Sherry. Sprinkle with 1 teaspoon brown sugar and ½ teaspoon salt. Cover and cook over gentle heat about 5 minutes, or until carrots are still crisp, but tender. This method may be used too with the little whole canned carrots or with cooked carrot sticks.

Wine Marinated Artichokes
(4 to 6 servings)

Be fussy about picking out unblemished artichokes for this dish. The artichokes are first cooked then put into a California Rosé marinade to enhance their natural delicious flavor. Serve these artichokes as the main part of a salad, or remove the choke and fill with a tiny shrimp or crab meat mixture to use as an opening course.

        4 to 6 medium artichokes
        1 cup California Rosé
    ½ cup salad oil
        1 tablespoon finely chopped onion
        1 teaspoon grated lemon peel
        2 tablespoons lemon juice
    ½ teaspoon each salt, tarragon leaves,
        monosodium glutamate
    ⅛ teaspoon pepper

To prepare artichokes: Wash, cut off stem at base and remove small bottom leaves. (If desired, trim tips of leaves and cut off about an inch from the top.) Stand artichokes upright in deep saucepan large enough to hold snugly; add ¼ teaspoon salt for each and pour in about 2 inches of boiling water. Cover and simmer gently about 35 minutes or until base can be pierced easily with fork. (Add a little more boiling water if needed during cooking.) Remove artichokes from pan and turn upside down to drain.

Make marinade by combining Rosé with remaining ingredients; pour over artichokes in pan and chill several hours or overnight. Serve marinade as dip for artichokes if you wish.

Easy Spinach Soufflé

(6 servings)

Don't let soufflés frighten you, just depend on this carefully tested recipe to see you through. It is interesting because it has a small amount of biscuit mix to help keep the soufflé elevated. A word of assurance, although soufflés do have to be served soon after they are baked, they will remain puffed up for 10 to 15 minutes if necessary.

    1 (12-oz.) package frozen chopped spinach,
      cooked according to directions on package
      or 1 cup chopped cooked fresh spinach
    ¾ cup milk
    ¼ cup biscuit mix
    ¼ cup California Dry Sherry
    ⅛ teaspoon nutmeg
    3 eggs, separated
    1 teaspoon salt
    ¼ teaspoon cream of tartar

Drain cooked spinach thoroughly, pressing out all excess water. In saucepan stir a little milk into biscuit mix to make a smooth paste; gradually add remainder of milk. Place over heat and cook until mixture boils and thickens then stir gradually into beaten egg yolks; blend in spinach. Add salt and cream of tartar to egg whites; beat until stiff. Fold in spinach mixture. Turn into ungreased (1-qt.) souffle dish or straight-sided casserole; set in pan of water and bake in moderate oven (350°) about 50 minutes or until knife inserted in center comes out clean. Serve at once from baking dish. Good with creamed chicken or turkey or with mushroom sauce.

To accompany this souffle: **California Dry Sauterne** *or the wine that goes with the main dish*

Broiled Tomatoes With Sherry. Tomatoes make a bright and delicious spot of interest on any luncheon or dinner plate. Cut medium large tomatoes crosswise into halves; pierce with fork and sprinkle generously with California Sherry. Season with salt, pepper and dried dill. Place under broiler for 5 to 7 minutes or until heated through. Combine equal parts mayonnaise and grated Cheddar cheese; put spoonful on each tomato, then return to broiler and brown lightly. Allow 1 to 2 halves per serving.

Green Beans in Cheese Sauce

(4 to 5 servings)

Green beans become much more important if they are served in a special smooth cheese sauce. Undiluted mushroom soup forms the basis of the sauce, then Parmesan cheese and a hint of white table wine such as California Sauterne or Chablis are added.

    1 (No. 2) can green beans, whole or cut
    ¼ cup California Dry Sauterne or other white table wine
    1 (10½-oz.) can condensed cream of mushroom soup,
      undiluted
    2 tablespoons grated Parmesan cheese

Drain liquid from beans; reserve liquid to use later in sauces and soups. In saucepan combine wine with undiluted mushroom soup and grated cheese; heat to boiling point, stirring constantly to smooth. Add beans; heat and serve in individual dishes. Beans would be good on the menu with minute steaks, juicy beef patties or frankfurters.

Asparagus with Wine Sauce

Treat asparagus in a royal manner with a special sauce.

Dressed-up Canned Sauce: Empty contents 1 (10½-oz.) can (1¼ cups) white sauce into saucepan and heat gently to boiling; stir in 3 or 4 tablespoons California Dry Sherry or a dry white table wine and a little grated Parmesan cheese. Heat well, then spoon over cooked stalks of asparagus. Sprinkle with toasted slivered almonds.

Hollandaise Sauce: Use 1 (6-oz.) can (¾ cup) Hollandaise sauce; heat, and stir in 2 tablespoons California Dry Sherry and 1 teaspoon lemon juice.

Sherried Cream Sauce: Melt 2 tablespoons butter in saucepan, stir in 2 tablespoons flour and cook briefly, being careful not to let flour brown. Add ¾ cup rich milk or part cream slowly, stirring to smooth. Add ¼ cup California Dry Sherry and bring just to boil. A spoonful of grated cheese, Parmesan or Cheddar, may be stirred in here too.

Red Cabbage and Rice

(10 servings)

While the spareribs or pot roast cooks along for an oven dinner, this excellent vegetable dish of red cabbage and rice can be cooking too. Since the amount of the recipe is generous, be assured that the cabbage is very good re-heated for a second appearance.

    1 medium head red cabbage, finely shredded
    3 green tart apples, peeled, cored and sliced
    1 cup sliced onions
    3 cups cooked rice
    ½ pound salt pork, diced
    1 tablespoon salt
    ½ teaspoon pepper
    ¼ teaspoon caraway seed
    1 (10½-oz.) can beef bouillon
    ½ cup California Burgundy, Claret or
       other red table wine

Combine cabbage, apples, onion, rice, salt pork, and seasonings. Turn into a greased (9 x 13 inch) baking dish. Combine bouillon and wine and pour over cabbage. Cover with foil and bake in moderate oven (350°) 1 hour.

To accompany this cabbage dish: **California Burgundy** *or* **Claret**

Spinach with Sour Cream

(4 to 5 servings)

Who could resist this fresh green spinach once they know how easy it is to prepare and how good it tastes? Serve it as a vegetable dish or use it as a sauce over baked fish, an omelet or soufflé.

    1½ pounds fresh spinach
    ½ cup dairy sour cream
    3 tablespoons California Medium Sherry
       Dash nutmeg

Cut stems from spinach while still tied in bunch. Wash leaves in warm water, cutting off remainder of stems. Place leaves in saucepan, add about ¼ cup boiling water, cover and cook about 6 minutes (enough for tender spinach). Drain very well, pressing water from spinach, and turn into blender. Add sour cream, Sherry and nutmeg; whirl until very smooth. Check seasonings and add a little salt and pepper if needed.

Creamy Sauterne Cabbage

(4 to 5 servings)

Since the cabbage is shredded, it takes only a few minutes to cook it to the point where it is tender, but just a bit crisp. That's the way you want it in this smooth Sauterne sauce.

    4 cups shredded raw cabbage
    2 cups boiling salted water
    1 (1-oz.) package white sauce mix
    ¾ cup milk
    ¼ cup California Medium Sauterne or
       other white table wine
    ½ teaspoon salt
       Pinch nutmeg

Cook cabbage, covered, in boiling salted water just until tender; drain. Empty white sauce mix into saucepan, slowly stir in milk, Sauterne, salt and nutmeg. Heat just to boiling, stirring constantly. Add drained cooked cabbage and heat gently a few minutes longer. Serve with baked ham, or braised tongue, or frankfurters.

Carrots in Dilled Wine Sauce

(5 to 6 servings)

Try this imaginative sauce on carrots; it perks them up and gives them the attention they deserve in the vegetable world.

    ½ teaspoon dried dill
    ½ cup California Dry Sauterne, Chablis or
       other white table wine
    2 teaspoons instant minced onion
    ½ cup chicken broth (canned, or bouillon cube in water)
    1 tablespoon cornstarch
    ¼ teaspoon garlic salt
       Drop or two Tabasco sauce
    1 tablespoon lemon juice
    3 cups hot cooked small carrots or large carrots,
       sliced or cut julienne

Melt butter in saucepan; add dill, Sauterne and onion. Combine broth with cornstarch and add to contents of saucepan along with salt, Tabasco and lemon juice. Cook over moderate heat stirring constantly until sauce thickens. Add carrots; lower heat and simmer 5 to 10 minutes before serving.

quick breads

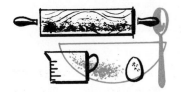    

Specialty breads made with wine have an extremely subtle flavor. Just as the alcohol of the wine vaporizes during the baking, so too does some of the flavor. Sherry is more dominant than any other wine in the baking process. Its characteristic caramel flavor survives the oven heat that dissipates others. As each new mix appears on the market, it creates an opportunity to try a new wine-flavored bread. Simply replace with wine part of the liquid specified on the package. But limit experiments to the baking powder type of bread. Wine and yeast are not compatible.

Sherry Orange Muffins
(12 muffins)

Hot breads of any kind make a breakfast or luncheon something special. These muffins, fragrant with nutmeg and California Sherry, are very easy to stir together with a mix. Or you can use your favorite muffin recipe and make the additions we suggest here.

> 1 (13¾-oz.) package muffin mix
> ¼ teaspoon nutmeg
> ½ cup chopped nutmeats
> ½ cup California Medium Sherry
> About ½ cup milk
> (see package directions for muffin mix)
> 1 egg
> 1 tablespoon grated orange peel
> 2 tablespoons melted butter or margarine

In mixing bowl combine muffin mix with nutmeg and nutmeats. Measure Sherry and add enough milk to equal liquid content given on package recipe. Combine with beaten egg, orange peel and melted butter or margarine and stir into mix lightly to blend all ingredients. Spoon into greased (or paper) muffin cups. Sprinkle tops generously with sugar and bake in a hot oven (425°) about 15 to 20 minutes or until done. Remove from pan; serve at once.

Biscuits in the Round
(8 servings)

Decorative and delicious is this biscuit creation, made with a mix and carefully proportioned amounts of herbs and cheese. California Sauterne is used as part of the liquid in the biscuits, adding not only flavor but a subtle tenderness.

> 2 cups biscuit mix
> ½ teaspoon crushed chervil or parsley
> ¼ teaspoon crushed sweet basil
> 1 cup grated sharp Cheddar cheese
> ⅓ cup California Dry Sauterne, Chablis or
> other white table wine
> ⅓ cup milk

Combine biscuit mix, herbs and cheese; add wine and milk. Stir briefly until dry ingredients are blended. Drop by large spoonfuls into well-greased 8-inch round layer cake pan (7 portions around the outer edge and 1 in the center will fit nicely). Bake in hot oven (425°) until biscuits are golden brown, about 12 to 15 minutes. Serve hot with butter.

NOTE: If you prefer, you can serve a creamed fish, eggs, meat or vegetable in the center of the ring, then squeeze biscuit No. 8 around the edge, instead of placing it in the center.

Joaquin Valley Raisin Scones
(6 servings)

No need to make a second call for breakfast once the aroma of these baking scones starts floating from the kitchen. Biscuit mix combines with California Sherry and raisins to give a fast and helpful start to early-bird baking. For an afternoon or an evening snack, cut them into 12 wedges. These scones are particularly good with a salad.

    ½ cup California Medium Sherry
    ½ cup dark or golden raisins
    1 teaspoon grated orange peel
    2 cups biscuit mix
    ¼ cup sugar
    ⅓ cup butter or margarine
    ¼ cup milk

Combine Sherry with raisins and orange peel in small saucepan; heat gently about 5 minutes until raisins are plump; cool. Meanwhile combine biscuit mix and sugar; cut in butter or margarine until in small pieces. Add cooled wine and raisins, then milk; stir until batter is just mixed (it will be rather lumpy). Turn into greased and floured 8-inch cake pan, spreading batter evenly. Mark with knife or scissors into 6 wedges. Bake in hot oven (425°) 20 to 25 minutes. Serve warm with butter.

Country Supper Bread
(8-inch square pan)

Packaged corn bread mix makes it very easy to put this unusual bread together in a hurry. California Sherry or Sauterne gives it that elusive something, making it outstanding. Of course, the sour cream and cheese topping add to its attraction too. If the baking pan is heated before the batter is poured in, the sides and bottom of the baked bread will be nicely browned.

    ½ cup chopped onion
    2 tablespoons butter or margarine
    1 (15-oz.) package corn-bread mix
    1 egg, beaten
    ½ cup California Medium Sherry or Medium Sauterne
      About ½ cup milk (see package directions)
    ½ cup dairy sour cream
    ½ to ¾ cup shredded Cheddar cheese

Sauté onion gently in butter until soft and transparent. Prepare corn bread mix according to directions given on package, using beaten egg, Sherry and enough milk to equal entire liquid content of directions on package. Pour into greased and heated pan; sprinkle with cooked onion. Combine sour cream with cheese, then spoon over top of batter and onion. Bake in a hot oven (400°) about 25 minutes or until done in center. Let cool briefly on rack; serve warm.

Casserole Corn Bread
(8 to 9 servings)

Serve this quick bread to accompany breakfast or supper dishes, or serve it as a base for creamed eggs, ham, chicken, vegetables or other creamed foods. Bake the bread in either a casserole (if you intend to spoon it out for the creamed dishes) or in a pan, to cut in squares.

    1 (15-oz.) package corn-bread mix
    2 tablespoons sugar (if you like a sweet corn bread)
    ¼ cup grated Parmesan cheese
    ½ teaspoon celery seed
    ½ cup California Medium Sauterne or
      other white table wine
    1 egg, beaten
    2 tablespoons melted butter or margarine

While mixing the corn-bread batter, heat lightly greased 8-inch square pan or 1½-quart casserole in oven. In mixing bowl combine corn-bread mix with sugar, cheese and celery seed. Measure wine; add enough milk to equal liquid measurement given on corn-bread mix package; combine wine, milk, beaten egg and melted butter. Add at once to cornmeal mix and stir until just combined. Pour into heated baking pan or casserole; bake in hot oven (425°) 30 to 35 minutes, or until bread tests done in center. Serve warm. Bread may be reheated if wrapped in foil or covered with heavy paper.

Toasted Cheese-Topped French Bread: Have 1 (6-oz.) cellophane-wrapped cheese roll (garlic-flavored or plain) at room temperature. Place in a bowl and mash with a fork. Blend in ¼ cup softened butter or margarine and ¼ cup California Sherry, beating until smooth. Cut a loaf of French bread lengthwise in halves, then slice crosswise, cutting down to the crust but not through it. Spread cut sides of bread with the cheese mixture; sprinkle with paprika. Just before serving, toast under the broiler until delicately browned.

Patio Cheese Bread
(1 long loaf)

Be sure to include this cheese loaf in your plans for your next barbecue event or informal buffet supper. It would be good to carry along on a picnic too. Wrap the prepared loaf in foil and place it on the grill to heat.

> 1 (5-oz.) jar processed American cheese spread
> ½ cup softened butter or margarine
> ¼ cup California Medium Sherry
> 2 tablespoons chopped parsley
> Crushed garlic (optional)
> 1 long loaf French bread

In a small bowl stir together cheese spread and butter; add Sherry gradually, stirring to blend well into smooth spread; add parsley and garlic. Slash a long loaf of French bread crosswise into thick slices, cutting down to bottom crust, but not through it. Spread slices with cheese-wine mixture. Slip loaf into paper bag and place on baking sheet. Heat in moderate oven (350°) about 20 minutes or until hot. Serve hot.

Sherried French Bread: Mix together ½ pound of shredded processed Swiss cheese, ¼ cup California Sherry, 1 slightly beaten egg, 1 teaspoon instant minced onion, 1 teaspoon prepared mustard and salt to taste. Cut a loaf of French bread in half lengthwise. Spread generously with cheese mixture. Bake in a hot oven (400°) 10 minutes.

Sherried Pancake or Waffle Syrup
(1½ cups syrup)

This special syrup designed for use on luncheon pancakes or waffles is a delightful way to use California Sherry. In a small saucepan combine 1 cup maple-blended syrup, ¼ cup butter or margarine and ¼ cup Medium Sherry. Heat slowly until butter melts, stirring occasionally. Serve hot with pancakes or waffles.

Cheddar Onion Muffins: Combine 2 cups biscuit mix, 1 cup grated Cheddar cheese, ⅓ cup finely chopped green onion and ¼ teaspoon seasoned salt. Stir in ¼ cup California Sauterne or other white table wine, 1 beaten egg and ½ cup milk. Spoon into greased muffin cups, filling about ⅔ full. Bake in hot oven (400°) 15 to 20 minutes. Serve hot.

Waffles with Cheese-Bacon Sauce
(4 servings)

This hearty sauce will be just right to make waffles a little more filling on the late breakfast or luncheon menu. Make your own waffles or, to save time, reheat the kind you find in the frozen food section.

> 1 (10½-oz.) can condensed cream of mushroom soup
> ¼ cup light cream
> ¼ cup California Chablis or other white table wine
> ½ cup grated American cheese
> 5 or 6 slices crisp cooked bacon
> Waffles

In saucepan blend together until smooth mushroom soup, cream and wine. Add cheese and heat slowly until cheese melts and mixture is well blended. Add bacon, crumbled into large pieces; heat a few minutes longer. Serve over hot waffles.

Pimiento Biscuits
(20 biscuits)

Hot biscuits are always welcome at the table, and quite easy to accomplish, thanks to biscuit mix. Make them ahead if you wish, and keep them covered with waxed paper or foil in the refrigerator until baking time. The little flecks of red pimiento and green onion make them most attractive.

> 2½ cups biscuit mix
> 2 tablespoons chopped pimiento
> 1 tablespoon chopped green onion
> ¼ cup melted butter or margarine
> ⅓ cup California Dry Sauterne, Chablis or other white table wine
> ⅓ cup milk
> Milk and coarse salt for top (optional)

Combine biscuit mix, pimiento and onion. Add butter, wine and milk, stirring to a soft dough. Turn out on board lightly sprinkled with biscuit mix; knead gently about 10 to 12 times. Roll dough out to ½-inch thickness and cut with 2½-inch cutter. Place on ungreased baking sheet, brush tops with milk and sprinkle with coarse salt, if desired. Bake in hot oven (425°) 10 to 12 minutes or until nicely browned and crusty.

Cardamom Loaf
(1 loaf)

The spice cardamom belongs to the ginger family and is a native of India. You will find it a delightful accent to your coffee cakes and breads. Here we use it with California Sherry in an easy-to-make quick bread. Slice the bread into thin slices and spread them with cream cheese for an afternoon or evening snack, or be more generous with your slices and present them at the breakfast table or at a salad luncheon.

    3 cups biscuit mix
    ¼ teaspoon ground cardamom
    ½ cup California Medium Sherry
    ½ cup milk
    ½ cup honey
    1 egg, beaten
    ½ teaspoon grated lemon peel

Combine biscuit mix and cardamom; blend remainder of ingredients together and add at once to biscuit mix, stirring just until blended. Turn into a well-greased 9 x 5 x 3-inch loaf pan. Bake in moderate oven (350°) 45 to 50 minutes or until done. Remove from pan and cool on rack.

Cucamonga Wine Ring
(6 to 8 servings)

California Sauterne and a small amount of oregano do such delightful things to this bread in the way of flavor. The Romano cheese gives it a golden brown, almost fluffy, crown. Bake it in a ring mold to make it look even more attractive, or bake it in an 8-inch cake pan.

    2⅓ cups biscuit mix
    2 tablespoons sugar
    ½ teaspoon crushed oregano
    1 tablespoon grated onion
    ¼ cup melted butter
    ⅓ cup California Dry Sauterne, Chablis or
       other white table wine
    1 egg, beaten
    ½ cup milk
    ¼ cup grated Romano cheese

In mixing bowl combine biscuit mix, sugar, oregano, and grated onion. Add melted butter, Sauterne, beaten egg and milk. Stir until well blended, then beat lightly and turn into well greased and floured 9-inch ring mold. Sprinkle with cheese. Bake in a hot oven (400°) 30 to 35 minutes. Remove from pan and cool on rack.

salads and salad dressings

Wine in a salad or salad dressing contributes a pleasant tartness, because of its mild acid content, in contrast to the sharpness of vinegar or lemon juice. It is particularly good with fruits. It is also useful in giving character to salad ingredients of mild flavor such as potatoes, chicken, and some fish and shellfish. Marinating these ingredients in wine before tossing them with the salad accomplishes the desired results. Of all the salads, those made with gelatin make the best use of wine. A table or dessert wine replaces some of the water, fruit or vegetable juice usually used in molded salads, and adds considerable distinction to the finished salad.

Sour Cream Potato Salad

(4 servings)

In your pursuit of easy cooking ideas try canned small, whole potatoes. They can be depended on in many ways, like this potato salad, for instance. Give the California Sauterne time to flavor the potato slices during chilling, then add the sour cream dressing.

    1 (1-lb.) can whole potatoes
    ½ cup chopped celery
    ¼ cup chopped green onion
    ½ cup chopped apple (optional)
    ¼ cup California Dry Sauterne or other white table wine
    1 teaspoon dried dill
    ½ cup dairy sour cream
      Salt and pepper to taste
      Paprika

Drain potatoes; slice into salad bowl. Add celery, onion and apple; pour wine over all, then toss lightly to mix. Cover bowl and refrigerate for an hour or more. Just before serving add dill to sour cream; pour over potatoes, stirring gently to coat. Sprinkle with paprika and serve.

♆ *To accompany this salad:* **California Sauterne**

Tuna Louis

(4 servings)

No emergency shelf can afford to be without tuna fish; there are so many uses for it. This salad is made especially interesting because of the dressing—California Sherry and chopped ripe olives are added to the usual mayonnaise and chili sauce. Serve this salad with hot corn bread sticks or muffins or heated thick slices of French bread.

      Shredded lettuce
    2 (7-oz.) cans flaked tuna
    1 cup finely diced celery
    ⅔ cup mayonnaise
    ⅓ cup chili sauce
    3 tablespoons California Medium Sherry
    3 tablespoons chopped ripe olives
      Tomato wedges
    2 hard-cooked eggs, cut in slices

Line chilled salad plates with lettuce. Combine tuna and celery and mound on lettuce. Cover with dressing made by mixing mayonnaise, chili sauce, wine and olives. Garnish with tomato wedges and egg slices.

♆ *To accompany this salad:* **California Sauterne or Chablis**

Tomatoes Rosé

(6 servings)

Use large well-ripened tomatoes for beautiful slices, and do take the time to peel them. Pour boiling water over the tomatoes, then cold water, and you will find the skins slip off easily.

    4 large tomatoes, peeled
    ¼ cup finely chopped celery
    ¼ cup finely chopped green onion
    1 (1-oz.) package Italian salad dressing mix
    3 tablespoons wine vinegar
    6 tablespoons salad oil
    ½ cup California Rosé
      Salt

Cut tomatoes across in thin slices. Arrange in shallow serving bowl. Combine all remaining ingredients, adding salt if desired. Pour over tomatoes and chill 1 hour or longer. Serve from bowl or arrange slices of tomato on crisp lettuce and spoon some of the dressing over top.

To accompany this salad: **California Rosé**

Zucchini Vinaigrette

(30 to 36 strips)

Choose your zucchini carefully for this salad or vegetable relish. It is important that the vegetable be young and tender. And give it only the briefest of cooking; it should be slightly crisp, that's all. You may find it best to cook the zucchini in a wide shallow frying pan or skillet.

    1 package Italian dressing mix
    2 tablespoons water
    ¼ cup white wine vinegar
    ¼ cup California Medium Sauterne or
      other white table wine
    ½ cup salad oil
    2 tablespoons each finely chopped green pepper,
      parsley, green onions
    3 tablespoons sweet pickle relish
    5 or 6 medium zucchini

Empty contents of package dressing mix into screw-top, pint jar; add water and shake well. Add vinegar, wine, and salad oil and shake jar about 30 seconds. Add remaining ingredients, except zucchini, and shake again. Cut ends from zucchini but do not peel. Slice each zucchini into 6 lengthwise strips and cook in boiling salted water about 3 minutes. Drain well and arrange in shallow dish or pan. Pour vinaigrette sauce over zucchini; marinate several hours or overnight. Serve on salad greens or on an antipasto tray.

To accompany this salad or relish: **California Riesling or Chablis**

Shrimp Remoulade

(4 to 5 servings)

You will have to try this salad before you believe how really good it tastes. Then you will want to have this sharp sauce and shrimp often for a main dish salad, served with hot muffins or narrow strips of home-made bread spread with sweet butter.

    3 hard-cooked eggs
    ½ teaspoon mustard
    1 teaspoon anchovy paste
    1 cup mayonnaise
    ⅓ cup California Burgundy or other red table wine
    ¼ teaspoon onion powder
    2 cups cooked small shrimp
    1 cup diced celery
    2 tablespoons finely chopped parsley
      Lettuce
      Paprika

Mash yolk of eggs with mustard and anchovy paste. Blend in mayonnaise, wine and onion powder. Add shrimp, celery and parsley. Chill. Heap in lettuce cups on chilled salad plates. Sprinkle sieved hard-cooked egg whites over top. Dust with paprika.

To accompany this salad: **California Rosé**

Vegetable Salad Mold

(6 servings)

    1 (3-oz.) package lemon-flavored gelatin
    1 cup hot water
    ¾ cup California Sauterne or other white table wine
    2 tablespoons lemon juice
    2 tablespoons sugar
      Dash of salt
    1 (10-oz.) package frozen mixed vegetables, cooked
      and drained
    ½ cup finely diced celery
    2 tablespoons each grated onion, chopped parsley

Dissolve gelatin in hot water; add wine, lemon juice, sugar and salt; stir well. Chill. When mixture begins to thicken, stir in remaining ingredients; spoon into 6 lightly oiled individual molds; chill until firm. Serve in lettuce cups; pass mayonnaise dressing.

To accompany this salad: **California Sauterne**

Bing Cherry and Port Mold
(8 servings)

California Port and cherries seem to have a natural affinity, not only of color but of flavor. Here we use them to make a handsome ring mold salad that is perfect to serve for a salad luncheon or a buffet. Poured into individual molds, they would be nice for dinner too. For variation, soften contents of a 3-ounce package of cream cheese and roll into small balls the size of marbles. Fold into gelatin with cherries.

    1 (1-lb.) can pitted Bing cherries
    2 tablespoons lemon juice
    1 (3-oz.) package cherry-flavored gelatin
    1 cup California Port
    12 salted pecan halves
    1 cup green grapes, halved

Drain cherries; reserve syrup. Pour syrup into measuring cup and add lemon juice and water to make 1 cup liquid; pour into small saucepan and heat to boiling; remove from heat. Stir in gelatin until dissolved; add Port. Arrange pecan halves in bottom of 1-quart ring mold. Add enough gelatin mixture so that pecans barely float; chill until set. Chill remaining gelatin mixture until it starts to thicken; fold in cherries and green grapes then pour into mold. Chill until firm, 4 or 5 hours or overnight. Unmold on bed of lettuce leaves, or surround with watercress. In center of ring, place bowl of Mayonnaise, lightened with whipped cream or dairy sour cream folded into it.

To accompany this salad: **California Chablis**

Avocado Mousse—Party Size
(16 to 20 servings)

This light, airy mold is generous enough for a party group such as a buffet supper. Or you might like to use it as an elegant offering for a patio affair. We used California Chablis to blend with the lime-flavored gelatin, but if you want a slightly sweeter mold, California Muscatel would be a good choice. For a smaller mold, simply use the 3-ounce package of gelatin and divide all the ingredients in half.

    1 (6-oz.) package lime-flavored gelatin
    1 teaspoon salt
    1⅓ cups boiling water
    ⅔ cup California Chablis or other white table wine
    1⅓ cups undiluted evaporated milk
    2 medium avocados
    2 tablespoons lemon juice
    ½ cup finely diced celery
    ½ cup chopped pecans
    ¼ cup finely chopped green pepper

Place gelatin and salt in large mixing bowl, add boiling water and stir until gelatin is completely dissolved then stir in wine. Chill to consistency of unbeaten egg white. Meanwhile, pour evaporated milk into ice cube tray; chill until fine ice crystals form around edges. Peel and dice avocados; mix with lemon juice. Beat thickened gelatin until frothy. Fold in avocado, celery, pecans and green pepper. Whip chilled evaporated milk until it is stiff and will hold a peak. Fold into gelatin mixture lightly but thoroughly. Turn into well-oiled 2½-quart mold; chill until set, about 4 to 5 hours. When ready to serve, unmold on serving platter and border with salad greens.

To accompany this salad: **California Chablis** *or* **Dry Sauterne**

Rosé Fruit Salad Dressing
(About 1 cup)

This is a cooked dressing, but it's quick and easy to make. Use it on almost any fruit salad. Vary it occasionally by folding whipped cream instead of sour cream into the chilled mixture.

    1 egg, beaten
    2 teaspoons cornstarch
    2 tablespoons honey
    ¼ teaspoon salt
    ½ teaspoon dry mustard
    ⅓ cup California Rosé
    ½ cup dairy sour cream

Combine all ingredients but sour cream in saucepan. Place over low heat and cook, stirring constantly until mixture clears and thickens. Cool thoroughly; fold in sour cream.

Avocado with Jellied Madrilene
(6 to 8 servings)

Use this salad as a first course, a gourmet opening for a special dinner. It is pretty and shimmering, and deserves the attention it would get when served alone. The soft gelatin must be well chilled. If you like a firmer gelatin, soften 1 teaspoon unflavored gelatin in 1 tablespoon lemon juice then dissolve over hot water and stir into madrilene before chilling.

    1 (12½-oz.) can consomme madrilene
    2 tablespoons California Dry Sherry
    1 tablespoon lemon juice
    3 or 4 unpeeled avocados, halved and pits removed
    1 cup dairy sour cream
    1 tablespoon chopped chives, dill or parsley

Blend madrilene, Sherry and lemon juice; chill until set. Stir carefully with fork; spoon into avocado half-shells. Combine sour cream with chives for garnish. Serve with Melba toast or special crackers.

To accompany this salad: **California Chablis**

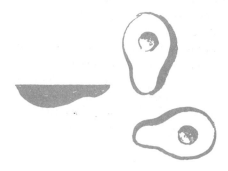

Cranberry Burgundy Salad
(4 to 6 servings)

We might call this a relish-salad for it has qualities that make it welcome either way. Good with meat or poultry, it is easy to put together and may be molded in one large mold or in individual containers.

    1 (3-oz.) package raspberry-flavored gelatin
    ½ cup boiling water
    ⅛ teaspoon salt
    ½ can jellied cranberry sauce
    ½ cup California Burgundy
    ½ cup finely chopped celery

Dissolve gelatin in boiling water; then add salt and cranberry sauce, stirring until well blended. Add wine; chill until mixture is slightly thickened. Fold in chopped celery. Pour into lightly greased 1-quart mold. Chill until firm.

To accompany this salad: **California Burgundy** *or* **Dry Sauterne**

Rosy Applesauce Mold
(6 servings)

Turn this mold out on a serving plate and garnish with a ring of canned or fresh fruits. Mixed salad fruits are especially attractive. Top with a spoonful of sour cream. To make the mold, heat 1 (1-lb.) can applesauce to boiling; remove from heat and stir in 1 (3-oz.) package raspberry-flavored gelatin, stirring to dissolve. Add 1 teaspoon grated orange peel, ½ cup California Port and ½ cup water. Pour into lightly oiled mold; chill.

Wine Marinated Vegetables
(4 to 6 servings)

Pour about ½ cup California Dry Sauterne over 2 or 3 cups hot cooked vegetables; cover and place in refrigerator overnight. When ready to serve, toss with well seasoned French dressing. Serve in lettuce cups with a little of the wine marinade.

Molded Waldorf Salad Muscatel
(5 to 6 servings)

You may use this basic gelatin for many fruit or vegetable combinations. Dissolve contents 1 (3-oz.) package lemon-flavored gelatin in 1¼ cups hot water. Add ½ cup California Muscatel or White Port, 1 tablespoon lemon juice and dash of salt; chill. When mixture starts to thicken fold in 1 cup diced apple, ½ cup finely diced celery and ½ cup chopped walnuts or pecans. Pour into 5 or 6 individual molds; chill until firm. Unmold on crisp salad greens and serve with mayonnaise.

Honey Wine Dressing

(About 1½ cups)

Plan to use this on your fruit salads. Don't forget to respect the power of garlic, and remove it once its flavor has been well established in the dressing.

- ¾ cup salad oil
- ¼ cup California Medium Sherry
- ¼ cup wine vinegar
- ⅓ cup honey
- 1 teaspoon each salt, dry mustard
- ½ teaspoon each paprika, celery seed
- 1 clove garlic

Combine all ingredients in jar or blender; shake or whirl contents until well blended. Store, covered, in refrigerator until needed, then shake again before using.

Golden Dressing

(About ¾ cup)

Use this dressing for mixed vegetables, coleslaw or sliced cucumbers. For deeper golden color, increase the prepared mustard content to 2 teaspoons.

- ¼ cup California Medium Sherry
- ¼ cup each dairy sour cream, mayonnaise
- 2 tablespoons sweet pickle juice
- ½ teaspoon prepared mustard
- ¼ teaspoon each salt, paprika
- ½ teaspoon mustard seed

Combine all ingredients and beat well; chill to blend flavors.

Fruit-flavored Salad Dressing: Mash or sieve 1 cup apricots; stir in ¼ cup California Sherry and a tablespoon lemon juice. Beat in 2 tablespoons mayonnaise and fold in 1 cup heavy cream, beaten stiff. A speck of salt and a drop of almond extract rounds out the flavors. You'll find this an excellent dressing on fresh or canned fruit salads.

Improve the flavor of Waldorf or cabbage salads with Sherry-flavored mayonnaise. Thin mayonnaise slightly with California Sherry and add a light sprinkle of nutmeg.

Pimiento Cheese Salad Dressing

(About 1 cup)

Use this dressing over hearts of lettuce or with any fruit or vegetable salad that takes kindly to a cheese flavor. With a fork, mash 1 (3-oz.) package pimiento cheese; gradually blend in ⅓ cup salad oil, 2 tablespoons lemon juice and ¼ cup California Medium Sherry, beating until mixture is smooth. Add 2 tablespoons chopped parsley, ½ teaspoon Worcestershire sauce and ¼ teaspoon each onion and garlic salts; mix well.

Apricot Sherry Dressing

(About 1 cup)

Here is a dressing that is golden and beautiful to serve with fruit and cottage cheese salad. Blend ½ cup apricot preserves with ¼ cup California Medium Sherry. Slowly beat in 1 tablespoon lemon juice, 3 tablespoons salad oil and ¼ teaspoon powdered ginger. Pour into container, cover and chill.

Favorite Salad Dressing

(About 1 cup)

Vary this good basic salad dressing by using different package dressing mixes, for both fruit and vegetable salads. Combine in a blender, or shake in a pint jar for thorough mixing.

¼ cup California Dry Sauterne or other white table wine
¼ cup white wine vinegar
1 (⅝-oz.) package French dressing mix
⅔ cup salad oil

Measure wine, vinegar and salad dressing mix into pint jar; cover and shake jar to blend ingredients; then add oil and shake thoroughly.

Additions to dressing: To half the amount of dressing add 1 hard-cooked egg, chopped and 1 tablespoon chopped parsley; or 2 tablespoons each chopped canned green chili and pimiento.

SAUCES ANd bASTES

Many of the sauces used by good cooks today are adaptations of the classic recipes of continental cuisine. Dehydrated mixes, pre-blended seasonings, chicken and meat stock concentrates—all hasten their preparation. Many other sauces are of modern inspiration, especially those for barbecue use. Wine is an important ingredient in all of them. It blends and mellows the other seasonings and adds its own characteristic flavor. In a marinating and basting sauce it has still another, more utilitarian, function. The mild acid of the wine tenderizes the meat. When a recipe calls for a table wine, it is both suitable and practical to serve the rest of the wine in the bottle as the accompanying beverage.

Burgundy Basting Sauce
(About 1½ cups)

There's quite an authoritative air about this sauce. In other words it is full strength in flavor and should be used on meats that can take it, like spareribs and beef, and possibly, duck. The powdered garlic and liquid smoke may be omitted if desired.

- ½ cup California Burgundy, or other red table wine
- ½ cup chili sauce
- 2 bouillon cubes, crumbled
- ¼ cup water
- 1 tablespoon grated onion
- 1 tablespoon Worcestershire sauce
- ⅛ teaspoon powdered garlic (optional)
- Few drops liquid smoke (optional)

In saucepan combine wine with remaining ingredients; bring to boil, then lower heat and simmer for about 5 minutes. Use sauce to baste beef, spareribs or duck while cooking.

To accompany meat with this sauce: **California Burgundy** *or* **Cabernet**

Wine Horseradish Sauce
(5 servings)

The best cooks are always mindful of the rules of vegetable cookery, that is, brief cooking and simple seasoning. However, for the sake of something different, it's a good idea to occasionally dress up vegetables with a sauce, perhaps like this one. Use it with green beans, asparagus or broccoli.

- ¼ cup California Sauterne, Chablis or other white table wine
- 1 package horseradish dip or seasoning mix
- 1 cup dairy sour cream
- 1 teaspoon seasoned salt
- 1 teaspoon seasoned pepper
- 2 to 3 cups cooked vegetables

Combine Sauterne with horseradish mix, let stand about 5 minutes. Stir into sour cream with seasoned salt and pepper. Serve on top of or combined with hot cooked vegetables.

To accompany this vegetable: **California Sauterne, Chablis** *or the wine that goes with the main dish*

Wine and Herb Barbecue Sauce
(About ½ cup)

Keep basting this simple wine sauce over the entree on the barbecue or rotisserie, such as turkey. There's enough of the sauce to enhance a 6- to 12-pound bird. The sauce does very well with other poultry and with lamb too. If the small clove of garlic is a bit strong for your taste, use half the amount or omit it entirely.

    ¼ cup California Sauterne or other white table wine
    ¼ cup melted butter or margarine
    1 small clove garlic, minced
    ½ teaspoon crushed rosemary leaves

Combine Sauterne with butter, garlic and rosemary; let stand at room temperature for several hours. Use as basting sauce for rotisseried roast turkey or other poultry or lamb.

To accompany meats served with this sauce: **California Sauterne** or **Rosé**

Cumberland Sauce
(About ¾ cup sauce)

Here's an old favorite for use with cold slices of venison, wild or domestic duck, but it's good too with cold chicken, turkey, or ham. The sauce is most decorative with its bright and sparkling color.

    ½ cup red currant jelly
    ⅓ cup California Port
    1 teaspoon orange peel cut in fine slivers
    ½ teaspoon prepared hot mustard

Place jelly in small saucepan and melt over low heat, stirring constantly; stir in Port and remainder of ingredients and when well blended remove from heat. Serve warm or chilled.

To accompany meat when this sauce is used: **California Rosé** or **Grey Riesling**

Cranberry Basting Sauce
(About 2½ cups)

There's a generous amount of basting sauce here, but you will use all of it if the ham or corned pork roast is a large one. Or you might use a portion of the sauce and keep the remainder in the refrigerator for future meat basting.

    1 (1-lb.) can whole cranberry sauce
    ½ cup brown sugar, firmly packed
    ½ cup California Dry Sherry

Combine all ingredients and spoon over surface of ham or corned pork the last half hour of baking time.

To accompany meat enhanced by this sauce: **California Rosé** or **Medium Sauterne**

Wine Barbecue Sauce
(About ¾ cup)

    ½ cup California Chablis or other white table wine
    ¼ cup salad oil
    1 small clove garlic, peeled and mashed
    2 tablespoons grated onion
    ½ teaspoon each salt, celery salt, black pepper
    ¼ teaspoon each powdered thyme, marjoram, rosemary

Combine Chablis with salad oil, garlic, onion and seasonings; chill several hours. Pour over cut-up turkey or chicken parts and marinate 2 or 3 hours, or overnight in refrigerator. Use to baste turkey or chicken during cooking period.

To accompany turkey or chicken with this sauce: **California Chablis** or **Sauterne**

Wine Currant Basting Sauce
(1¼ cups)

This bright sweet-tart sauce was created to use on turkey, but we found it was agreeably helpful on lamb and veal roasts, too. The amount is enough for a 6- to 12-pound turkey or an average size roast.

    ¾ cup California Dry Sherry
    ¼ cup butter or margarine
    ¼ cup currant jelly
    1½ teaspoons salt

In a small saucepan combine Sherry with butter, jelly and salt; simmer gently for 10 minutes. Baste meat with sauce during the last 30 minutes of cooking time. After roast is taken from the pan, skim fat from sauce and juices and serve as is or slightly thickened.

To accompany roast or turkey served with this sauce: **California Dry Sauterne** or **Dry Semillon**

For a quick, unusual sauce blend ¼ cup California Chablis, and ¼ cup light cream into contents of 1 (10½-oz.) can of asparagus soup, undiluted. Into this sauce go ingredients for a fast supper or lunch creation: 4 quartered, hard-cooked eggs and ½ cup cooked vegetables; tuna fish and peas; dried chipped beef or left over meats with vegetable combinations. Heat and serve over buttered toast points or squares of corn bread.

Easy Mushroom Sauce
(About 1½ cups)

If you have a can of cream of mushroom soup on hand you are never at a loss for a quick dress-up sauce, such as this one. Use it on ordinary meat loaf, quick minute steak or an omelet.

¼ cup California Sauterne, or other white table wine
1 (10½-oz.) can condensed cream of mushroom soup, undiluted
¼ teaspoon Worcestershire sauce
Dash of mace or nutmeg

In a small saucepan combine wine with other ingredients and heat to boiling. Remove from heat and serve at once.

To accompany a dish enhanced by this sauce: **California Claret** *or* **Chablis**

Quick Sherry Cheese Sauce
(1½ cups)

Cheddar cheese soup in a can is a natural for an easy cheese sauce, especially when it is combined with California Dry Sherry, then seasoned with bits of pimiento and green onion. Spoon it over grilled hamburgers, frankfurters, meat loaf, or omelets. Good to dress up toasted chicken sandwiches.

¼ cup California Dry Sherry
1 (11-oz.) can condensed Cheddar cheese soup
1 tablespoon chopped pimiento
1 tablespoon chopped green onion

Blend Sherry and undiluted soup together in saucepan; add pimiento and green onion. Heat gently, stirring now and then, until piping hot.

To accompany meat with Sherry Cheese Sauce: **California Claret** *or* **Dry Sauterne**

Red Wine Sauce
(About 2½ cups)

California Port and cranberry sauce with just a hint of spice make an excellent sauce or relish to serve with lamb or venison. If meat is to be served hot, then the wine sauce should be heated too.

¼ cup California Port
3 tablespoons sugar
Grated peel 1 lemon
1 teaspoon cinnamon
12 cloves
1 (1-lb.) can whole cranberry sauce

In saucepan combine Port, sugar, lemon peel, cinnamon and cloves; simmer about 5 minutes; remove cloves. Add cranberry sauce and stir to blend well. Serve warm.

To accompany lamb or venison roast: **California Claret** *or* **Sauvignon Blanc**

Sherry Cherry Sauce
(About 2 cups)

1 (1-lb.) can dark sweet cherries
¼ cup California Medium Sherry
1 cup orange juice
2 tablespoons lemon juice
1 teaspoon dry mustard
1 tablespoon finely chopped green onion
1 tablespoon cornstarch
1 teaspoon sugar
½ teaspoon grated orange peel

Drain and pit cherries; save syrup and use in hot mulled wine or other beverage. In saucepan combine Sherry with orange and lemon juices, mustard, onion, cornstarch and sugar; place over heat and cook, stirring constantly until sauce boils and thickens. Stir in pitted cherries and orange peel; heat a few minutes longer. Serve hot with roast duck, ham, or pork.

To accompany meat with Sherry Cherry Sauce: **California Rosé** *or* **Chablis**

Buttery Mushroom Wine Sauce
(About 2 cups)

Whole mushroom caps in this wine sauce make it most luxurious. It tastes wonderful with California Burgundy helping to blend the herbs together. California Rosé or Chablis may be used in place of the Burgundy if you wish.

½ cup California Burgundy
1 (6-oz.) can broiled-in-butter whole mushroom crowns
⅛ teaspoon dried dill
1 tablespoon instant minced onion
1 teaspoon garlic-flavored red wine vinegar
¼ cup tomato catsup
1 teaspoon kitchen bouquet
2 teaspoons cornstarch
1 tablespoon cold water

In saucepan combine wine with mushrooms, dill, onions, vinegar, catsup and kitchen bouquet; heat slowly to boiling. Blend cornstarch with cold water and stir into sauce; simmer about 5 minutes until sauce thickens slightly and clears. Spoon over grilled steaks or other meat. Sprinkle with finely chopped fresh parsley if desired.

To accompany meat with this sauce: **California Burgundy** *or* **Rosé**

All Purpose Barbecue Sauce
(About 3 cups)

Keep some of this sauce on hand in the refrigerator for use whenever you decide to barbecue. This wine sauce is rich and browns quickly, so be sure to grill poultry and meat slowly and not too close to the coals.

    1 cup California Rosé, Sauterne or Burgundy
    1 (14-oz.) bottle tomato catsup
    2 bouillon cubes, crumbled
    ¼ cup wine vinegar
    2 tablespoons soy sauce
    2 tablespoons honey or brown sugar
    ½ teaspoon garlic salt
    ⅓ cup salad oil

In saucepan combine wine with remaining ingredients; heat to boiling then reduce heat and simmer about 5 minutes. Use this sauce to brush over chicken, steak or chops while broiling or grilling over charcoal. Spoon remaining baste over cooked meat or poultry as a sauce when serving.

To accompany meat basted with this sauce: **California Rosé** *or a red table wine*

Pineapple Burgundy Sauce
(About 2 cups)

Slices of ham or corned pork will taste even better if they are accompanied by this smart wine sauce, perfectly combined with California Burgundy and crushed pineapple. There's something of the sweet and sour flavor put in by the wine vinegar and brown sugar. This sauce is good on hot or cold tongue too.

    1 cup California Burgundy
    ½ cup brown sugar, firmly packed
    2 tablespoons wine vinegar
    1 (8½-oz.) can crushed pineapple
    1 teaspoon dry mustard
    1 tablespoon cornstarch
    1 tablespoon dripping from baked ham, or butter

In saucepan stir together Burgundy, sugar and vinegar; bring to boil, then lower heat and simmer for 10 to 15 minutes. Blend undrained pineapple with mustard and cornstarch; add to wine mixture and simmer, stirring until sauce is clear and thickened, about 5 minutes. Stir in drippings or butter. Serve hot.

To accompany meat with this sauce: **California Burgundy** *or* **Rosé**

desserts

However good the dessert, it just can't help but be better for the close companionship of wine, both in it and with it. Wine adds the unexpected, brings out natural flavor, gives life and excitement to even the most unassuming offering. The simplest dessert is a glass of wine, chosen from the California dessert wines, Sherry, Port, Tokay, Muscatel or Angelica. Serve the wine with an imaginative cheese tray, carefully selected thin cookies, pound cake, or fruits. Or take a happy shortcut in dessert preparation and use wine to combine convenience foods as suggested in these recipes.

Filbert Wine Cake
(9-inch cake)

Intriguing because it's so different is this syrup glaze on a light cake. Use a baker's sponge-type cake, or whip up one of your easy ones. Present the cake as a whole on a special plate as mid-afternoon or evening refreshment in company with glasses of wine.

- ¾ cup filberts
- 1½ cups sugar
- ½ cup California Port
- ½ cup chopped maraschino cherries
- 1 (9-inch) sponge-type cake

Spread filberts in shallow baking pan; toast in hot oven (400°) 10 to 15 minutes, stirring occasionally. Remove from heat and cool slightly, then chop medium fine. Place sugar in heavy skillet and stir constantly over medium heat until sugar melts and carmelizes. Remove from heat and slowly stir in wine from one side of the pan. (Be careful not to let the steam burn you.) Return to heat and cook gently a few moments until syrup is well blended with wine. Take from heat and stir in cherries and filberts. Pour over cake on serving plate. Cool, spooning occasionally with syrup as it runs off.

To accompany this cake: **California Port** or **Cream Sherry**

Peach Lemon Dream Cake
(12 servings)

The perfect dessert for a special dinner, perhaps a buffet where the cake may be presented for admiration before it is cut. Use sliced peaches, fresh, frozen or canned. Or think how good it would be with fresh or frozen strawberries. But always use California Sherry to add that special flavor to the filling. You can buy the angel food cake or bake it yourself.

- 1 (3½-oz.) package lemon pudding mix
- ½ cup California Sherry
- 1 (10-inch) angel food cake
- 2 cups sliced peaches, drained
- 1 cup heavy cream
- 1 tablespoon powdered sugar
- ½ teaspoon vanilla

Make pudding according to package directions, substituting ½ cup Sherry for ½ cup water. Cool. Cut angel food cake horizontally to make 4 equal layers. Combine cooled pudding with peach slices; spread about 1 cup filling between each of the 3 layers and on top of cake. Whip cream, with powdered sugar and vanilla, until stiff enough to spread over top and sides of cake. Chill.

To accompany this cake: **California Champagne,** *demi-sec or sec; or a* **Light Sweet Muscat**

Dark Raisin Cake
(10-inch cake)

There's a generous amount of raisins in this dark, fruity cake. It's handsome, easy to make and good to keep on hand for it stores very well. The raisins are simmered in California Sherry and Brandy, then allowed to plump up in the wine and absorb all the good flavors. Time allowing, you can let the raisins stand overnight or several days in the refrigerator.

    ½ cup California Sherry
    ¼ cup California Brandy
    2 cups seedless raisins
    ½ cup softened shortening
    1½ cups sugar
    2 eggs
    1½ cups applesauce
    3 cups sifted all-purpose flour
    ¼ cup cocoa
    1½ teaspoons baking soda
    1 teaspoon each salt, cinnamon
    ¼ teaspoon cloves

In saucepan add Sherry and Brandy to raisins; cover and simmer over low heat 5 minutes. Remove from heat and let stand. Cream shortening and sugar until blended; beat in eggs and applesauce. Sift together flour and dry ingredients; add at once to batter and beat until smooth. Sir in prepared raisins. Spoon batter into well-greased and floured 10-inch tube pan (put paper on the bottom). Bake in a moderate oven (350°) 65 minutes, or until done. Remove from oven, cool about 5 minutes, then take from pan and cool on rack. Dust top generously with sifted powdered sugar.

To accompany this cake: **California Port** *or* **Muscatel**

Quick Fruit Desserts: If you're looking for a quick and easy last minute dessert, try this. Drizzle California sweet Sherry on a mixture of orange slices and grapefruit sections. Dot with butter and sprinkle lightly with brown sugar. Place under the broiler for a few moments, until lightly browned. This light dessert can be served plain or topped with dairy sour cream.

Dress-Up Sauce for Custard and Pudding: Here's a quick, ruby-colored sauce to dress up baked custards or bread pudding. Blend a package of frozen raspberries with ⅓ cup currant jelly, ¼ cup California Port and a tablespoon of cornstarch. Add a light pinch of salt and a drop or two of almond extract. Cook, stirring until thickened. Strain and store covered until ready to use.

Fresh Fruits in Wine Add Few Dessert Calories: For a fresh, low-calorie approach to the dessert course, fruits marinated in wine are a delicious answer. As each fruit comes into season, try serving it with a compatible wine—perhaps a dry red, white or Rosé wine, sometimes sweetened a little with honey or sugar. Port, the fruity dessert wine produced in California, is especially good with fruits, starting with early strawberries and moving right on through the seasons to winter pears.

Pears Poached in White Wine: Peel 6 pears, leaving fruit whole with stems intact. Combine 1 cup each California Sauterne or other white table wine, sugar and water; add 1½ teaspoons cloves and 2 tablespoons lemon juice. Bring to a boil, lower heat and simmer 5 minutes. Add pears to hot syrup; poach just until tender, basting and turning carefully. Remove from heat; lift pears to serving dish and allow to cool. Spoon cooled syrup over pears, cover and chill several hours. Serve the poached pears with a little of the syrup and cream cheese beaten until soft and fluffy with a little additional wine and a grating of orange or lemon rind.

Quick Cheese Cake
(12 x 8 inches)

Easy as 1–2–3 is this delightfully flavored, smoothly elegant cheese cake, and there's no baking required. In addition to possessing all the attributes a gourmet would demand in a dessert, it is simple to create and can be varied by a number of different fruit toppings.

    1 cup graham cracker crumbs
    2 tablespoons sugar
    3 tablespoons softened butter or margarine
    ¾ cup cold milk
    2 (2-oz.) packages whipped topping mix
    ¼ cup California Cream Sherry
    ¼ cup sugar
    2 (3-oz.) packages cream cheese
    1 (1-lb. 5-oz.) can cherry pie filling

Rub together graham cracker crumbs, sugar and butter or margarine; pat into bottom of 12 x 8-inch pan. Add milk to whipped topping mix and beat until topping is light and fluffy and just holds its shape. With the same beater in a small bowl, beat Sherry and ¼ cup sugar into cream cheese; fold carefully into topping mix, and spread in pan over crumbs. Pour pie filling over top of cheese mixture and chill in refrigerator several hours or overnight.

To accompany this cheese cake: **California Cream Sherry, Port** *or* **Muscatel**

Toddy Gingerbread
(8 to 10 servings)

Sherry and spice and everything nice are in this mix-it-quick dessert. While it bakes, turn your attention to making the Creamy Sherry Sauce to be served warm with the pudding. Simple, but a good blend of flavors.

 1 (14½-oz.) package gingerbread mix
 ¼ cup California Sherry
 ¾ cup water
 1 (3½-oz.) can flaked coconut

Prepare gingerbread according to package directions using ¼ cup Sherry and ¾ cup water for liquid specified. Add half the coconut to the batter. Turn batter into 9-inch square pan; sprinkle remaining coconut on top. Or turn batter into well-greased ring or other fancy mold sprinkled with remaining coconut (batter should fill mold ½ to ⅔ full). Bake in moderate oven (350°) about 30 minutes or until cake-pudding is done. Serve warm with a special sauce made with California Sherry.

Creamy Sherry Sauce: Combine 1 cup sugar, ½ cup butter or margarine, ¼ cup light cream and ⅛ teaspoon salt. Heat slowly to boiling, stirring now and then. Add ¼ cup Sherry and 1 teaspoon grated lemon rind. Heat slightly to blend flavors. Makes about 1⅓ cups sauce.

To accompany this dessert: **California Sherry** *or* **Muscatel**

Sherry Chiffon Cake
(10-inch tube cake)

A delightfully subtle wine flavor results when California Cream Sherry is used in making a chiffon cake from a package mix. Use ½ cup Sherry for part of the liquid called for and follow directions on the package. Then glaze the cooled cake with a thin icing make by combining 1 cup sifted powdered sugar with 2 or 3 tablespoons Sherry. For a different cake of excellent flavor, use California Muscatel instead of the Sherry.

Brandied Orange Cake. Quick to make and highly satisfactory is this cake made with an orange cake package mix and California Brandy. Follow the directions on the package for making the cake, using ½ cup Brandy for part of the liquid called for. Bake as directed. Sprinkle the baked cake with sifted powdered sugar or spread a thin frosting on the cooled cake, using ⅓ cup orange marmalade, 1 tablespoon Brandy and about 1½ cups sifted powdered sugar. You may use California Sherry or Muscatel in this cake too.

DeLuxe Cheese Cake
(10 to 12 servings)

This delectable sweet-sharp flavored cheese cake looks impressive and tastes even more so. California Sherry blends with the filling and topping ingredients to make it ever so smooth and inviting. Easy to make too. Lacking the spring-form pan, line a deep (at least 2½ inches) 8-inch pan with aluminum foil, pressing it in carefully. When ready to serve, lift the whole well-chilled cheese cake out of the pan.

First make the crust: Crush 1½ cups graham crackers until very fine; add ½ cup melted butter and mix well. Press into bottom and up on sides of an 8-inch spring-form pan.

Then make filling:

 2 (8-oz.) packages cream cheese
 1 cup sugar
 3 eggs
 1 teaspoon lemon juice
 ¼ cup California Sherry

Combine all of these ingredients and beat until smooth. (Very nice in blender.) Pour into crumb lined pan and bake in slow oven (300°) 40 to 45 minutes or until firm. Pull out on oven rack and spread on *Sherry Topping.* Return to oven and bake for another 10 minutes. Cool; and, to insure full flavor, refrigerate overnight.

Sherry Topping: Stir together 1 cup dairy sour cream, 2 tablespoons sifted powdered sugar and 1 tablespoon California Sherry.

To accompany this dessert: **California Medium** *or* **Cream Sherry, Sweet Sauterne** *or* **Port**

Prune Cake with Penuche Frosting
(13 x 9 inch)

Usually a spice cake starts out with a long list of ingredients, rather frightening if time is limited for cake making. Here we use a spice cake mix, dairy sour cream, cut up, cooked prunes and some California Port (goes so well with prunes). For another short cut use the junior baby food prunes instead of cooking your own, if you wish.

    1 (1-lb. 2½-oz.) package spice cake mix
    2 eggs
    ½ cup dairy sour cream
    1 cup cooked, cut up prunes
    ½ cup California Port

Place spice cake mix in bowl; add eggs, sour cream, prune pulp and Port. Beat with electric beater about 2 minutes, or until batter is well blended. Pour into lightly greased and floured 13 x 9-inch pan. Bake in moderate oven (350°) 40 minutes or until done. Place on rack to cool. Frost cake in pan with Penuche Frosting.

Penuche Frosting: In saucepan combine ½ cup dairy sour cream with 1 cup brown sugar, firmly packed. Place over heat and stir to dissolve sugar. Bring to boil, stirring occasionally; cook about 3 minutes. Remove from heat, cool to lukewarm; beat in ⅓ cup **sifted** powdered sugar; beat to spreading consistency. Spread on cake.

To accompany this cake: **California Port** *or* **Cream Sherry**

Serve small cantaloupe halves with a spooning of California Muscatel in the cavity. For top flavor, prick the inside of the melon with tines of a fork, pour in the wine and chill an hour before serving.

For refreshing warm weather desserts, combine one or more of the fresh fruits in season with a sweet Sherry from California. Just pour the Sherry over the fruits and let stand for an hour or longer. A simple yet sophisticated dessert for summer parties.

Marinated Fruit Compote: For those who like a light yet elegant dessert, a fruit compote marinated in wine is a good choice. Marinate canned cling peach slices, halved fresh strawberries and chunks of pineapple in California Sherry for several hours. These fruit flavors blend nicely with shortbread cookies.

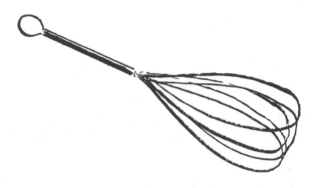

Peach Upside Down Cake
(12 servings)

When dinner seems to be on the skimpy side, bolster it up with this fruit and cake combination. Use sliced cling peaches, they're firmer and hold their pretty shape better. And marvel at the unexpected flavor combination that happens when the warm Sherry Custard Sauce is spooned over all.

    ⅓ cup butter or margarine
    1 cup brown sugar, firmly packed
    3 tablespoons California Dry Sherry
    1 (1-lb.) can sliced cling peaches, well drained
    1 (1-lb. 3-oz.) package sour cream fudge cake mix

Melt butter or margarine in a 13 x 9-inch pan. Measure in brown sugar and 2 tablespoons of Sherry; stir to combine. Arrange drained peach slices over mixture. Prepare cake mix as directed on package; pour over fruit. Bake in moderate oven (350°) 40 to 45 minutes or until done (top springs back when touched with finger). Cool cake in pan for 5 minutes; invert on flat serving plate. Sprinkle fruit surface with remaining 1 tablespoon Sherry. Serve warm with Sherry Custard Sauce.

Sherry Custard Sauce: In medium saucepan combine 2 slightly beaten eggs, 2 cups milk; beat with a wire whisk to blend; add ⅓ cup sugar and 2 tablespoons California Dry Sherry. Cook over medium heat, stirring constantly, until sauce thickens, about 5 minutes. Do not boil. Serve warm.

To accompany this dish: **California Medium** *or* **Cream Sherry**

Banana Cream Crunch
(6 to 8 servings)

Packaged mixes lend a hand in speeding up the preparation of this impressive chilled dessert. Made ahead and served at leisure, this Sherry-flavored creation will be sure to receive a warm welcome, either at dinner or perhaps for an afternoon dessert-only affair.

⅓ cup butter or margarine
1 (9- or 9½-oz.) package yellow cake mix
1 (3¾-oz.) package instant vanilla pudding mix
1½ cups milk
¼ cup California Sherry
½ cup heavy cream
2 small bananas
Nutmeg

Cut butter into cake mix until particles are very fine. Press mixture against bottom and sides of rectangular baking dish (about 6 x 10 x 2 inches). Bake in moderate oven (350°) about 20 minutes or until very lightly browned; cool. Combine instant pudding mix and milk; beat slowly with rotary beater about 1 minute, until mixture thickens. Stir in Sherry; let stand a few minutes until set. Whip cream until stiff and fold into pudding. Turn part of pudding into baked crust. Top with sliced bananas. Cover with remaining pudding and sprinkle with nutmeg. Chill 4 or 5 hours or overnight to allow crust to soften slightly.

To accompany this dessert: **California Cream Sherry, Sweet Sauterne** *or* **Sweet Semillon.**

Orange and Port Jelly
(About 6 medium glasses)

Keep a few glasses of this good wine-flavored jelly on hand for all sorts of uses in garnishing such desserts as custards, tapioca or other bland puddings. Use a small portion to brighten a spoonful of whipped cream or on the mayonnaise for a fruit salad. A California Dry Sherry does well in this jelly too.

3 cups sugar
½ cup water
1 cup California White Port
1 (6-oz.) can concentrated orange juice, undiluted
2 tablespoons lemon juice
½ bottle fruit pectin

Measure sugar and water into a large saucepan and mix well. Place over high heat, bring to a full rolling boil and boil hard 1 minute, stirring constantly. Remove from heat; stir in wine and fruit juices. Add fruit pectin; mix well. Pour quickly into glasses. Cover at once with ⅛ inch hot paraffin.

Cream Fruit Cocktail Pie
(6 to 8 servings)

Festive enough for the most important occasion is this make-ahead company pie, sparked with a white table wine—we used California Sauterne, but you might like to vary it with one of the California Sherries or Muscatel.

1 (3-oz.) package lemon-flavored gelatin
¾ cup hot water
2 tablespoons lemon juice
⅓ cup white table wine
¼ teaspoon salt
1 pint vanilla ice cream
1 (1-lb. 14-oz.) can fruit cocktail, well drained
1 (9-inch) baked pastry shell

Dissolve gelatin in hot water; add lemon juice, wine and salt. Add ice cream by spoonfuls and stir until melted. Chill until thickened, 15 to 20 minutes. Set aside a little fruit cocktail for garnish. Fold remainder into gelatin mixture. Turn into baked pastry shell and chill until firm, 2 hours or longer. Garnish with remaining fruit cocktail.

To accompany this pie: **Sweet Sauterne** *or* **Pink Champagne**

Pastel Wine Cake
(1 10-inch cake)

There's no mystery about making this handsome cake, and the variations in color and flavor seem almost endless. We use a cake mix and fruit-flavored gelatin, blending it together with wine. It makes a most pleasing product, something like a pound cake that's fine in texture, delicately firm (not fluffy) and very good to eat.

1 (1-lb. 2½-oz.) package yellow or white cake mix
1 (3-oz.) package raspberry-flavored gelatin
¾ cup California Sherry
½ cup salad oil
4 eggs, unbeaten

Combine all ingredients in bowl and beat for about 3 minutes with electric beater. Pour into lightly greased and floured 10-inch tube pan (you may want to put a ring of paper in the bottom) and bake in moderate oven (350°) for 55 to 60 minutes. Remove from oven, let stand 5 minutes, then turn out on cake rack. When cool, spread with thin Sherry Glaze.

Sherry Glaze: In a small saucepan heat together ⅓ cup Sherry and 2 tablespoons butter or margarine. Remove from heat and stir in gradually 2 cups sifted powdered sugar. When cooled and slightly thickened, spread over top of cake.

To accompany this cake: **California Cream Sherry** *or* **Port**

Napa Valley Cake
(13 x 9 inch cake)

Transform a plain but delicious cake into a conversation piece with this special Sherry topping. A yellow or white cake mix gives a head start in the easy mixing and baking. While the cake is still warm, puncture it all over the top with a knife and pour on a syrup made of California Sherry and sugar, with just a trace of instant coffee. Later everyone will be delighted with the Sherry flavor of the cake.

  1 (1-lb. 2½-oz.) package yellow or white cake mix
  ½ cup California Cream Sherry
  ½ cup sugar
  1 teaspoon instant coffee
    Sifted powdered sugar

Line bottom 13 x 9-inch pan with foil or paper; grease and flour well. Prepare cake from mix, according to package directions and pour into prepared pan; bake. Remove cake from pan and cool on rack about 10 minutes. In saucepan combine Sherry with sugar and instant coffee; bring to boil and cook about 3 minutes, until syrupy. With sharp knife cut deep slits over surface of cake or pierce with fork; pour Sherry syrup slowly over cake, allowing it to penetrate. Sift powdered sugar generously over top. Sprinkle additional sugar on just before serving.

To accompany this cake: **California Cream Sherry** *or* **California Port**

Gingerbread with Sherry-Lemon Sauce: Gingerbread made from a packaged mix becomes elegant company dessert when served with a Sherry-lemon sauce. Blend ½ cup sugar, 1 tablespoon cornstarch, ¾ cup water, ¼ cup California Sherry together in a small saucepan. Boil until thickened. Blend in a tablespoon butter and lemon juice and 2 teaspoons grated lemon rind. Serve hot over squares of warm gingerbread.

Gingerbread: Spicy gingerbread with a creamy wine-flavored topping is a real taste pleaser. Blend 3 or 4 tablespoons California Sherry into a 3-ounce package cream cheese. Add enough powdered sugar to make a soft, fluffy mixture—about 2½ cups. Serve over squares of warm gingerbread made with ½ cup chopped salted peanuts added to the batter before baking.

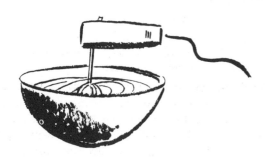

Sherry Chiffon Pie
(6 to 8 servings)

Confidence in preparing a successful dinner is knowing there is a light and lovely pie like this one waiting in the refrigerator for dessert time. Make it in the morning, or the night before, because the filling does need time to set and let the flavor of the California Sherry permeate it well.

  1 envelope unflavored gelatin
  ¼ cup cold water
  ½ cup hot water
  ½ cup sugar
  ½ cup California Medium Sherry
  2 tablespoons lemon juice
  1 cup evaporated milk, chilled
  1 (9-inch) graham cracker shell
    Flaked coconut

In small bowl of electric mixer, soften gelatin in cold water; dissolve in hot water. Stir in sugar, Sherry and lemon juice; chill until mixture thickens to consistency of unbeaten egg whites. Add chilled evaporated milk slowly to gelatin-Sherry mixture while beating at low speed. When all is added, increase to highest speed and whip until mixture doubles in volume. Turn into crumb crust. Chill until completely set, at least 2 hours. Garnish top with flaked coconut.

To make graham cracker shell: Blend 1½ cups graham cracker crumbs with ⅓ cup melted butter; press firm and evenly over bottom and sides of 9-inch pie pan. Chill.

To accompany this dish: **California Cream Sherry** *or* **Sweet Sauterne**

Apple Pie with Port
(6 to 8 servings)

California Port, apples and cheese are always a winning combination, but put them together to create this dessert and you have one of the best apple pies. Because the apple filling is cooked before it goes into the pastry, the baking time is cut in about half.

Cheese Pastry:

    2 cups sifted all-purpose flour
    1 teaspoon salt
    ⅔ cup shortening
    ¾ cup (3-oz.) shredded sharp Cheddar cheese
    5 to 6 tablespoons cold water

Mix flour, salt and shortening with pastry blender until mixture resembles coarse meal. Stir in cheese; add water gradually and mix lightly with fork. Divide pastry in half and roll out to fit 9-inch pie pan. Roll second half of pastry and cut into 10 ½-inch strips.

Port-Apple Filling:

    ¾ cup sugar
    2 tablespoons corn starch
    ⅓ cup apple juice
    ⅓ cup California Port
    1 tablespoon butter or margarine
       Few drops red food coloring
    5 medium cooking apples, peeled and sliced
      (about 5 cups)

In large saucepan mix together sugar and cornstarch. Stir in apple juice, Port, butter or margarine and food coloring. Cook over medium heat until mixture boils. Add apples and cook gently until barely tender. Spoon into pastry lined pan; weave pastry strips across filling to make lattice top. Bake in hot oven (425°) 30 minutes. Serve warm with ice cream, if desired.

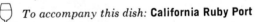 *To accompany this dish:* **California Ruby Port**

Apple Cobbler: Deep dish apple cobbler is a favorite cold weather dessert. Slice apples to make 1 quart into a baking dish. Mix with ¼ cup sugar, ½ teaspoon cinnamon and a sprinkle of salt. Dot with butter; pour on ¼ cup California Sherry. Top with a pastry crust and bake as usual.

Sherry Nutmeg Whip Topping
(1 cup)

It may look like familiar whipped cream, but the taste is something much more subtle and exciting. The topping is really quite simple, add a little California Sherry and a flick of nutmeg to the cream and let it chill well before beating. Use it to top fruit desserts.

    ½ cup heavy cream
    1 tablespoon California Sherry
    ¼ teaspoon nutmeg
    1 tablespoon powdered sugar
    ¼ teaspoon vanilla

Combine heavy cream, Sherry and nutmeg and allow to stand about thirty minutes before whipping. Add sugar and vanilla extract; whip with a rotary beater until thick. Spread evenly over top of blueberry or apple pie. Chill until serving time.

Cranberry Wine Chiffon Pie
(6 to 8 servings)

It's easy enough to produce this beautifully pink-tinted dessert that has a definite party air. Jellied cranberry sauce and California Port blend together as good flavor partners. Do a little planning ahead, like baking the pastry shell, and the rest is accomplished quickly.

    1 (1-lb.) can jellied cranberry sauce
    1 (3-oz.) package orange-flavored gelatin
    ½ cup California Port
    1 tablespoon grated orange peel
      Dash of salt
    2 eggs whites
    2 tablespoons sugar
    1 cup heavy cream
    1 (9-inch) baked pastry shell

Place cranberry sauce in saucepan and crush with fork. Simmer while adding orange-flavored gelatin. Stir until dissolved. Remove from heat; add Port, orange peel and salt; cool. Chill until mixture begins to thicken. Beat egg whites until stiff, gradually beating in sugar. Fold into cranberry mixture. Whip half of the cream and blend in gently. Spoon into baked pastry shell. Chill until firm. Before serving, decorate with the remainder of cream, whipped and slightly sweetened.

To accompany this dish: **California Tawny Port**

Strawberry Port Pie

(9-inch pie)

½ cup California Port
¾ cup water
1 (3-oz.) package strawberry-flavored gelatin
1 (10-oz.) package frozen sliced strawberries
2 teaspoons lemon juice
1 (3-oz.) package cream cheese
1 tablespoon milk
1 (9-inch) baked pie shell
    Whipped cream

Heat Port and water to simmering. Remove from heat; add gelatin and stir until dissolved. Drop in frozen block of strawberries and let thaw, breaking up block with fork to hasten process; add lemon juice. Chill until mixture begins to thicken. Meantime, whip cream cheese and milk together with fork; spread evenly over bottom of pie shell. Pour in partially thickened gelatin mixture; chill several hours or overnight until firm. Garnish with whipped cream before serving.

 *To accompany this dessert:* **California Ruby Port**

Sherry-Glazed Apple Pie

(9-inch pie)

For the pie shell, use your own pastry recipe based on 1½ cups all-purpose flour (or a prepared pastry mix) adding ½ cup grated American cheese.

1 (1-lb. 9-oz.) can prepared apple pie filling
1 (9-inch) baked pie shell
2 teaspoons unflavored gelatin
2 tablespoons water
½ cup apple jelly
½ cup strained lemon juice
    Pinch of salt
⅓ cup California Sherry
    Ginger-Cheese

Turn pie filling into baked pastry shell. Stir gelatin into water. Turn jelly, lemon juice and salt into a small saucepan; bring to a boil, stirring. Add gelatin and stir to dissolve; add Sherry. Cool until mixture begins to thicken slightly; then, spoon over apples in pastry shell. Chill until set. Serve topped with spoonful of Ginger-Cheese.

Ginger-Cheese: Beat 1 (8-oz.) package cream cheese with enough Sherry to soften. Add 1 or 2 tablespoons chopped preserved ginger.

To accompany this dessert: **California Cream Sherry or Port**

Honey Sherried Crunch Pie

(9-inch pie)

Elegance is the keynote in this beautifully smooth and creamy pie, delicately flavored with California Sherry and honey. Crushed peanut brittle patted gently over the top of the filling, is the surprise ingredient.

1 tablespoon unflavored gelatin
½ cup California Medium Sherry
1 (3¼-oz.) vanilla pudding and pie filling (not instant)
1½ cups milk
¼ cup honey
1 cup heavy cream
1 (9-inch) baked pie shell
1 cup coarsely crushed peanut brittle

Soften gelatin in Sherry. Prepare pudding mix according to directions on the package, using 1½ cups milk as liquid. Remove cooked filling from heat, add softened gelatin and stir until dissolved; stir in honey. Cool filling completely, about 1 hour, and when partially thickened, fold in cream, whipped until stiffened. Spoon into pie shell. Cover top with crushed peanut brittle, patting down with hand. This pie cuts to perfection if it has been chilled several hours or overnight.

To accompany this dish: **California Medium Sherry**

Cream Puff Fantasy

(6 servings)

Most impressive to present to guests, but really easy and quick to make, these cream puffs are filled with ice cream and sauced with a sparkling combination of cherries and California Port. Pick up the cream puffs at your bakery, or make your own puffs from a standard recipe. They can be made at any time, even frozen and later popped into the oven for a moment to crisp.

1 (10-oz.) package quick-thaw frozen cherries
⅓ cup California Port
1 tablespoon sugar
1½ teaspoons cornstarch
    Few grains salt
6 baked cream puff shells
1 to 1½ pints vanilla or coffee ice cream

Thaw cherries as directed on package. Drain off the rich syrup and combine with Port, sugar, cornstarch and salt in a small saucepan. Cook and stir over high heat until sauce boils, thickens and clears. Remove from heat and add cherries. Serve warm or cool over cream puffs filled with ice cream.

To accompany this dessert: **California Medium or Cream Sherry**

California Raisin Tartlets
(18 3-inch tarts)

⅔ cup seedless raisins, coarsely chopped
¼ cup California Medium Sherry
2 teaspoons unflavored gelatin
½ cup orange juice
3 eggs, well beaten
⅔ cup sugar
1 tablespoon lemon juice
⅛ teaspoon salt
½ cup finely chopped raw cranberries
1 cup heavy cream
18 (3-inch) baked tart shells

Pour Sherry over raisins and set aside. In a saucepan soften gelatin in orange juice; then add eggs, sugar, lemon juice and salt. Cook over moderate heat, stirring until gelatin dissolves and mixture thickens. Remove from heat and stir in raisins. Cool. When filling begins to thicken, fold in cranberries and cream whipped until stiff. Pile high into tart shells. Chill until firm.

To accompany these tartlets: **California Port, Muscatel, Medium** or **Cream Sherry**

Banana Coconut Rolls
(4 servings)

Briefly, this fruit concoction wins its way because it is quick and easy to make, and very good to eat. An added attraction is that the banana roll recipe is basic, with a choice of two good wine sauces, both using California Dry Sherry.

4 medium ripe bananas
2 tablespoons lemon juice
½ cup flaked coconut

Peel and cut bananas crosswise into halves and place in greased baking dish. Brush with lemon juice and sprinkle with coconut. Bake in moderate oven (375°) 15 to 20 minutes until coconut is browned and bananas are easily pierced with fork. Serve with either one of the hot wine sauces below.

Sherry Egg Nog Sauce: Beat ½ cup heavy cream until it holds its shape. With the same beater, beat 1 egg well; gradually beat in ½ cup sugar, beating until creamy. Blend in 3 tablespoons California Dry Sherry. Fold in stiffly beaten cream and a dash of cinnamon.

Apricot Sherry Sauce: In small saucepan combine ¼ cup California Dry Sherry with 1 cup apricot preserves, ¼ cup sugar and a dash of salt; bring to boil, stirring gently. Remove from heat and serve hot.

To accompany this dish: **California Cream Sherry** or **Muscatel**

Chocolate Wine Sauce
(2 cups)

It's the little unexpected hint of something slightly different in taste that counts. Here we make the pleasure of good chocolate even better by adding a judicious amount of California Port. Keep this sauce on hand to spark ordinary desserts—chilled if you like, or heated. The warm sauce will be slightly thinner.

1 (1-lb.) can milk chocolate fudge topping
½ cup California Port

Pour fudge topping into a medium bowl; gradually stir in Port, beating well to blend. Cover and store in refrigerator.

Superb Chocolate Torte
(10 to 12 servings)

1 (6-oz.) package semi-sweet chocolate morsels
1 cup sugar
½ cup softened butter
½ teaspoon salt
6 eggs, separated
¼ cup plus 4-6 tablespoons California Muscatel
1½ cups blanched almonds, ground
½ cup fine, dry bread crumbs

Melt chocolate morsels over hot, not boiling, water; cool. Combine sugar, butter and salt and beat until creamy. Add egg yolks one at a time and continue beating well after each addition. Blend in cooled melted chocolate, Muscatel, almonds and dry crumbs. Beat egg whites until they are stiff enough to hold a point when the beater is pulled up through them; fold gently but thoroughly into chocolate mixture. Pour into 8-inch spring-form pan, greased and dusted with fine crumbs. Bake in moderate oven (350°) 60 minutes. Remove from heat and while still warm drizzle 4 to 6 tablespoons Muscatel over top. Cool thoroughly before serving or store in refrigerator, tightly covered. Dust with sifted powdered sugar or decorate with whipped cream before serving.

To accompany this dessert: **California Cream Sherry** or **Muscatel**

Beat cream cheese smooth with California Sherry. Stir in sour cream just until mixture mounds softly on a spoon. Spoon into chilled canned peach halves and sprinkle with toasted coconut. Goes well with your favorite cookies.

Broiled Coconut Cream Pudding
(5 to 6 servings)

1½ cups cold milk
½ cup California Chablis, Sauterne, or other white table wine
⅛ teaspoon salt
1 (3¾-oz.) package instant coconut cream pudding mix
Pound cake slices or lady fingers
Brown sugar
Flaked coconut

Measure milk, wine and salt into mixing bowl. Add instant coconut pudding mix. Beat slowly with egg beater 1 minute or until blended. Let stand until pudding begins to thicken. Arrange pound cake or lady fingers in a large or individual heat-proof serving dishes. Spoon coconut pudding over top. When ready to serve, sprinkle each dish with brown sugar and coconut. Run under the broiler until topping bubbles.

To accompany this dessert: **California Sec Champagne**

A dessert idea: Grate soft Cheddar cheese and mix with a little California Sherry or Port. Shape into small balls and roll in chopped salted almonds. Serve with fruit and small glasses of dessert wine.

Thin canned fudge or butterscotch sauce with a little California Sherry. Heat and serve as a thin sauce over well-chilled canned pears, squares of plain cake, vanilla pudding or the old standby, ice cream.

Zabaglione
(8 servings)

Brief and to the point is this way with a traditional Italian Custard, light and rich. Now that egg nog is available in cans, this quick Zabaglione can be a year-around dessert. Use California Medium or Cream Sherry in place of the Marsala if you wish.

1 (1-qt.) can egg nog
2 eggs, slightly beaten
2 tablespoons Marsala

Pour egg nog into top of double boiler; heat over hot, not boiling, water. Stir a little of the hot egg nog into beaten eggs, then pour into remaining hot egg nog, and cook gently, stirring constantly until mixture coats a metal spoon, about 5 minutes. Remove from over water; stir in wine. Pour into 8 sherbet glasses. Cover tops with waxed paper. Chill.

To accompany this pudding: **California Medium** *or* **Cream Sherry** *make a delightful partner for this custard*

Frozen Raisin Tortoni
(6 servings)

There's joy in using whipped cream in a dessert as it insures delicate smoothness and richness. This tortoni has these qualities plus a light handling of California Sherry and raisins to make it different. Lacking individual molds, use paper baking cups for freezing containers. When time to serve, be sure to garnish with a few macaroon crumbs, a hint of cream topping and perhaps a festive bit of candied fruit.

½ cup seedless raisins
2 tablespoons California Medium Sherry
1 egg, separated
½ cup milk
⅓ cup sugar
1 teaspoon unflavored gelatin
¼ teaspoon salt
½ cup almond macaroon crumbs
1 cup heavy cream

Chop raisins lightly; add Sherry. In saucepan combine lightly beaten egg yolk and milk; stir in sugar mixed with gelatin and salt. Cook over very low heat, stirring constantly, until mixture coats spoon. Remove from heat and stir in macaroon crumbs. Cool. Beat egg white stiff, then with same beater, beat cream until stiff. Fold egg white and cream into cooled custard; fold in raisins and wine. Turn into individual molds; freeze until firm.

To accompany this dish: **California Muscatel** *or* **Sweet Sauterne**

Frozen Sherry Cream Glacé
(6 servings)

Each little piece of candied fruit stands out like a jewel in this impressive to look at but certainly easy-to-make dessert. Just combine 1 quart slightly softened vanilla ice cream with ½ cup California Sherry and 1 cup prepared glace (candied) fruit. Spoon into refrigerator freezing tray; freeze until mushy. Stir well, then continue freezing until firm.

Rich Sherry Trifle
(6 servings)

There's no dessert so typically English as a trifle, and quite good it is too. This new method makes it possible to prepare the dessert easily and quickly. And if it is served beautifully (here is where a lovely cut glass or thin modern glass bowl comes in), even a trifle achieves its full gourmet potential. This recipe may be tailored to your taste. Use ½ cup of California Sherry if you like a full wine character and ¼ cup Sherry for a more subtle taste.

    1 (15-oz.) can sweetened condensed milk
    2 cups cold water
    4 egg yolks, slightly beaten
    1 teaspoon vanilla or almond extract
    24 macaroons, broken into large pieces
    ¼ to ½ cup California Sherry
       Currant, Strawberry or Raspberry Jelly

Combine sweetened condensed milk, water and slightly beaten egg yolks in top of double boiler. Cook over hot water, stirring constantly, just until mixture coats a spoon. Remove from heat; cool quickly. Stir in extract. Place macaroons in bottom of medium glass serving bowl. Pour Sherry over macaroons and allow to soak into macaroon pieces, stirring lightly to distribute the wine. Remove ½ cup macaroons. Gently spoon cooled custard mixture on top of crumbs in serving bowl. Garnish with spoonfuls of jelly and remaining macaroon pieces. Chill in refrigerator until very cold, about 3 hours. Serve chilled.

 To accompany this dessert: **California Cream Sherry**

Banana Nut Trifle
(6 servings)

Distinctive California Sherry comes through with delicate insistence as it blends all the other ingredients in this old favorite dessert made modern. We used Dry Sherry here, but there's no reason why you can't use Medium or Cream Sherry and expect an equally good result and slight change in flavor. Packaged vanilla or banana pudding and pie filling mix may be used instead of the egg custard sauce.

    24 macaroons or 1 (12-oz.) package pound cake
       cut in 1-inch cubes
    ½ cup California Dry Sherry
    3 egg yolks, beaten
    1 cup sugar
    ⅛ teaspoon salt
    2 large bananas, sliced
    2 tablespoons lemon juice
    2 cups whipped cream or whipped topping mix
    ½ cup almonds, blanched and sliced

Place macaroons or cubed pound cake in serving dish; sprinkle with ¼ cup of the Sherry. In top of double boiler, beat egg yolks until very thick; beat in sugar and salt. Stir in remaining Sherry. Place over hot water and cook, stirring constantly until thick. Pour over macaroons or pound cake. Chill. Slice bananas and coat with lemon juice. Top cake mixture with bananas and whipped cream. Sprinkle with sliced almonds. Chill well before serving.

 To accompany this dish: **California Cream Sherry**

Rosy Red Peach Rice Cream
(6 servings)

Easy as can be to create is this dandy dessert from ordinary on-the-shelf or in-the-freezer ingredients. Raspberries color the peaches and California Muscatel lends its sweet richness. Rice never had it so good.

    1 (1-lb. 13-oz.) can sliced cling peaches
    ¼ cup California Muscatel
    2 teaspoons vanilla
    1 (10-oz.) package frozen raspberries, thawed
    3 cups cold cooked rice
    1 cup heavy cream

Drain peaches. Pour syrup into small saucepan, add Muscatel and 1 teaspoon vanilla; place over heat and boil until thick. Pour over thawed raspberries and peaches in bowl. Chill. Whip cream; fold in rice and remaining vanilla. Spoon into serving dishes. Top with red peaches.

To accompany this dessert: A chilled **California Muscatel** *would be the obvious one to serve. But you could also consider a* **California Rosé,** *one on the slightly sweet side. Its color will just about match the dessert.*

Raisin Angel Pudding
(8 servings)

Slices of angel food cake and California Sherry have always been more or less companionable served as a quick dessert or at any quiet talk exchange. So it's not unusual to go a step further and make a dessert using these two, plus a few additional ingredients. The result is a light, airy soufflé-type dessert, good after a filling meal. And the nice Sherry touch is there, right in the raisins.

    ¼ cup California Medium or Cream Sherry
    1 cup seedless raisins
    ¼ teaspoon grated orange peel
    1 tablespoon lemon juice
    4 egg whites
    ¼ teaspoon salt
    ½ cup sugar
    3 or 4 cups angel food cake pieces

Pour Sherry over raisins, orange peel, and lemon juice. Cover and let stand 3 or 4 hours or overnight. Add salt to egg whites, and beat to soft peaks. Gradually beat in sugar to make meringue. Fold cake pieces into meringue, then sherried raisins. Spoon mixture into 1½-quart soufflé dish or casserole. Bake in moderate oven (350°) about 25 minutes. Serve warm.

To accompany this dish: **California Cream Sherry**

Strawberry Mousse
(5 servings)

Light and delicately touched with strawberries and California Port this frozen creamy mousse deserves the best in elegant surroundings. Spoon it into long-stemmed sherbet glasses and serve it with little crisp wafer cookies. Frozen raspberries may be used instead of strawberries. However, be sure to press raspberries through a sieve to take out the seeds.

    1 (10-oz.) package frozen sliced strawberries
    16 marshmallows
    ⅓ cup California Port
    1 cup dairy sour cream
    ⅛ teaspoon salt

Allow strawberries to thaw completely and crush thoroughly. Cut marshmallows in quarters, combine with wine and stir over very low heat until marshmallows are completely melted; cool. Stir in strawberries, sour cream and salt. Turn into refrigerator tray and freeze until barely firm.

To accompany this dessert: **California Pink Champagne or Ruby Port**

Wine Milk Chocolate Mousse
(8 servings)

Any party hostess will be pleased with this frozen beauty, not only because the dessert can be made with such ease, but it can be put together the evening before and requires no thought until serving time.

    1 cup milk chocolate chips
    ¼ cup California Muscatel
    2 eggs, beaten
    1 cup heavy cream

Melt milk chocolate chips with Muscatel in the top of a double boiler over hot, not boiling, water, stirring until smooth. Blend in beaten eggs rapidly. Cook, stirring constantly, for 2 minutes, then remove from heat and cool. Whip cream until stiff and fold in wine-chocolate mixture. Pour into refrigerator tray; freeze until firm. Cut into squares to serve.

To accompany this dessert: **California Muscatel.**

Drench lightly sugared raspberries with California Rosé wine. Chill and serve with thin crisp cookies for a light and lovely dessert.

Sherry Cherry Cream
(4 servings)

    1 cup heavy cream
    2 tablespoons brown sugar, firmly packed
    2 tablespoons California Medium or Cream Sherry
    1 tablespoon grated orange peel
    2 egg whites (room temperature)
    1 (8-oz.) jar red maraschino cherries,
        drained and chopped

Whip heavy cream until soft peaks form, gradually adding sugar and Sherry. Fold in orange peel. Whip egg whites until stiff but not dry. Fold into cream mixture along with cherries. Spoon into parfait glasses or dessert dishes; chill until serving time.

To accompany this dessert: **California Medium** *or* **Cream Sherry, Muscatel,** *or* **Pink Champagne.** *These wines provide pleasurable sipping with and after this dessert.*

Marinate frozen or fresh pineapple cubes in California sweet Sherry. Spoon into sherbets and top with sour cream mixed with a little chopped candied ginger.

Strawberries a l'Imperatrice
(6 to 8 servings)

The French created this original classic dessert, and are justly proud of it. We have taken a few liberties by way of short-cuts to simplify the recipe, but we have been careful to retain its legendary delicate texture and taste. Use California Cream Sherry to accent the flavor of fresh or frozen strawberries.

    ¾ cup long grain rice
    1 quart milk
    ½ teaspoon salt
    1¼ cups sugar
    1 teaspoon vanilla
    1 tablespoon unflavored gelatin
    ½ cup California Cream Sherry
    1 cup heavy cream
    3 cups whole strawberries, fresh or frozen

Combine rice, milk, salt and ¾ cup of the sugar. Cook over low heat (or boiling water) until very soft and creamy. Force mixture through a fine sieve or smooth in a blender. Add vanilla. Soften gelatin in ¼ cup Cream Sherry and stir into hot rice to dissolve. Cool to lukewarm. Fold in cream (beaten until stiff) and turn mixture into an 8-inch ring mold. Chill until well set, about 1 hour. Meantime, place strawberries in bowl and pour remaining Sherry over fruit; let stand for at least a half hour. Unmold rice ring onto a cold serving plate; fill center with Sherried Strawberries, reserving a few choice berries for garnish on the ring.

To accompany this dessert: **California Sec Champagne or Cream Sherry.** *The Champagne may be white or pink*

Strawberry Wine Cream
(6 to 8 servings)

A subtle touch of wine can boost the flavor of something as delicious as strawberries with cream. Take your choice of a sweet wine, such as Haut Sauterne or Cream Sherry to add to both berries and cream.

    2 pints fresh strawberries, hulled but left whole
      California Haut Sauterne or Cream Sherry
    2 tablespoons sifted powdered sugar
    1 cup heavy cream

Place prepared strawberries in bowl; sprinkle with 2 or 3 tablespoons wine; chill. When ready to serve, stir berries gently and spoon into dessert glasses. Top with Wine Cream.

Wine Cream: Add powdered sugar to heavy cream; whip until stiff enough to hold shape. Very carefully fold in 2 tablespoons of either Sauterne or Sherry.

To accompany this dessert: **California Haut Sauterne or Cream Sherry or Port**

Cranberry Wine Marlow
(4 servings)

    ½ cup jellied cranberry sauce
    ½ cup California Burgundy
    32 marshmallows, cut in quarters
    2 teaspoons lemon juice
    ½ cup heavy cream

Place cranberry sauce and Burgundy in saucepan; crush sauce with fork, or beat with rotary beater until smooth; heat to boiling. Pour over marshmallows in bowl and stir until marshmallows are almost melted; add lemon juice; chill. When mixture begins to thicken, fold in cream, whipped until stiff. Spoon into sherbet glasses and chill until firm. Before serving garnish with spoonful of whipped cream and a bit of cranberry sauce.

To accompany this dish: **California Muscatel or Champagne**

Golden State Rice Pudding
(10 servings)

    5 cups milk
    1 cup uncooked rice
    ½ teaspoon salt
    ¼ cup heavy cream
    ¼ cup butter or margarine
    ½ cup orange marmalade

Heat milk in 3-quart saucepan. When bubbles start to form around edges, add rice and salt gradually, stirring until it comes to a full boil. Cover saucepan with tight lid and simmer about 50 minutes. Remove rice from heat and add cream and butter or margarine. Fold in orange marmalade. Spoon into serving dishes. Serve warm with Sherried Marmalade Sauce.

Sherried Marmalade Sauce: In a small saucepan pour ⅓ cup California Medium or Cream Sherry; add 1 cup orange marmalade and place over low heat. Stir gently and when marmalade is melted, remove from heat and add ½ cup nuts, chopped fine. Serve warm over rice pudding.

To accompany this pudding: **California Medium or Cream Sherry, Muscatel or Tokay**

Squire's Pudding
(6 servings)

Despite the masculine label given this wine dessert we like to view it as something to be served as a real fancy party creation for the girls. Make it ahead of time, keep in the refrigerator and decorate with candied fruit and almond garnish. Sherry gives it that special accent.

1 (1-lb. 2½-oz.) package whipping cream cake mix
½ cup California Medium Sherry
1⅓ cups strawberry jelly
2 (2¾-oz.) packages custard mix
1 package vanilla whipped refrigerator frosting mix
Candied fruit or maraschino cherries
Slivered blanched almonds

Following package directions prepare cake mix; bake in two well-greased and lightly floured 9-inch round layer pans. Cool about 15 minutes in pans; remove to wire racks. Split each layer and sprinkle cut side with about 2 tablespoons Sherry; spread each with ⅓ cup jelly. Prepare both packages of custard mix according to package directions.
To assemble: Use a large shallow bowl or serving plate with sides. Pour in about ⅓ cup warm custard mix; place a cake layer, jelly side up, in custard and top with about ⅔ cup custard. Repeat layers of cake and custard (there will be about ¾ cup for each layer). Refrigerate over night or at least 6 hours. Prepare whipped refrigerator frosting as directed, and spread about 1½ cups over top of dessert; use remainder frosting in pastry tube to decorate edges. Garnish with candied fruits and almonds.

To accompany this dessert: **California Cream Sherry** or **Muscatel.** *Imagine how beautifully a glass of California Cream Sherry or Muscatel blends with this dessert, especially for a ladies' luncheon*

Marshmallow Fruit Cake
(6 servings)

The last of the holiday fruit cake disappears into a very good dessert when combined with California Muscatel and marshmallows. Small portions of applesauce or prune cake might be used in this way too, or soft fruit cookies.

¼ cup California Muscatel
2 cups fruit cake cubes, cut about ½ inch
1½ cups miniature marshmallows
¼ teaspoon nutmeg
½ cup heavy cream, whipped

Combine Muscatel with fruit cake cubes, marshmallows, nutmeg and whipped cream, folding gently. Allow to stand several hours or overnight before serving.

To accompany this dessert: **California Cream Sherry**

Angel Parfait
(6 servings)

1 tablespoon unflavored gelatin
¼ cup cold water
½ cup boiling water
½ cup honey
¼ cup California Medium Sherry
1 cup heavy cream, whipped
6 macaroons or candied cherries for garnish

Soften gelatin in cold water; dissolve in boiling water. Add honey and Sherry. Chill until mixture mounds on spoon. Whip cream until it holds its shape; fold into gelatin mixture. Spoon into parfait or sherbet glasses. Dip macaroons into additional Sherry and top each parfait. Chill. (If dessert is to be refrigerated several days, do not add macaroons until serving time.) A candied cherry adds a gay note.

To accompany this dessert: **California Cream Sherry** *Pour this sweet Sherry, chilled or at room temperature*

Frozen Fruit Crème
(6 to 8 servings)

This creamy fruit combination, beautifully colored and flavored by California Port, has a dual personality. Use it as a lovely pink dessert, or present it as a dessert salad for a special luncheon.

1 cup California Port
1 (3-oz.) package raspberry-flavored gelatin
1 (8½-oz.) can pineapple tidbits
⅛ teaspoon salt
½ cup mayonnaise or dairy sour cream
2 cups non-dairy whipped topping mix
1 banana, peeled, cut in half lengthwise, sliced
1 cup miniature marshmallows (optional)
¼ cup sliced maraschino cherries (optional)

Heat Port; add gelatin and stir until dissolved. Remove from heat, add syrup drained from pineapple; add salt. Cool. Chill quickly in ice water until mixture begins to thicken. Stir mayonnaise or sour cream until smooth; fold into gelatin and chill again a few minutes, if necessary. Fold in topping mix, whipped according to package directions. Fold banana slices, marshmallows and cherries into creamy mixture. Turn into a 5-cup mold, individual molds or pan for freezing. Freeze firm. When ready to serve, unmold and garnish as desired.

To accompany this dessert: **California Port** or **Medium** or **Cream Sherry**

Cranberry Wine Dessert Mold
(6 servings)

Just a little something, light and not too rich, but certainly pink and attractive, and distinctive. You can thank California Port and cranberry sauce for this. Let it take shape in individual portions or a small fancy mold. For an extra flourish use a spoonful of dairy sour cream on the top instead of the usual garnish.

    1 (3-oz.) package raspberry-flavored gelatin
    ¾ cup hot water
    1 (1-lb.) can jellied cranberry sauce
    ¾ cup California Port

Dissolve gelatin in hot water. Press jellied cranberry sauce through sieve and add to gelatin. Stir in Port. Pour into mold and chill until firm. Serve with chilled custard sauce or a rosette of whipped cream.

To accompany this dessert: **California Port**

Cherries in Wine Gelatin
(5 to 6 servings)

Looking for something easy to make—a little different—a dessert with a party air? Then consider this delightful wine gelatin, filled with dark, sweet cherries and topped with a golden custard sauce, made double-quick with a package mix.

    1 (8-oz.) can pitted dark, sweet cherries
    1 (3-oz.) package cherry or black cherry-flavored gelatin
    1 cup hot water
    Cherry syrup plus California Port to make 1 cup liquid

Drain cherries well, saving all syrup in measuring cup. Add enough Port to syrup to make 1 full cup liquid. Place gelatin in medium bowl and add hot water, stirring to dissolve well. Stir in cherry syrup and Port. Chill to consistency of unbeaten egg whites. Cut cherries into halves; fold into gelatin, then spoon into individual molds. Chill until set, about 2 hours. When ready to serve, unmold and top with cold Cinnamon Custard Sauce.

Cinnamon Custard Sauce: Pour 1 cup chilled evaporated milk into medium bowl. Empty in 1 package instant vanilla pudding mix; beat slowly with rotary beater until well blended, about 1 minute. Stir in ¼ teaspoon *each* grated orange peel and cinnamon. Chill until ready to serve. Makes 2 cups sauce.

To accompany this dessert: **California Sherry** or **Sweet Sauterne.** *This deep red wine gelatin becomes more impressive by color contrast alongside these brilliant wines.*

Glazed Apples Rosé
(4 servings)

    3 large cooking apples
    ½ cup California Rosé
    1 tablespoon lemon juice
    ⅓ cup sugar
    ⅛ teaspoon cinnamon
    ⅛ teaspoon mace or nutmeg
    Pinch salt
    2 tablespoons orange marmalade or apricot jam

Pare apples, quarter and remove cores. Combine Rosé, lemon juice, sugar, spices and salt in skillet and heat to simmering. Add apples, cover and poach gently until transparent and tender, about 20 minutes. Remove apples, add marmalade to liquid remaining in pan and heat, stirring until marmalade is melted. Spoon over apples. Serve warm or chilled, plain or with cream.

To accompany this dessert: **California Haut Sauterne** *or* **Rosé**

Rocky Road Pudding
(6 servings)

You can depend on winning favorable reception for chocolate pudding every time, but make a few additions, including a small amount of California Sherry, and see what happens. Please do not use the instant pudding mix in this recipe, for it doesn't thicken properly.

    1 (4-oz.) package chocolate pudding and pie filling mix
    1½ cups milk
    ¼ cup California Sherry
    1 cup marshmallow pieces
    ½ cup chopped walnuts
    ½ cup heavy cream, whipped

Combine pudding and pie filling mix with milk and Sherry and cook according to package directions. Cool, stirring occasionally. Stir in marshmallow pieces, nuts and cream which has been whipped. Spoon into sherbet glasses; chill. Garnish with additional whipped cream, if desired.

To accompany this dessert: **California Sherry** *or* **Muscatel**

Fruit Compote with Port
(6 servings)

Unusual because it is served warm, this very good combination of pineapple chunks and dark cherries is enhanced by California Port. Save the fruit syrups from the drained fruits and later add them to wine, making an excellent baste for ham or corned pork. It's good in wine punches too.

    1 (1-lb. 12-oz.) jar dark sweet pitted cherries
    1 (14-oz.) can pineapple chunks
    ½ cup California Port
    ½ cup dairy sour cream
      Brown sugar

Place drained cherries in a shallow baking dish and top with drained pineapple chunks. Drizzle wine over the fruit. Cover and bake in moderate oven (350°) for 20 minutes. Serve hot. Stir sour cream until fluffy; spoon over each serving. Sprinkle brown sugar over sour cream.

To accompany this compote: **California Port**

Sherried Peach Bavarian
(4 to 6 servings)

Because it is made with dairy sour cream this Bavarian seems lighter and not so rich as the usual dessert of this type. California Sherry adds to the piquant flavor of the mold, and you might like to sprinkle additional Sherry on the thawing (or fresh) sliced peaches. The mold should not be too high; a ring mold or small molds for each serving are recommended.

    1 envelope unflavored gelatin
    ¼ cup cold water
    1 cup light cream
    ¾ cup sugar
    ⅛ teaspoon salt
    1 cup dairy sour cream
    ¼ cup California Sherry
    1 teaspoon lemon juice
    1 (12-oz.) package frozen, sliced peaches, thawed and
      sprinkled with 1 teaspoon lemon juice

Soften gelatin in cold water about 5 minutes. Heat cream but do not boil; remove from heat and add sugar, salt and gelatin. Stir until gelatin is completely dissolved (mixture will look curdled). Chill until slightly thickened. Beat sour cream lightly, then fold into slightly thickened gelatin along with Sherry and 1 teaspoon lemon juice. Pour into a 1-quart ring mold. Chill until firm, about 3 hours. Unmold on serving plate and fill center with sliced peaches.

To accompany this dessert: **California Cream Sherry**

Fruits in Champagne
(6 servings)

    1½ cups sliced peaches
      2 tablespoons lemon juice
     ½ cup pineapple chunks
     ½ cup Bing cherries, halved
     ¼ cup seedless green grapes
     ½ cup strawberries
     ⅓ cup sugar
       California Champagne, chilled
       Mint leaves
      1 box paper-thin rolled cookies

Peel peaches; sprinkle with lemon juice to prevent discoloration. Add remaining fruits and sugar; chill in refrigerator until serving time. Arrange fruits in long-stemmed sherbet glasses. Fill glasses with Champagne. Garnish with mint leaves.

To accompany this dessert: **California Port**

Peaches in Honey and Wine
(2 pints)

Keep a jar or two of these honey-sweet peaches on hand to answer a quick dessert call. Serve the fruit with ice cream, or on a slice of pound cake. The extra syrup may be used to glaze ham or corned pork, or to sweeten hot or cold wine punches. The jars of peaches need not be sealed, just covered to keep in the refrigerator.

    1 cup honey
    ¾ cup California Muscatel
    ½ cup lemon juice
    6 whole cloves
    2 inches stick cinnamon
    1 (1-lb. 13-oz.) can drained cling peach halves
    ⅛ teaspoon vanilla

In saucepan combine honey, wine and lemon juice; add spices. Simmer over low heat stirring occasionally about 10 minutes. Add drained peaches and cook gently 10 to 15 minutes or until fruit is glazed. With slotted spoon, lift out fruit and place in jars. Continue to cook syrup until fairly thick. Add vanilla. Pour syrup over fruit. Place in refrigerator or seal.

To accompany this dessert: **California Cream Sherry or Muscatel**

Spiced Peach Champagne Cup
(6 servings)

Another delightfully refreshing fruit and wine dessert might be the closing chapter to a good, robust roast beef dinner. Be sure to use large glasses so that you may be generous with the California Champagne.

> 1 (1-lb. 14-oz.) can whole spiced peaches
> 1 large bottle chilled California Champagne
> 6 slices lime (optional)

Chill peaches in can. Spoon about 3 tablespoons spiced syrup into each 6- or 8-oz. glass. Place spiced peach in each and fill glass with chilled Champagne, about ⅓ cup. Garnish with fresh lime slices, if desired; serve with a spoon.

To accompany this fruit cup: **California Light Muscatel**

Sherry Coconut Mousse
(12 servings)

> 1 tablespoon unflavored gelatin
> 2 tablespoons water
> ¾ cup milk
> ¼ cup California Medium or Cream Sherry
> ⅔ cup sugar
> ¼ teaspoon salt
> 1 tablespoon butter or margarine
> 1⅓ cups flake coconut
> 2 envelopes whipped topping mix

In small bowl soften gelatin in water. Heat milk, but do not boil, and pour into bowl, stirring until gelatin is dissolved. Stir in Sherry, sugar and salt. Chill until slightly thickened. Meantime, melt butter or margarine in skillet over medium heat and add coconut, stirring until coconut is delicately browned. Crush slightly. Fold 1 cup coconut into slightly thickened gelatin mixture. Prepare topping mix according to directions on package and fold into gelatin. Spoon into individual soufflé cups. Freeze until firm, at least 3 hours. Use rest of coconut for garnish.

To accompany this dessert: **California Sparkling Muscat, Champagne** *sec* **or Muscatel**

Ported Fruit Medley
(2 cups)

This is an attractive sauce to use in a variety of ways. Serve it over a scoop of ice cream placed on a waffle section, or use as a topping for baked custard, slices of plain or toasted angel food or chiffon cake.

> 1 (1-lb.) can salad fruits
> ½ cup California Port
> ¼ cup sugar
> ¼ teaspoon salt
> 2 tablespoons cornstarch
> Red food coloring
> 1 banana, peeled and sliced

Drain syrup from fruits into a small saucepan (will be about ¾ cup). Blend about ⅓ cup of Port with sugar, salt and cornstarch. Add to fruit syrup. Cook and stir over high heat until sauce boils, thickens and clears. Remove from heat and stir remaining Port and a drop or two of red coloring into the thick sauce. Pour over drained fruits; cool. When ready to use, fold banana into sauce.

To accompany this dessert: **California Port**

Orange-Wine Charlotte
(6 servings)

> 1 cup orange juice
> ½ cup water
> 1 (3-oz.) package orange-flavored gelatin
> 2 tablespoons sugar
> ½ cup California Muscatel
> 1 tablespoon lemon juice
> Dash of salt
> ½ cup heavy cream, whipped
> ½ cup diced orange sections

Heat orange juice and water to simmering. Add gelatin and sugar and stir until dissolved. Remove from heat; add wine, lemon juice and salt. Pour 1 cup of this mixture into a mold that has been rinsed with cold water; chill until firm. Meantime, chill remaining gelatin mixture until it begins to thicken. Beat with a rotary or electric beater until frothy. Fold in whipped cream and orange sections, blending gently but thoroughly. Pour this gelatin-cream mixture on top of the firm gelatin; chill until cream layer is firm. Unmold and garnish with additional orange sections, if desired. Serve with whipped cream.

To accompany this dessert: **California Sparkling Muscat, Champagne** *sec* **or Muscatel**

St. Helena Fruit Cup
(6 servings)

For a full impact of blended flavor be sure to let this California Port and fruit compote refrigerate for several hours before spooning it into stemmed sherbet glasses. And as an additional refreshing note, top each serving with a scoop of lemon ice.

- 1 (1-lb. 14-oz.) can purple plums
- 1 (1-lb. 13-oz.) can peach halves
- 1 tablespoon canned lemon juice
- ⅔ cup California Port

Combine 1 cup syrup from plums with drained plums and peaches, lemon juice and Port. Chill several hours to blend flavors, mixing gently once or twice.

♀ *To accompany this fruit cup:* **California Sweet Sauterne** *or* **Muscatel**

Peaches Diane
(6 to 8 servings)

- ½ cup mild flavored honey
- 1 (12-oz.) jar peach or apricot jelly
- ¼ cup California Medium or Sweet Sherry
- 6-8 fresh freestone peaches, peeled and sliced
- 1 qt. vanilla or pistachio ice cream

In a small saucepan combine honey with jelly. Heat, stirring constantly, until jelly is melted; add wine. Remove from heat; cool; then pour over sliced peaches and chill thoroughly. Spoon sauce over scoops of ice cream.

♀ *To accompany this dessert:* **California Champagne** *or* **Muscatel**

Figs Continental
(6 to 8 servings)

Simple to make and simply delicious to eat are dried figs prepared and served like this. In saucepan combine 1 pound dried figs, ½ teaspoon grated lemon peel, 1 tablespoon lemon juice, ½ cup sugar and 1 cup California Sauterne. Bring to boil; cover pan and simmer for 5 minutes. Remove from heat and let stand, still covered, for at least 15 minutes. Serve warm or chilled with a spoonful of dairy sour cream.

Fruits in Wine Sauce
(4 servings)

Use this refreshing fruit and wine combination as a topping over ice cream, puddings or any simple cake dessert. Or, serve it as a chilled compote. Thaw 1 (10-oz.) package quick thaw fruit as directed on package, pour into serving bowl and add 2 tablespoons of any California dessert wine such as Madeira, Marsala, or Port; stir gently to blend. Keep in refrigerator until ready to use.

Prunes in Wine

Easy and delicious, prunes respond with enthusiasm to wine treatment. Their wrinkles smooth out and their flavor blends with the wine to become something decidedly good.

Prunes in California Sherry: Select large tender dried prunes. Let them stand in California Sherry for several days in a covered jar or crock. Serve them as they are, or pit and stuff with nuts or brandied fruits. They're an excellent relish with poultry and game dishes. Stuffed with cream cheese these shiny black prunes are a good addition to fruit salad plates.

Prunes in California Claret or Burgundy: Soak about 24 large prunes over night in 1¼ cups Claret or Burgundy and ¼ cup water; cook gently in this liquid until tender, about 25 minutes. Add ⅓ cup sugar and cook 5 minutes longer. Add few drops vanilla extract if desired. Chill thoroughly. Serve as dessert with a spoonful of whipped cream. Serves 4 to 6.

Prunes in California Port: Cover dried prunes with equal parts of Port and water. Simmer about 15 minutes over gentle heat; cover and chill overnight. Serve with a little of the juice. Makes an elegant dessert served with a topping of dairy sour cream. Or use to decorate a simple dessert such as custard or tapioca pudding.

Wine Cranberry Sundae Topping
(8 servings)

Simply beautiful to look at, this sparkling crimson sauce dipped generously over plain vanilla ice cream is good to eat and easy to make. Turn out contents of 1 (1-lb.) can jellied cranberry sauce into small bowl; crush and stir with fork; stir in ⅓ cup California Port. Let stand for a while to give everything a chance to blend. Spoon over vanilla ice cream.

Sherried Pots de Crème
(6 servings)

Custard cups do very well for containers if you do not have the intriguing small pots de creme cups.

- ⅓ cup sugar
- 1 tablespoon cornstarch
- ¼ teaspoon salt
- ½ cup cold water
- 1¼ cups evaporated milk
- 1 (6-oz.) package semi-sweet chocolate pieces
- 2 tablespoons California Medium or Cream Sherry
- 2 teaspoons vanilla

In 1-quart saucepan mix sugar, cornstarch and salt. Stir in gradually, water and evaporated milk. Cook and stir over medium heat until mixture thickens and begins to bubble. Remove from heat, add chocolate pieces, Sherry and vanilla. Stir until chocolate melts completely, then beat with rotary beater or wire whip until smooth. Pour into pots de creme or custard cups. Chill.

To accompany this dessert: **California Sherry, Medium** *or* **Cream** *seems so right here*

Port Wine Bon Bons
(About 32 balls, 1½" size)

They are really unbaked cookies, these smooth-tasting little round morsels, lightly dusted with sugar. To achieve balls of even size, start with a tablespoonful of firmly packed mixture; roll it briskly between the palms and drop into the sugar for coating.

- 1 (6-oz.) package, or 1 cup, semi-sweet chocolate bits
- ½ cup sugar
- 3 tablespoons corn syrup
- ⅓ cup California Port
- 2½ cups finely crushed vanilla wafer (about 5 dozen) crumbs
- 1 cup finely chopped walnuts

In medium saucepan melt chocolate bits over hot but not boiling water. Remove from water and stir in sugar, corn syrup and Port. Stir in vanilla wafer crumbs and chopped nuts; mix well. Form into 1½-inch balls; roll each in granulated or powdered sugar (spread sugar in a shallow soup bowl). Let ripen in a covered container; 3 to 4 weeks is not too long as these bon bons improve in flavor upon standing.

To accompany these cookies: **California Port.** *For an afternoon refreshment these bon bons go well with Port.*

Crème Brulée
(6 servings)

An elegant ending for a fine meal, is this custard dessert with its rich, crisp topping. The custard is made from a mix, combined with California Sherry and heavy cream, and the brown sugar top is put under the broiler to crisp. Don't make it too far in advance—no more than 3 or 4 hours before serving.

- 1 (3-oz.) package egg custard mix
- 1 cup heavy cream
- ½ cup California Cream Sherry
- ½ cup milk
- ¾ cup light brown sugar

Make custard following package directions using Sherry, heavy cream and milk for liquid. Pour into 8-inch pie pan. Chill. Push brown sugar through sieve over the surface of the custard; pat down very lightly. Broil 3½ to 4 inches from the source of heat about 2 minutes or until sugar is melted and bubbly. Remove from heat and cool. Break crust into serving pieces by tapping lightly with back of spoon. Chill until ready to serve.

To accompany this custard: **California Cream Sherry**

Sherry Pralines
(About 18 medium pralines)

Candy lovers will be impressed by the professional appearance of these good nutty pralines, but even more delighted with their added Sherry flavor. Use all brown sugar for a praline darker in color. Drop candy on 6-inch squares of aluminum foil or waxed paper for individual wrapping.

- 1 cup light brown sugar
- 1 cup granulated sugar
- Few grains salt
- ⅔ cup evaporated milk
- 1 tablespoon butter or margarine
- 2 cups (½ lb.) pecan halves
- 2 tablespoons California Dry Sherry

In medium saucepan mix sugars, salt, evaporated milk and butter or margarine. Stir over low heat until sugar is dissolved. Add pecans and cook over medium heat to soft ball stage (234°). Remove from heat, measure Sherry onto surface of candy, but do not stir in; let cool 5 minutes. Beat until mixture begins to thicken and to coat nuts lightly. Drop rapidly from tablespoon onto buttered baking sheet; let stand until cold and set. Wrap pralines separately in waxed paper or foil.

To accompany this candy: **California Medium** *or* **Cream Sherry**

Chantilly Rice Pudding
(6 servings)

The Sherried dates in this recipe can be made any time and kept in refrigerator. Use whole pitted dates done this way for a delightful sweet or as an addition to fruit salads. This is a light, creamy pudding.

- ¾ cup packaged precooked rice
- ¾ cup hot water
- ½ teaspoon grated orange rind
- 1 (3¼-oz.) package regular vanilla pudding mix
- ¼ teaspoon salt
- 1 cup milk
- ⅓ cup California Sherry
- ½ or 1 cup whipping cream
- Sherried Dates

Measure rice, water and orange rind into saucepan. Bring to boil. Remove from heat, cover and let stand 10 minutes. Add pudding mix, salt and milk. Cook, stirring, until mixture comes to a full boil and thickens. Add Sherry and cook a minute longer. Remove from heat and cool, then cover and refrigerate until well chilled. When ready to serve, fold in stiffly beaten cream and spoon into serving dishes. Top with Sherried Dates.

Sherried Dates: Cut 1½ cups pitted dates in large pieces and turn into a jar with cover. Heat ⅓ cup California Sherry with 1 tablespoon brown sugar and dash of cinnamon to boiling. Pour over dates. Cover jar and refrigerate overnight. Turn jar back and forth a few times to distribute syrup.

♀ *To accompany this dessert:* **California Cream Sherry**

Chocolate Sherry Cookies
(About 4 dozen)

Certainly simple and easy to make, these dark and delicious little drop cookies are especially good to keep on hand for an afternoon or evening companion to a glass of California Sherry.

- 1 (13½-oz.) all-purpose cookie mix
- ¼ cup California Sherry
- 1 egg, beaten
- ½ teaspoon cinnamon
- ¼ teaspoon nutmeg
- 1 (6-oz.) package semi-sweet chocolate bits

Combine cookie mix with Sherry, beaten egg and spices. Melt semi-sweet chocolate bits over hot, but not boiling water; blend into cookie batter. Drop by rounded teaspoonfuls onto lightly greased baking sheet. Bake in moderate oven (375°) 8 to 10 minutes.

♀ *To accompany these cookies:* **California Medium or Cream Sherry or California Champagne,** *such as sec or demi-sec*

Crepes Suzette
(6 servings)

Guests will enjoy a bit of show-off at dessert time, particularly when it is done with grace and ease and the end result is so good to eat. Make the crepes ahead of time and keep them in the refrigerator. When ready to serve, heat briefly in chafing dish. Sometimes crepes change their contours, and are folded in quarters, rather than rolled.

- 4 eggs, slightly beaten
- 2 cups milk
- 6 tablespoons butter or margarine, melted
- 1½ cups pancake mix

In mixing bowl combine eggs, milk and melted butter or margarine; blend in pancake mix, beating until smooth. Heat a small 6½-inch skillet; butter lightly. Pour in a scant ¼ cup of batter, tilting pan to spread the batter; turn when edges start to dry. Fold immediately and place in chafing dish. Makes 12 to 14 crepes.

Make sauce: Blend together in small saucepan ½ cup butter or margarine, ½ cup sifted powdered sugar, 1 tablespoon grated orange peel and ⅓ cup orange juice. Heat to boiling; pour over rolled crepes. Immediately add ¼ cup California Brandy; ignite to flame crepes. Baste crepes with flaming sauce and serve.

♀ *To accompany this dish:* **California Champagne** *or* **Sherry**

Mocha Sherry Brownie Squares
(36 small cookies)

These brownies are made with a mix but dressed up with the addition of California Sherry and instant coffee powder. Use the number of eggs required to make fudgy or cake-like brownies, as directed on the package. After baking, sprinkle top lightly with a little sifted powdered sugar if you wish; just a tablespoon in a sieve will do it easily.

- 1 (1-lb.) package fudge brownie mix
- 1 teaspoon instant coffee powder
- ½ teaspoon cinnamon
- ¼ cup California Sherry
- 1 or 2 eggs
- ½ cup chopped nuts

Stir all ingredients, except nuts, together until blended to stiff batter. Add nuts. Turn into greased 9-inch square pan. Bake in moderate oven (350°) for 25 to 30 minutes. Cool thoroughly in pan before cutting into small squares.

♀ *To accompany these cookies:* **California Cream Sherry**

Meringues with Mincemeat Wine Sauce

(8 servings)

Try this to fully appreciate the very good combination of crisp meringue shells, ice cream and a bold sauce made of mincemeat and California Port. Clearly it's easy enough to keep the makings of this dessert on hand for all kinds of inspired servings. A frosting mix converts easily into the shells, ready to store indefinitely, and the sauce needs only a short re-heating to be at its best.

Mincemeat Wine Sauce: Thin 1 cup prepared mincemeat with ½ cup California Ruby Port. Heat and serve.

Crisp Meringue Shells: In small mixer bowl blend ⅓ cup boiling water, 1 package white frosting mix (dry mix) and ⅓ cup sifted powdered sugar. Beat at high speed in mixer for 3 to 5 minutes until mixture is thick and holds very stiff peaks. Scrape sides and bottom of bowl occasionally. Drop about ⅓ cup meringue, for each shell, onto baking sheet covered with aluminum foil or brown paper. Shape centers with back of spoon. Bake in slow oven (275°) 45 minutes. Turn off heat, but do not open oven door, and let meringues dry out for 45 minutes longer. When ready to serve, fill with ice cream and top with Mincemeat Wine Sauce.

To accompany this dessert: **California Ruby Port** or **Muscatel**

Spicey Burgundy Sauce

(6 servings)

Perfect as a hot sauce to serve over slices of apple pie, or apple dumplings or even gingerbread. Heat ½ cup California Burgundy or other red table wine such as California Cabernet or Claret to simmering; add ½ cup cinnamon red-hot candies and 1 tablespoon shredded lemon peel. Remove from heat, but keep warm, stirring frequently until candies are completely dissolved.

Ported Cherry Sundae

(6 servings)

Spoon this warm sauce over mounds of vanilla ice cream, or use it to good advantage over slices of fruit cake or tapioca pudding. In a small saucepan combine contents 1 (1-lb. 5-oz.) can prepared cherry pie filling with ½ cup California Port and ½ cup orange marmalade; stir over medium heat until mixture is hot and well blended. Keep warm until ready to serve.

Sherried Prune Sauce

(10 to 12 servings)

Prunes, encouraged by California Sherry, have unusual appeal in this dessert sauce. You will find it very easy to put together—good to keep on hand for ice cream, custard, rice and bread puddings.

    1 pound dried prunes
    ½ cup sugar
    ½ teaspoon cinnamon
    ½ cup California Medium Sherry
    2 tablespoons rum

Place prunes in small bowl; cover with cold water and chill in refrigerator overnight. Drain prunes and reserve 1 cup liquid. Halve prunes and pit. Combine sugar, cinnamon and prune liquid; bring to boil and simmer 5 minutes. Add prunes, Sherry and rum. Chill. Spoon over vanilla ice cream. Sprinkle with toasted slivered almonds.

To accompany desserts made with this sauce: **California Cream Sherry**

Sherry Pecan Sauce

(About 2 cups)

California Sherry always pairs so well with brown sugar, as it does here in this nicely worked out, smooth sauce with crunchy pecans.

    1½ cups brown sugar, firmly packed
    ⅔ cup light corn syrup
    ½ cup water
    ⅔ cup evaporated milk
    2 tablespoons California Medium Sherry
    ½ cup chopped pecans

In medium saucepan combine sugar, corn syrup and water. Bring to boil, stirring constantly, and cook about 5 minutes over medium heat. Remove from heat. Cool 5 minutes, then stir in evaporated milk, Sherry and pecans. Serve warm or chilled.

If you plan to store this sauce, don't add pecans, as they tend to soften when held any length of time.

To accompany desserts enhanced with this sauce: **California Cream Sherry**

WiNE TASTiNG PARTY

There's an interesting way to meet new wines. It's the wine tasting party —a popular idea that originated in California and is showing up all over America.

Wine tasting parties are appropriate at various times of day and in all kinds of settings—from the living room to the great outdoors. Very little equipment is required. You'll need a selection of wines, about one half of a fifth-gallon bottle per guest. (That is the total amount of wine per person, not of each kind.) You'll also need a glass for each person attending, some pitchers of water for rinsing glasses between tastes and a container in which guests can pour out the water they've used for rinsing glasses.

Bread and cheese are the traditional food accompaniments at a wine tasting party. A cube of bread and a chunk of mild cheese refresh the palate between wines. Other finger foods may be served also.

The Point of the Party—Discovery

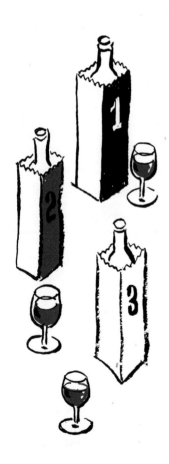

The wines are the most important part of a wine tasting party, and there is a great variety to choose from. Since discovery is the point of the party, you'll want to provide some wines your guests may not have tried before. A red, a white, a rosé, and an appetizer or dessert wine are good choices. Or a tasting only of reds or whites can be interesting. Before dinner, an appetizer wine tasting party is in order, where Sherry, Vermouth, and Natural Flavored wines are tasted. A dessert wine tasting after dinner or in the afternoon might feature Cream Sherry, Port, Angelica, Muscatel, or other dessert wines. Pound cake, fruit and cookies would be good food accompaniments for this kind of tasting.

Tasting games can be a happy part of wine tasting parties. Guests may taste three wines blindfolded, and try to name the one wine which is unlike the other two, solely by aroma and taste. In preparation for this game the hostess pours two glasses of wine from one bottle and one glass from another. Still another "blind man's no-bluff" calls for an attempt to identify a red, a white, and a rosé wine while blindfolded. When all the wines are the same temperature, this can be quite a trick.

What to Look For

For tasting games and for wine tasting of any sort, the three areas to examine in wine are color, aroma, and flavor. By holding wine up to the light you can observe the color, the rich red tones or the delicate gold-greens. A good deep sniff or two with nose right in the glass will reveal the wine aroma to you. If you swirl the wine a bit in the glass before you inhale, you'll release the wine's aroma and make your sniffing more rewarding. When actually tasting the wine, roll it around on your tongue to get a full impression of the flavor. And pay attention to the taste left in your mouth by the wine.

All of these tasting techniques have been borrowed from professional wine tasters and removed to a party atmosphere. They're easy. And they're fun, making a wine tasting party one of the most congenial events you can offer your guests.

TO YOUR Health

Wine has been considered healthful by many through the centuries. Modern medical research has confirmed the benefits. For example, this statement: "There is no doubt at all that the moderate use of wine while eating is the pleasantest and probably the most effective tranquilizer known to medical men."

That is the view of Dr. Russel V. Lee, Clinical Professor of Medicine Emeritus at the Stanford University School of Medicine. He is one of the hundreds of physicians around the world who have been studying the relationships between the use of wine and our health.

Wine Is a Food

A discussion of wine and health centers on two major points. First, that wine is a food. It provides food energy for work and for body maintenance, a basic requirement of any food. Second, that wine, under most circumstances, not only is good, it is good for you.

We know, as men have known for thousands of years, that wine can relax us and make us more sociable. Research in the past couple of decades backs us up with mountains of scientific data. A noted physician puts the cold facts into warmer sentiments: Wine, he said, can give a "cerebral sense of richness," and a "more serene state of consciousness."

The old Prohibition-era myths are largely dispelled in our more knowledgeable generation. Most doctors today think of wine as they do of other items they prescribe — a valuable addition to the diet under proper conditions and in the proper amounts.

An Aid to Health

Wine, of course, is prescribed as a release from emotional tension, especially for the elderly and for people on reducing diets. It frequently is given to persons suffering from heart disease, where wine can reduce discomfort and perhaps prevent attacks of angina pectoris.

Dry table wine also is prescribed in the diets of many diabetics, and wine is used to combat insomnia and in prevention of hardening of the arteries.

When it is improperly used, any alcoholic beverage — like any other food, sunshine or penicillin — loses its healthful and social benefits.

For most of us, wine is a pleasure, not a prescription. The fact that it acts as a gentle tranquilizer, that it contains calories, carbohydrates, vitamins and minerals, and that it is widely used as a therapeutic agent, is a bonus.

We would rather think about how a wine makes a meal more festive than that wine is an aid to digestion. And so we should.

But it is good to know that there is a little extra dividend when we raise our glasses of wine in a toast — "to your health."

THE TRADITIONS
...GUIDES NOT RULES

Some Helpful Guides

Most of us have heard that old and inflexible "rule" that insists on red wine with red meat, white wine with fish, fowl and white meat.

The truth is, that statement is old but neither inflexible nor a rule. It is a tradition, broken with great regularity by independent thinkers with individual tastes. The red-with-red tradition still is with us because many wine drinkers agree and conform to it.

Red Table Wines

If you want to try traditional combinations of red table wines and meats, you want a robust Burgundy (or Pinot Noir) with game and roast beef. A Claret (or Cabernet Sauvignon) with broiled steak, and perhaps a Chianti (or Barbera) with spaghetti.

White Table Wines

With fish and such seafoods as crab, lobster, shrimp and oysters, a crisp, dry, white wine such as a Chablis, Chardonnay, Pinot Blanc or Rhine Wine is recommended. These same seafoods, when creamed or sauced, can take a slightly sweeter wine, such as Sauterne or Chenin Blanc.

With pink meats such as ham, pork and veal, a pink wine — Rosé — is a natural companion. Slightly sweet white wines also are recommended.

Appetizer and Dessert Wines

The traditional wine with appetizers and creamed soups is Dry or Cocktail Sherry. With cheese, nuts or fruit after dinner, Port is the customary choice, with Muscatel, Cream Sherry and Tokay close runners up. The "light" (12 per cent) wine most often associated with dessert is Sweet Sauterne (or Haut Sauterne). The dessert wines also are often used *in desserts*, as topping for fresh fruit, ice cream and pastries.

Champagne

Champagne is the one wine nobody tries to limit to a particular time or food. It *is* true the drier Champagnes (Natural, Brut) are preferred before and with dinner, and the sweeter types (called Extra Dry and Sec) with dessert and in the evening. But any Champagne is appropriate and festive at any time of day and with any combination of foods.

Flavored Wines

The flavored wines, including Vermouth, are associated with the cocktail hour. More and more people are enjoying these wines as their before-dinner drink, plain, chilled, over ice, or in a tall drink with soda.

Many of the flavored wines are known by proprietary names, in the European tradition. Several of the major California wine producers market wines with fruit, herb and spice flavors under original labels. Other winemakers do the same with table wines, identifying the wine with their company instead of with a particular type or variety of grape.

Order of Serving

Traditionalists also say there is an order in which wines should be enjoyed. From the lightest to the fullest-bodied, they say; from white to red and from dry to sweet. They advise that this order will be more pleasing to the palate for the wine still to come — assuming more than one wine at a sitting.

Probably the most telling argument the non-conformists have is that the vast majority of the world's wine drinkers enjoy a single wine — their local product — with all their meals, all their lives. They like it that way, and would laugh at anybody who told them they were wrong.

choosing wines

Most of us have our first dinner with wine in a restaurant or when visiting friends. Next, we try it at home. For a while we run over to the neighborhood retailer whenever we want a bottle of wine with dinner.

As we use more wine, and become more at home with it, the majority of us have two reactions — we want to know more about it and we want to have wine on hand for dinners and parties, and for cooking.

Buy What You Like

There is an all-purpose rule for buying wines — "buy what you like." First, you probably will want to cover the five classes — red table wine, white table wine, sparkling wine, dessert wine and appetizer wine. Then you can experiment within each of the classifications.

Whether or not you buy them all at once, this kind of breakdown is a representative starter set: Three red table wines, perhaps a mellow red or vino type, a Burgundy and a Zinfandel. Three whites, such as Riesling, a Sauterne and a Chablis. A bottle of California Rosé, either a varietal Grenache or a Vin Rosé. A bottle of Dry (Cocktail) or Medium Dry Sherry, one of Port, two of Vermouth (a Dry and a Sweet) and a bottle of Champagne.

Your retailer may have other suggestions, based on whether your taste is for dry or sweeter wines, for red or for white, and on the number of wines you buy. Depending on the kind of wines you select, this assortment can cost you anywhere from a modest $12 to several times that. With California wines, which range in price from about 75¢ a fifth to a top of $5 or so for the more expensive Champagnes, the cost will be surprisingly low.

Try Different Wines

The "secret" is experimentation. Find out which wines *you* like, in different price ranges, of different types, and from different wine districts. For instance, check out the wines that are sold in gallon and half-gallon containers. These can be decanted (poured gently) into smaller bottles for serving at the table and keeping. Try some of the varietals, too. Most wines can be purchased in half-bottles (tenth size), especially suitable for small families who want to sample many different wines.

keeping wines

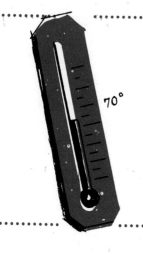

Suppose you have just accumulated a dozen or so bottles of wines at home and you have to do something with them. Must you have a dim cellar, complete with cobwebs and creaking hinges? Modern householders—and experts—laugh at such a notion. Wine can be kept over long periods in any area that is not brightly lighted and has a relatively cool (less than 70°) and a constant temperature. On a closet shelf, for example, or a kitchen cabinet or in a stairwell.

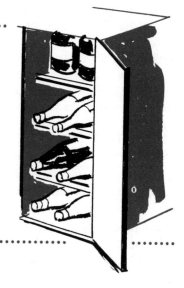

Most people agree that light and heat *do* affect wine, but not to the extent once thought. And modern and sanitary production methods have made the wines of California sound and stable. Most of us, even if we intend to keep wine for several years, make do with a cool, dark place with an area for wines with corks to lie on their sides. Bottles with metal or plastic screwcaps can lie down or stand upright — there is no cork to dry out and let air in. So can Champagne with plastic closures.

Wines can be refrigerated for many weeks with no ill effects. After table wines have been opened, leftover wines should be reclosed tightly and put in the refrigerator. They will be palatable for several days. Dessert and appetizer wines, more hardy than their table wine cousins because their higher alcohol content preserves them, should keep well for a month or more after being opened.

GUIDE TO WINE TYPES
CHARACTERISTICS—PRONUNCIATION

Appetizer Wines

Sherry (dry to sweet)

Vermouth (dry or sweet) (vur-mooth')

Special Natural Wines

Red Table Wines

Burgundy (dry)

Barbera *(bar-bair'a)*
Charbono *(shar-bo'-no)*
Gamay *(gah-may)*
Pinot Noir *(pea-no no-ahr')*
Red Pinot *(pea-no)*

Rosé (pink; dry to sweet) (roh-zay')

Claret (dry)
Cabernet *(kab-er-nay')*
Cabernet Sauvignon *(so-vee-nyonh)*
Grignolino *(green-yo-leen'-oh)*
Zinfandel *(zin'-fan-dell)*

Vino Rosso (semi-sweet) or **Mellow Red** (vee-no-ross-o)

Others:
Red Chianti *(dry) (kee-ahn'tee)*

White Table Wines

Chablis (dry) (sha-blee')
Pinot Chardonnay *(pea-no shar-doh-nay')*
Folle Blanche *(fohl blon-sh)*
Pinot Blanc *(pea-no blanh)*
Chenin Blanc *(shen-in blanh)*

White Pinot *(pea-no)*

Sauterne (dry to sweet) (so-tairn')
Sauvignon Blanc *(so-vee-nyonh-blanh)*
Semillon *(say'mee-yonh)*
Haut *(oh)* or Chateau *(shah-toh')*

Rhine Wine (dry)
Riesling *(reez'-ling)*
Sylvaner *(sil-vah'ner)*
Traminer *(trah-mee'-ner)*

Others:
White Chianti *(dry) (kee-ahn'-tee)*
Light Muscat *(dry to sweet)*

Sweet Dessert Wines

Port (Red, White or Tawny)

Tokay (toh-kay')

Muscatel (Gold, Red or Black) (muss-kah-tell')
Muscat Frontignan *(fron-teen-yawn)*

Others:
Angelica *(an-jell'-ee-cah)*
Madeira *(mah-day'rah)*
Marsala *(mahr-sah'lah)*
Sweet or Cream Sherry

Sparkling Wines

Champagne (Gold or Pink) (sham-pain')
Brut *(very dry) (brewt)*
Sec *(semi-dry) (sehk)*
Extra Dry *(Sweet)*

Sparkling Burgundy (semi-sweet to sweet)
Others:
Sparkling Muscat *(sweet)*
Sparkling Rosé *(dry to semi-sweet)*

brands used in testing recipes

A number of companies producing convenience foods and other ingredients were requested to send us recipes using their products in wine cooking. The response was generous. These products were used by our home economist in testing the recipes. The producers, their products and their brands used in testing are listed below, along with the recipe titles as they appear in the index of this book.

The Borden Co., 350 Madison Ave., New York, N.Y. 10017: Instant Nonfat Dry Milk used in "Star Syllabub" and "Hearty Cold Chicken Soup." Eagle Brand Sweetened Condensed Milk used in "Rich Sherry Trifle." Canned Egg Nog used in "Zabaglione." Evaporated Milk and Pasteurized Process Gruyere Cheese Slices used in "Lamb Chops in Potato Cheese Sauce." Wyler's Chicken Bouillon Cubes, Sweet Pepper Flakes, and Minced Onion used in "Hearty Cold Chicken Soup." Wyler's Dehydrated Instant Minced Onions, Bouillon Cube-no salt added, and Aunt Jane's Sour Pickle used in "Pork Chops with Piquant Sauce."

Betty Crocker Kitchens, 9200 Wayzata Blvd., Minneapolis, Minn. 55440: Fluffy White Frosting Mix used in "Meringues with Mincemeat Wine Sauce."

Frito-Lay, Inc., P.O. Box 35034, Dallas, Texas 75235: Corn Chips used in "Crunchy Creamed Chicken."

General Foods Kitchens, 250 North St., White Plains, N.Y.: Birds Eye Concentrate for Lemonade and Strawberry Halves used in "Wine Lemonade Punch." Sliced Peaches used in "Sherried Peach Bavarian." Certo Fruit Pectin used in "Orange and Port Jelly," "Claret Cranberry Jelly," and "Minted Wine Jelly." Birds Eye Quick Thaw Fruit used in "Fruits in Wine Sauce." Good Seasons Garlic Salad Dressing Mix used in "Marinated Roast Beef." Old Fashion French Salad Dressing Mix used in "Roast Wild Duck." Minute Rice used in "Veal and Rice Buffet." Bakers Angel Flake Coconut and Dream Whip Whipped Topping Mix used in "Sherry Coconut Mousse."

Green Giant Co., 8000 Normandale Blvd., Minneapolis, Minn. 55431: Whole Mushrooms Frozen in Butter Sauce used in "Savory Mushrooms Hors D'oeuvre." Le Sueur Brand Little Baby Early Peas Frozen in Butter Sauce used in "Seafood En Coquille." Sliced Mushrooms used in "Easy Stroganoff." Le Sueur Brand Small Early Peas used in "Potage Boula."

Hershey Chocolate Corp., 19 E. Chocolate Ave., Hershey, Penna. 17033: Milk Chocolate Chips used in "Wine Milk Chocolate Mousse." Milk Chocolate Fudge Topping used in "Chocolate Wine Sauce."

Lawry's Home Economics Patio Kitchens, 568 San Fernando Rd., Los Angeles, Calif. 90065: Private Blend Garlic Salt used in "California Marinated Mushrooms." Seasoned Salt used in "Pickled Eggs," "Halibut with Shrimp Sauce," "Cioppino," "Beef Burgundy Flambé," "California Beef Stew," "Butterfly Leg of Lamb," and "Continental Lasagna." Seasoned Pepper used in "Pickled Eggs," "Cioppino," "California Beef Stew," and "Continental Lasagna." Italian Dressing Mix used in "Butterfly Leg of Lamb," and "Zucchini Vinaigrette." Spaghetti Sauce Mix used in "Cioppino." Beef Stew Seasoning Mix used in "Beef Burgundy Flambé."

McCormick & Co., Inc., 414 Light St., Baltimore, Md. 21202: McCormick or Schilling Season-All or Bon Appetit used in "Barbecued Chicken Legs" and "Spanish Padre Chicken." Black Pepper used in "Barbecued Chicken Legs" and "Spanish Padre Chicken." Nutmeg used in "Spanish Padre Chicken" and "Modesto Turkey with Waffles." Dry Mustard used in "Spanish Padre Chicken" and "Modesto Turkey with Waffles." Barbecue Spice, Onion Juice, Garlic Powder or Garlic Salt and MSG used in "Barbecued Chicken Legs" and "Pepper Steaks with Sherried Sauce." Celery Flakes and Sweet Pepper Flakes used in "Spanish Padre Chicken." Chicken Seasoned Stock Base, White Pepper and Poultry Seasoning used in "Modesto Turkey with Waffles." Coarse Grind Black Pepper used in "Pepper Steaks with Sherried Sauce."

The Nestlé Corp., Inc., 100 Bloomingdale Rd., White Plains, N.Y. 10605: Wispride Blue Cheese Spread used in "Blue Cheese Wine Spread." Nestea Instant Tea used in "Sherried Tea Flip." Semi-Sweet Chocolate Morsels used in "Chocolate Sherry Cookies," "Port Wine Bon Bons," and "Superb Chocolate Torte." C & B Red Currant Jelly used in "Cumberland Sauce."

Ocean Spray Cranberries, Inc., Main St., Hanson, Mass. 02341: Jellied Cranberry Sauce used in "Cranberry Wine Dessert Mold," "Cranberry Wine Marlow," "Wine Cranberry Sundae Topping," "Cranberry Burgundy Salad," and "Cranberry Apple Wine Sherbet." Whole Cranberry Sauce used in "Cranberry Basting Sauce" and "Red Wine Sauce."

Oscar Mayer & Co., P.O. Box 1409, Madison, Wisc. 53701: Bacon used in "Rumaki." Little Wieners, Little Smokies, Little Cheese Smokies and Little Pure Beef Franks used in "Sausage Sampling Fondue."

Pepperidge Farm, Inc., Westport Ave., Norwalk, Conn.: Pirouettes used in "Fruits in Champagne."

Pet, Inc., Arcade Bldg., St. Louis, Mo. 63166: Evaporated Milk used in "Crab Dip Elegante," "Swiss Dip Sonoma," "Cheese Rarebit," "Sherried Pots de Creme," "Last Minute Shrimp Newburg," and "Roman Veal Rolls." Laura Scudder's Zippy Horseradish Dip Mix and Tortilla Chips used in "Hot Cheese and Sauterne Dip." Also contributed "Apple Pie with Port."

The Pillsbury Co., 608 Second Ave., Minneapolis, Minn.: Funny Face Drink Mix used in "Sauterne Sparkle." Extra Light Pancake Mix used in "Crepes Suzette." Sour Cream Fudge Cake Mix used in "Peach Upside Down Cake," and "Whipping Cream Cake Mix." Vanilla Whipped Refrigerator Frosting Mix used in "Squire's Pudding." Flaky Baking Powder or Buttermilk Biscuits used in "Lobster Special." All Purpose Flour used in "Sacramento Skillet Duck" and "Pheasant in Gourmet Sauce." Also contributed "Chicken Breasts in Sour Cream" and "Bing Cherry and Port Mold."

Checkerboard Kitchens, Ralston Purina Co., Checkerboard Sq., St. Louis, Mo. 63199: Honeysuckle Giblet Gravy and Sliced Turkey used in "Turkey Nero Sandwiches." Turkey Roast used in "Turkey Thermidor" and "Turkey with Wine Sauce." Also contributed "Burgundy Pear Poultry Garnish."

Rath Packing Co., Sycamore and Elm, Waterloo, Iowa: Braunsweiger or Liver Sausage and Black Hawk Bacon used in "Braunsweiger Paté." Hickory Smoked Ham used in "Artichoke Ham Casserole." Smoked with Hickory Canned Ham used in "Sherry Walnut Ham."

Reynolds Metals Co., 19 E. 47 St., New York, N.Y. 10017: Reynolds Wrap used to prepare "Fish Fillets with Shrimp Sauce," "Fish Poached in White Wine," "Sole Bonne Femme," "Delicious and Easy Pot Roast," "Pot Roast Superior," "Glaze for Baked Ham," "Braised Leg of Lamb," "Veal Marengo," "Breast of Chicken Eugenie," "Chicken and Mushrooms" and "Italian Chicken in Foil."

Planters Peanuts, Standards Brands, Inc., 625 Madison Ave., New Aork, N.Y. 10022: Peanut Oil used in "Fish and Tomato Bake," "Braised Prawns," "Chicken with Riesling," "Roast Duckling with Orange Sauce," and "Green Pepper Hamburgers."

United Fruit Co., Prudential Center, Boston, Mass. 02199: Chiquita Bananas used in "Banana Coconut Rolls" and "Banana Nut Trifle." Sara Lee Pound Cake used in "Banana Nut Trifle."

Contributors not Specifying Brands

Special thanks are due to the following for contributing non-brand recipes including their products:

American Institute of Baking, Artichoke Advisory Board, Brussels Sprouts Advisory Board, California Avocado Advisory Board, California Beef Council, California Honey Advisory Board, California Raisin Advisory Board, Cling Peach Advisory Board, Dried

Fig Advisory Board, Evaporated Milk Association, International Shrimp Council, National Canners Association, National Dairy Council, Poultry and Egg National Board, Prune Advisory Board, Rice Council for Market Development, Strawberry Advisory Board.

index of Recipes